1994

A Question of Identity

A Question of Identity

WOMEN, SCIENCE, AND LITERATURE

edited by Marina Benjamin

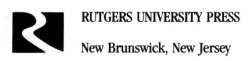

RUTGERS UNIVERSITY PRESS

New Brunswick, New Jersey

Library of Congress Cataloging-in-Publication Data
A Question of identity : women, science, and literature / edited by
  Marina Benjamin.
      p.   cm.
    Includes bibliographical references and index.
    ISBN 0-8135-1982-9 (cloth)—ISBN 0-8135-1983-7 (paper)
    1. Women in literature.   2. Women in science.   3. Human
reproductive technology—Social aspects.   4. Sex differences—Social
aspects.   5. Gender identity—Social aspects.   6. Feminism.
I. Benjamin, Marina.
PN56.W64Q47   1993
809'.93352042—dc20   92-38796
                                                                         CIP

British Cataloging-in-Publication information available

For my parents

Contents

Acknowledgments

As with most edited collections the making of this volume has been something of an uphill struggle, but one that was nonetheless smoothed by the generous support of friends and colleagues, and one that was certainly worthwhile. No one could want a more committed, resourceful, and enthusiastic editor than Leslie Mitchner, and I would like to thank her for her wonderful work on this collection. I would also like to express my gratitude to the all the contributors for entering into the spirit of the collection and producing such stimulating essays. My own contribution benefited enormously from the comments and criticisms of Elaine Showalter, Roy Porter, and Francis Spufford: to all three I would like to extend thanks and appreciation. I am indebted also to Lucinda Montefiore, who initially backed the book behind the idea, and to Ornella Moscucci, Catherine Crawford, Mary Ann Hushlak, and Jenni Calder, whose advice I sought at various stages of its development.

Notes on Contributors

MARINA BENJAMIN was educated at Cambridge University. She is now a freelance writer and journalist living and working in London. She is the editor of *Science and Sensibility: Gender and Scientific Enquiry, 1780–1945* (Basil Blackwell, 1991) and the author of several articles on eighteenth-century history of science, as well as numerous newspaper features.

JENNI CALDER was educated in the United States and England and has degrees from the Universities of Cambridge and London. After twelve years as a freelance author and teacher, in 1978 she joined the National Museums of Scotland, where she is now head of publications. She continues to lecture in various parts of the world and has recently completed a book on Margaret Oliphant's work. Publications include *Women and Marriage in Nineteenth-century Fiction* (Thames and Hudson, 1976), *Heros, from Byron to Guevara* (Hamilton, 1988), *The Victorian Home* (Batsford, 1977), and *RLS: A Life Study* (H. Hamilton, 1980). She is currently working on a biography of Naomi Mitchison.

TESS COSSLETT is a senior lecturer in the Department of English, University of Lancaster, where she teaches mainly nineteenth-century and women writers courses and contributes to an interdisciplinary Women's Studies Part One course. She took her undergraduate and graduate degrees at Oxford. Her previous publications are *The "Scientific Movement" and Victorian Literature* (Harvester and St. Martins, 1982), (ed.) *Science and Religion in the Nineteenth Century* (Cambridge, 1984), and *Woman to Woman: Female Friendship in Victorian Fiction* (Harvester and Humanities Press, 1988). She is now working on the representation of childbirth by twentieth-century women writers, about which she has several articles in print or forthcoming, which may form the basis of another book.

N. KATHERINE HAYLES is Professor of English at the University of California at Los Angeles. Her publications include *Chaos and Order: Complex Dynamics in Literature and Science* (University of Chicago Press, 1991), *Chaos Bound: Orderly Disorder in Contemporary Literature and Science* (Cornell University Press, 1990), and *The Cosmic Web: Scientific Field Models and Literary Strategies* (Cornell University Press, 1984). She is currently at work on a book entitled *Virtual Bodies: Writing the Posthuman*.

JOHN MULLAN is a lecturer in English at Fitzwilliam College, Cambridge. He is the author of *Sentiment and Sociability: The Language of Feeling in the Eighteenth Century* (Oxford University Press, 1988). He is currently editing an anthology of eighteenth-century popular culture.

MARIE MULVEY ROBERTS is a lecturer in literary studies at the University of the West of England, Bristol. She is the author of *British Poets and Secret Societies* (Croom Helm, 1986) and *Gothic Immortals: The Fiction of the Brotherhood of the Rosy Cross* (Routledge, 1990). She also co-edited *Explorations in Medicine* (Gower, 1987), the forthcoming *Literature and Medicine during the Eighteenth Century* (Routledge), and *Secret Texts: The Literature of Secret Societies* (A.M.S.). At present she is editing a series of women's texts for Thoemmes, Routledge and *Out of the Night: Writings from Death Row* for the New Clarion Press.

LONDA SCHIEBINGER is a professor of history and women's studies at the Pennsylvania State University. She is author of *The Mind Has No Sex? Women in the Origins of Modern Science* (Harvard University Press, 1989) and *Nature's Body: Gender in the Making of Modern Science* (Beacon Press, 1993). She is currently writing a book on gender in contemporary scientific culture and a cultural history of the breast.

SALLY SHUTTLEWORTH is a senior lecturer in the School of English, University of Leeds. She is the author of *George Eliot and Nineteenth-century Science: The Make-believe of a Beginning* (Cambridge University Press, 1984) and co-editor, with John Christie, of *Nature Transfigured: Science and Literature, 1700–1900* (Manchester University Press, 1989) and, with Mary Jacobus and Evelyn Fox Keller, of *Body/*

Politics: Women and the Discourses of Science (Routledge, 1990). She is currently engaged on a study of Charlotte Brontë's fiction in the light of nineteenth-century medical and psychological discourse.

SUSAN SQUIER has a Ph.D. in English literature from Stanford University and is an associate professor of English at the State University of New York at Stony Brook, where she teaches modern literature and feminist theory and criticism. She is the author of *Virginia Woolf and London: The Sexual Politics of the City* (University of North Carolina Press, 1985), editor of *Women Writers and the City: Essays in Feminist Literary Criticism* (University of Tennessee Press, 1984), and co-editor of *Arms and the Woman: War, Gender, and Literary Representation* (University of North Carolina Press, 1989). The recipient of a Fulbright Senior Research Scholar Fellowship to Melbourne, Australia, for 1990–1991, she is currently working on a study of the representational origins of reproductive technology in the works of modern writers, about which she has several articles forthcoming or in print.

SYLVANA TOMASELLI was a research fellow at Newnham College, Cambridge 1985–1988), where she is now based. She is an intellectual historian working predominantly on the seventeenth and eighteenth centuries. Her publications include a translation of Jacques Lacan's *Seminar II: The Ego in Freud's Theory and in Psychoanalytic Technique* (Cambridge University Press and Norton, 1988). She edited *Rape: An Historical and Social Enquiry* (Basil Blackwell, 1986) and *The Dialectics of Friendship* (Routledge, 1989) with Roy Porter. She has contributed to a number of reference works on the Enlightenment and other subjects. Her book *Seduction and Civilisation: An Enlightenment Perspective on the History of Woman* will be published by Weidenfeld and Nicolson. She is also editing Mary Wollstonecraft's *Vindication of the Rights of Woman* for Cambridge University Press.

A Question of Identity

A Question of Identity

Marina Benjamin

> Imaginatively she is of the highest importance; practically she is completely insignificant. She pervades poetry from cover to cover; she is all but absent from history. She dominates the lives of kings and conquerors in fiction; in fact she was the slave of any boy whose parents forced a ring upon her finger. Some of the most inspired words, some of the most profound thoughts in literature fall from her lips; in real life she could hardly read, could hardly spell, and was the property of her husband.
>
> Virginia Woolf, *A Room of One's Own*

Some sixty years on, and for all the material changes that have taken place in women's position in society, it is surprisingly easy to sympathize with Virginia Woolf's ultimately futile quest for the essential oil of womanhood, to succumb to the temptation to search for it among dusty books and partial histories and to attempt to extract nuggets of truth about woman from the worlds of literature and psychology. Perhaps after all Woolf was right in thinking that what truth we may glean of woman from her various presences and absences lies somewhere between life and the printed page. Yet it seems to me that the problem is less a matter of where we look and more a matter of how the question is framed. While we might still ask "Who is woman, what is she?"—to paraphrase Shakespeare on the enigmatic Sylvia—we now do so with an awareness that the difficulty of defining what woman is and of thereby characterizing a subjective female identity is a critical problem for contemporary feminism. While the category of woman is central to any feminist discourse, the concept of woman remains notoriously difficult for feminists to formulate precisely, because it is overdetermined by the constructions of patriarchal culture where male power is predicated on defining woman as Other and as Object.

While feminist theorists are eloquent on the difficulties of conceptualizing woman, a rather more evocative approach can be found in the work of American photographer Cindy Sherman, who since the late 1970s has consistently confronted the problem of female identity.

Sherman provides no ready-made solution to this problem. Indeed, part of her appeal is that her photographs seem to dramatize the lack of any straightforward answers throwing the problem into bold relief; taken as a whole they convey a near-frenzied search for a female identity that proves, like the philosopher's stone, to be frustratingly elusive. Sherman's technique is to place her own body in the conventions of advertising and film, eliding herself with images of women created for the mass market in an elaborate parody of the loss of self. In the past she has drawn on genres as varied as the love story and the surrealist film, revealing, chameleon-like, a new surface of woman in each photograph—from housewife to siren, from model to grotesque—while her most recent work daringly re-creates the paintings of Old Masters.

The photograph reproduced here (fig. 1), recalling the kind of 1950s "girly" calendar in which Marilyn Monroe made a famous appearance, is typical of Sherman's output in the late 1970s and early 1980s. It forms part of a substantial series of black-and-white work that offers snatched glimpses of women. Snatched, because many of the photographs give the impression of having been stolen, the result of intruding on a private moment: there's a woman crouching on the kitchen floor beside newly dropped shopping, a woman seemingly the worse for drink stepping out onto a patio as if caught by paparazzi, a self-absorbed woman standing in her underwear in a bathroom, and so on. (Interestingly, in none of these photographs is Sherman nude; the identity she confronts is not a matter of anatomy.) Sherman's use of black and white reveals a certain cynicism about the intrusiveness of the mass-market media she deals with; her abstraction of woman from the real world of color is grimly analogous to the way in which mass-market media abstract types from real women. Even the label given to this series, "Untitled Film Stills," addresses the tendency of these media to depersonalize their objects and distance them from the real. When Sherman did introduce color into her self-portraits, it served to depict emotional as well as physical states of being, contradiction as well as equanimity, and verisimilitude rather than veracity. Among other things, she evoked the fear of a battered wife, the loneliness of a junkie, and the faraway gaze of adolescent love.

Presented with this cornucopia of femininity, we might reasonably suppose that Sherman is concerned to affirm female identity as fluid and plural rather than fixed and monolithic. But as Whitney Chadwick points out, Sherman's role-playing constitutes a challenge to "the masculine desire to fix the woman in a stable and stabilizing identity." Yet this is only part of the story. While Sherman invites the

FIG. 1.   *Cindy Sherman, Untitled film still, 1979, black-and-white photograph, 10 × 8 in. (Courtesy of Metro Pictures, New York)*

viewer to indulge this masculine desire, she manages at the same time to deny its gratification, because although her photographs are always self-portraits, "they never reveal anything about Cindy Sherman the person and her image functions only as an object of contemplation for the gazes of others."[1] Sherman thus opens up a gap between the objective representation of women and their subjective identity and so highlights woman's resistance to definition. Throughout her work she exposes only a constituted self—a self composed entirely from the repertoire of cultural images of women. In this way she reveals herself while concealing her identity, and suggests authenticity while intending deception. Moreover, by denying us access to the individual woman, Sherman highlights a taken-for-granted double vision that is at work whenever we rely on well-defined, general categories of woman as a means of knowing specific women. Such double vision effectively collapses the individual into the collective identity of woman.

Cindy Sherman's work may appear to be an unlikely choice for flagshipping a volume whose concerns are with women, science, and literature and whose chronological focus extends over the best part of three hundred years. But far from being removed from the concerns of this collection, it admirably captures the meeting point of many of the contributions. As a comment on the issue of gendered identity formation, its significance is twofold. In the sheer multiplicity of male-constructed images of woman that it mobilizes, Sherman's work stresses the diversity and temporality of what it is that Western patriarchal culture deems woman to be. At the same time, the silences in her work speak volumes, casting doubt on whether it is possible to represent a subjective female identity at all. With respect to chronology, this collection points to the continued relevance of major currents of Enlightenment thought: notably, science's persistent need to define, explain, and categorize woman, and our enduring reliance on the distinction between subject and object as a basis for distinguishing the typically male world of knowers from the world of the known, which is all too frequently symbolized by woman. In their deliberate conflation of subject and object, Sherman's self-portraits lend immediacy to the problems attendant on the struggle to define woman as subject not object, and therefore as the author of her own existence.

Any attempt to (re)position woman as subject or agent must first expose the man-made ontologies that posit an exclusive identification of woman with object as synthetic constructions belonging to a given historical space and moment. But it must also challenge the dominant humanist philosophy of the autonomous subject that designates agency as the power to transcend nature's mandates. Such a conception of subjecthood is embodied in those discourses that cast woman as object and man as subject in the first place. Only by understanding how the equation of woman and object has been formulated in different discourses at different times and in different cultures can we arrive at an understanding of female subjectivity that does not simply mirror the male subject position of the self-determining individual.

On one level, it is not difficult to demonstrate that women are indeed subjects or agents; they are after all authors of texts, of ideas, of political and religious movements, of science, and of subversion. The products of their labor are all around us. The same can be said about women past; the evidence of feminist historians is, in an important sense, incontrovertible—we know that such women lived and breathed and worked; we can read their letters, novels, and diaries; we know about their families, friends, and patrons, their hopes, fears, and disappointments. But is this enough? Certainly the very notion of treating women as subjects runs against the grain of traditional historical approaches; however, in the absence of evaluation the historical fact of women's authorship throws no light on the relationship between author and authority. In order to explore this relationship we need to be able to square the variety of subject positions that have been assumed by particular women, over time and in different discourses, with the object positions that have been thrust upon woman as a category. This is a theoretical as well as historical problem, and one to which Mary Poovey has already drawn attention. To put it in her terms, the problem is how to relate *women* as real, historical agents or subjects to *woman*—the objectified and historically specific cultural representation of the female that, she suggests, "mediates the relationship of women and men to every individual, concrete woman." While Cindy Sherman purposefully conflates women with woman to great effect, Poovey complains that much feminist criticism unwittingly indulges the same slippage only to generate confusion. Poovey's point, however, is not merely to scold; her intention is rather to express the need to theorize both "how women have been able to enter discourses from which they have been initially excluded so as to begin to represent themselves, and how to read texts that mark the passage of women from objects of another's discourse to women as subjects of their own."[2] Mapping the relationship between women and woman is a program that grafts comfortably onto attempts to erode the distinction between subject and object. And because of the vast wealth of material that can be put at the disposal of this program, it invites contributions from the entire spectrum of the humanities, from history and anthropology to art and literary criticism to sociology and economics. At present we have only the barest outlines of such a map, and it is one of the goals of this volume to begin to synthesize some of its topographical features.

The importance of the dichotomy between women as subjects and objects of human experience should not be underestimated; it is so deeply entrenched in our culture that even the feminist criticism that has sought to reconcile its constituent halves has by and large continued to reproduce it. We need only glance across the women's studies shelves of the local bookshop to see that the fundamental bifurcation between subject and object has been materially realized with its object-weighted asymmetry intact. Broadly speaking, we find on the one hand studies of women as active agents of historical change; biographies and dictionaries; explorations of female subcultures in education, science, politics, and religion; a rich and wide selection of works devoted to women's contribution to literature; and a rapidly increasing number of works that address the gendered division of labor in the professions. Some are more sophisticated than others, some more controversial, and some, like Ivy Pinchbeck's *Women Workers and the Industrial Revolution, 1750–1850,* Ray Strachey's *The Cause: A Short History of the Women's Movement in Great Britain,* and Dale Spender's *Women of Ideas,* have come to dwell in the pantheon of "classics." On the other hand, we find comparatively more studies of women as passive objects of historical change, empty vessels into which cultural value is simply poured. The metaphorical meanings invested in woman have been elaborated by writers as different as Carolyn Merchant and co-authors Sandra M. Gilbert and Susan Gubar.[3] But perhaps the greatest impact of such studies derives from those that deal with the representation of women in visual media; among the more memorable works of this kind are Marina Warner's *Monuments and Maidens,* Judith Williamson's *Consuming Passions,* Susanne Kappeler's *The Pornography of Representation,* and Bram Dijkstra's *Idols of Perversity.*

What these latter studies reveal time and time again is that woman, the transparent, objectified, historical construct, has taken on mythic qualities, the power to represent things that are not herself, from ships, countries, and abstract values like justice and truth, to Nature

Herself. Here lies the key to the malleability of woman, to the cultural insistence on (re)molding her to form public statues, emblems of war and peace, or icons of modern advertising and pornography. Ludmilla Jordanova, who has recently been concerned to establish how "women's bodies permit cultural investment in them," stresses the role of myth, metaphor, and personification as devices that transport woman from present reality into a distanced realm. She further points out that the use of the female body to personify abstract qualities implies that "it is a ready substratum onto which shared values and collective commitments can be projected, even if these have not been consciously articulated."[4] In cultures where men have taken on the power of naming, thereby assuming the public role of manufacturing culture from textual and visual languages—and that is most cultures—they have added woman to their vocabulary. It is because woman has been inscribed with the sum of human experience that women's minds and bodies can be regarded as legible. It follows that reading women's minds and bodies tells us a great deal about a culture.

Of all the tools with which woman has been named, science has been invested with privileged authority. In the first place, science claims the power to naturalize, that is, to ground the knowledge it produces in nature. In speaking for the natural—the world that is real or material, organic, and innate—science assumes a position outside of man-made culture, which it thereby represents as artifice. Moreover, science carries the authority of objectivity within itself; science has been constructed in the "elite" and "popular" imaginations in opposition and as a corrective to the subjectivity of literature and the arts. Its practitioners, popularizers, and critics have, as a matter of course, equated scientific knowledge with true knowledge as if the process of developing scientific theories or distilling facts out of artifacts were immune to the fingerprints of human involvement. Uncertainty theories in quantum physics went some way toward dissociating science from truth. They even acknowledged that experimental knowledge was the result of experiential conditions. But while modern physics turned science into a metaphor for reality, it claimed that science was the best metaphor we had. Although science's power to name has been challenged in recent years by sociologists of science, revisionist historians, and cultural critics, who unite in insisting on the social character of all knowledge claims, issues of gender have not been given due prominence. The political, religious, or class interests of scientists, yet not their gender interests, are assumed to color how they see. The fact that the majority of the Royal Society's early fellowship was Protestant, for example, has been considered more significant than the fact that the entire fellowship was male. By overlooking the relationship between masculinity and knowledge production, the new science criticism fails to deal with how intimately gender is bound in with subjecthood. The result is that while science's power to name is effectively compromised, men's power to name remains unchallenged.

Feminist critics of science, by contrast, seek to problematize the masculine character of science. They argue that science, perhaps more than any other area of cultural production, has been and continues to be dominated by men largely because manliness is so thoroughly imbricated in scientific methods and values. Science is tightly bound to the popular hallmarks of masculinity—objectivity, rationality, truth, progress, exploration, and power. Indeed, it is no less bound to aspects of masculinity, particularly of male sexuality, that many men today regard as less than flattering; unclothing, conquering, dominating, penetrating, and even raping have served as the most prevalent metaphors for scientific inquiry.[5] While the scientific subject is supremely male, the scientific object par excellence is female. Feminists have explored how science has persistently flexed its muscles on woman, rigorously exercising the significance of gender difference. Within the bio-medical sciences, special priority has been placed on taxonomizing woman, that is, determining both the specific characteristics of the sex and the multilayered and intricate weave of relations between the sexes.[6] The designation of woman as object is equally insistent on a symbolic level, where the association of woman with the passive world of inanimate matter has long been articulated through an identification of nature as female. It is nowhere more evident than in the natural sciences that the more *woman* is objectified, the less empowered to act, at least theoretically, are *women*. As a consequence of their ideological and material exclusion from scientific societies, professions, and institutions, women have been conspicuous by their absence in the development of science, and the few who throughout the centuries have been conspicuous by their presence have more often than not had to conceal their individual gender identity behind the protective shield of womanly ideals.[7] Because the history of science—its practices, languages, and imagery—manifestly enhances the polarization between women as subjects and objects of civilization, it provides a particularly suitable platform on which to build an inquiry into the relationship between women and woman.

Although scientific interest in the bodies and minds of women can be traced back to ancient Greece, science's isolation of woman as a category has its origins in the Enlightenment with the emergence of the science of woman. The science of woman is therefore a useful point of departure for an examination of the architecture of the relationship between women and woman, but it is not a topic to be treated lightly, since there is some dispute about what it comprised: a recent book by Ornella Moscucci bears the title *The Science of Woman: Gynaecology and Gender in England, 1800–1929,* while Sylvana Tomaselli's contribution to the literature, the first essay in this volume, has nothing whatsoever to do with gynecology.[8] More than nomenclature is at stake. Moscucci and Tomaselli are concerned with rather different conceptual problems, not to mention historical periods: while the former draws together the various medical and quasi-medical sciences that converged in the mid-nineteenth century under the umbrella of gynecology, the latter is concerned with a much more nebulous concretization of scientific and literary interest in woman that dates from the mid-eighteenth century and that was conceived in the shadow of what David Hume called the "Science of Man." How then should the science of woman be characterized? Is it a homogeneous or heterogeneous science? Is it constituted by one discourse or several?

Looking for the science of woman as a finite historical entity bound in time within a specific discourse is liable to lead to a characterization riddled with contradictions; the eighteenth-century science of woman bears as little relation to gynecology as the science of man bears to anthropology. However, if we explore several nonlinear and partially overlapping discursive practices that centered on woman, we will find more than one generic definition of the science of woman. This is not to complicate the matter; quite the contrary, this process enables us to discern three more or less distinct stages or phases in the development of the science of woman. In chronological sequence these are the emergence of a science of woman that mirrored the project of the science of man, a more amorphous grouping of principally medical and predominantly French discourses best described as natural histories of woman, and a more streamlined professional discourse of gynecology. As the science of woman is traced through these phases, an increasing emphasis on physiology and anatomy becomes evident; in other words, to the modern mind it becomes more recognizable as a science. This is because the meaning of science was itself narrowed and refined as the science of woman evolved and moved through its various stages, so that the more undiluted scientific discourses on woman came to prominence in the Victorian era while the less scientific discourses either fell into disuse or were absorbed into other disciplines.

The men and women of the Enlightenment who wrote specifically about woman—the Comte de Buffon, Lady Mary Wortley Montagu, Denis Diderot, Lord Kames, Madame de Staël, Madame de Genlis, Antoine-Léonard Thomas, and William Alexander, to name but a few—ambitiously tackled the scientific, legal, educational, and anthropological history of woman. They concerned themselves with a wide range of issues: the education of women, their employments and amusements, what they read, what they wore, what qualities constituted their virtues and vices, how women behaved in savage and civilized societies, how their physical attributes fitted them for particular roles, what sort of civil rights they should be accorded, whether they were better off in the society of their own sex or the other, whether or not they should own property or be permitted to bring lawsuits against their husbands. These writers were part descriptive and part normative, part literary and part scientific, part anthropocentric and part theocentric. This is a heterogeneous corpus, with contributions scattered here and there—within travel writings, educational treatises, or inquiries into the human condition—as well as among essays, sketches, or histories complete in themselves.

Tomaselli acknowledges the difficulty of using this literature to gain an overall perspective on the science of woman, but she nonetheless points to a distinction between these writers and those who may be regarded as their predecessors, namely, that they self-consciously linked their undertaking to the project of the science of man. They wanted to do for woman what Rousseau had done for man: "Historians of woman wanted to tell her story as he had told his. They wanted to come to terms with her nature, as he had unravelled his nature. As it was, history stood half-written; human nature half-examined; half the species shrouded in darkness." As it turned out, the history of woman was less the other side of the coin than the same side of a different coin, in that the unfolding story was one of men's tyranny over women. Sometimes this theme was merely alluded to: recounting her visit to the women of a Turkish harem, Lady Mary Wortley Montagu remarked, "I was at last forc'd to open my skirt and shew them my stays, which satisfy'd 'em very well, for I saw they believ'd I was so lock'd up in that machine that it was not in my own power to open it, which contrivance they attributed to my Husband." More often than not, it was stated outright: William Alexander, addressing his male readership, aptly summed up the tension inherent in the science of woman when he claimed that women "have in all periods, and almost in all countries, been, by our sex, constantly oppressed and adored."[9] These writers protested vociferously against men's oppression of women and agreed that civilization heralded the righting of this wrong. They saw themselves as champions of female emancipation. Paradoxically their work only served to facilitate a conceptual shift in the understanding of women's oppression from implicating the tyranny of men to implicating the tyranny of their ovaries. With this move the burden of women's oppression was lifted from the shoulders of man and transferred to the workings of the female body.

The scientific basis of the science of woman extends beyond its genealogical relationship to the science of man. The Enlightenment writers in question were preoccupied with the systematic categorization of women according to race, nationality, culture, and class. Their spirit of investigation was genuinely scientific in that they sought to attain true knowledge of the condition of woman, casting an eye back over women's history while simultaneously eyeing the future and the progress they hoped it would bring. Moreover, as Tomaselli argues, wherever possible they grounded their arguments in natural law and so made predictability a feature of their narratives. The natural history of woman shared these scientific aims to the extent that to force a rigid three-stage model of the science of woman becomes a nonsense; Alexander's history of woman, in particular, bears equal generic relation to the science of man as it does to natural history. A broad brush stroke rather than a fine line separates the natural history of woman from a more interdisciplinary science of woman. The fluidity of this separation is considerable, since writers like Buffon and Rousseau, as well as Alexander, owed a considerable debt to natural history—the science that combined interest in the anatomy, life cycles, and climatic variations found in any given species of the animal or vegetable kingdoms. They compared the physical attributes of women cross-culturally, they discussed puberty, reproduction, and motherhood, and they took pains to express the diversity of female gender roles in relation to the environment. Their comparisons between the behavior of Western, Eastern, and, often, Eskimo women have a parallel in the natural-historical comparison of flora and fauna in temperate, hot, or cold climates. Perhaps more important, the science of woman shared with natural history an emphasis on specular knowledge: natural history was an observational rather than experimental science; it was based on detailed observation and recording of the natural world, the collection and collation of data, and the synthesis of conceptual systems that classified the living world according to a pattern of strict hierarchy. Through the science of woman, women were subjected to the scrutiny of the scientific eye and transformed from companions of mankind into beings that presented yet another species for the "male gaze" to rest upon.

The natural histories of woman produced by Enlightenment bio-medical writers generated increasing interest in the biological differences between man and woman. But while woman's nature became a matter of biological anomaly and subsequently, in the nineteenth century, gynecology, an analogous science of masculinity or andrology never left the ground.[10] The notion that woman and man are fashioned from different stuff has a history as old as the species itself; the Bible tells us woman was begot of Adam's rib, placing her at one earthbound remove from the divine handiwork that formed her mate. Aristotle and Galen inform us that she is colder and more humid than man, and medical men of the seventeenth century agreed with Thomas Sydenham that female tissue was "less closely knit and less firm" than that of the male. We will see that this theme takes on new significance in the Enlightenment, that of modeling woman as the being "in which the principle of life and all illness is eminently manifested."[11] Women were believed to be inherently weaker than men, and therefore more sensitive, but the concept of sensitivity was double-edged, since as well as constituting the essential quality of life, sensitivity predisposed women to illness. In short, woman embodied human pathology.

Perhaps the best-known of these natural histories is Pierre Roussel's *Système physique et moral de la femme* (1775). As a physician, Roussel drew on comparative anatomy to demonstrate that woman's solid tissues were "spongy and soft" compared to man's. But this was not all; "the vessels, the nerves, the fleshy fibres, tendinous and ligamentous," which are "more slender, more small, more delicate and more supple that those of which the body of man is composed," reveal to us "the passive state for which nature destines her." A passivity of mind as well as body was recommended, since Roussel claimed that "the gentle passions are the most familiar to woman because they are the most analogous to her physical constitution."[12] Here, Roussel followed Rousseau, providing biological justification for his theory of sexual complementarity, which defined male and female ideals as opposite and complementary: for instance, "women have more wit, men more genius; women observe and men reason." William Alexander, also a physician, echoed, "Each sex has its peculiar qualities, and is fitted by the Author of nature for accomplishing different purposes."[13] In effect these natural histories grounded the refinement that the nonmedical writers on woman had ascribed to civilization in biology.

A striking feature of these texts is the teleological ease with which they link woman's physical and behavioral virtues. By invoking the concept of teleology to describe what is here being said about woman, I am referring less to its original meaning of final causes (although this is certainly evident), and more to the sense of teleology as "narrative drive," for this gives rise to a literary dimension, the notion of telling a story with a plot resolution in mind. Modern science has learned to disguise its teleology, and, as the essays in this volume demonstrate, literary analysis serves as a useful means of uncovering it. A further aspect of these writings that we have come not to associate with modern science is their aesthetic imperative. Roussel presents his case thus; having asserted that the cellular tissue, found in far greater quantities in the female than in the male, modifies the structure and sensibility of cells, he goes on to claim that it "gives the limbs of woman their uniform and polished surface, their roundness, and the gracious contours that those of man cannot and must not have. . . . One may say that in woman nature has done everything for the graces and the pleasures."[14] This aesthetic, like the teleological drive, serves to prescribe as well as describe. Alexander, for example, insisted that women who despise the charms of their own sex "soon become the roughest and most uncultivated of the human species"; boldness, courage, and other "beauties" of the male sex would represent defects in woman.[15] The politics of pleasure runs deeper still, since the aesthetic demand of harmonizing natural law with the laws of society meant that the penalty paid by women who transgressed social law had a biological correlate. Roussel warned that in women "excessive work wastes and deforms the organs, in destroying, by repeated compressions, that cellular substance which contributes to the beauty of their contours and complexion."[16] It followed that for women, the price of making a bid for independence by indulging in bodily or mental labor was a heavy one, implicating all manner of monstrosities—physical deformity, mental pathology, and social ostracism.

The grounding of female beauty in anatomical differences between woman and man was further extended in the nineteenth century, as disciplines like phrenology, craniometry, and gynecology increasingly anchored the essence of femininity to an ideal that was biologically weak and childlike and behaviorally passive and domestic. Indeed, the applauding of female passivity reached an extreme within Victorian idealizations of femininity as invalidity. Science promoted the notion that the quintessential woman was typified by the numerous middle-class ladies who spent their adult lives confined to the sickbed or prostrate on the couch afflicted by vapors or consumption.[17] It is tempting to read the bio-aesthetics of invalidity as a realization, if not a materialization, of the pathological prognoses implicit in the Enlightenment science of woman. More important perhaps is the need for a recognition that once woman is bio-aesthetically defined as uniquely passive, almost any construction of female agency can be regarded as a dangerous flirtation with monstrosity. Sally Shuttleworth's essay on the discourses of sensation fiction and psychology explores the bio-aesthetics of gender difference in relation to conceptions of selfhood and mental stability and reveals that sensation fiction conventionally depicted economic or sexual ambition in women as a signifier of pending insanity. Yet she argues that the genre was also subversively deployed to suggest that excessive femininity, in its repression of individuality and overemphasis on passivity, was itself a path to insanity. Sensation novels offered a cynical picture of society in which women were forced to tread a precipitously narrow margin of social legitimacy; if they strayed too far from prescribed feminine ideals, in whatever direction, mental pathology became their fate.

It would be rash to suggest that the relationship between what science has said about woman from the Enlightenment to the present day is a linear one, yet certain important continuities and recurring themes invite comment. One need only reflect on the bio-aesthetic imagery of monstrosity that today's popular press borrows from sociobiology in order to characterize (and caricature) controversial feminists, single mothers, women who have several sexual partners as opposed to one, or women who chose artificial insemination as an initiator of pregnancy.[18] Women with independent bodies and minds are still, it seems, perceived as a threat to social stability. Today, as in the nineteenth century, reproduction is a prime site of contestation over the meaning of femininity. With the development of ever more sophisticated methods of bio-technology, reproduction has assumed privileged status in the discourses of capitalism and economics. Sociobiology in particular has spun stories around reproduction that read, teleologically, like a lesson in investment strategy and the politics of human management.[19] The essays in this volume that deal with the theme of reproduction reveal a keen awareness of the links between reproduction and capitalist power strategies. Marie Roberts and Susan Squier explore the disastrous consequences of a male appropriation of reproduction both in the literal sense, of creating life or meddling with the reproductive process, and metaphorically, as the ultimate slight on female creativity brought about by aligning the forces of reproduction with those of production. The persistence of the Victorian notion of woman as a reproductive machine subject to regulation by male technological expertise is taken up by Tess Cosslett, who studies the novels of two contemporary women writers who deal with the effects of technological intervention on pregnant women's self-perception.

Exploring how the scientific objectification of woman bears on the process of conceptualizing female agency is evidently a matter of political urgency. In particular, such objectification provides a backdrop against which to evaluate the emancipatory nature of the activities of women, past and present. What may appear to the contemporary mind as a conservative action may in context reappear as a liberating one. Given the degree of ideological and material constraint placed on *woman,* we could be forgiven for thinking it a marvel that *women* could meaningfully act in the world at all. A historical appreciation of specific constructions of gendered subjectivity goes a long way toward reassessing what at any given time constitutes female resistance, protest, and dissent.

To take a nineteenth-century example, it is clear that although women were socially and biologically identified with the private world of domesticity within an emerging ideology of separate spheres, woman's physical and mental inferiority to man was counterbalanced by long-held beliefs in woman's innate moral or spiritual superiority. Woman's moral superiority to man was encoded in her physiology, in the extreme sensitivity of her nervous system, which gave rise to her refined sensibilities. And it was given religious validation by evangelical crusaders like Hannah More and Thomas Gisborne, who defined woman's moral worth as a product of her domestic confinement. Woman was considered to be in the full flourish of femininity in the service of home, husband, and children.[20] Women drew on domesticity, the joys of motherhood, and the influence it accorded them in justifying public activity. By remaining within the accepted bounds of femininity, women could exploit their domestic autonomy by actively feminizing areas of public culture that could be construed as extensions of the domestic sphere, such as writing, teaching, and philanthropy. I have argued elsewhere that such strategies enabled women to enter male-dominated scientific discourses with impunity.[21] Jenni Calder's essay in this volume provides, by contrast, an example of how respectable women could draw on specific formulations of sexual difference to voice antiscientific opinions. Calder shows how Mrs. Oliphant invoked established views on gendered ways of seeing to subvert the social values attached to rational, masculine scientific observation. Another area where it became possible for women to subvert formal codes of gender identity was Victorian spiritualism. The appeal of understanding the upsurge of spiritualism and mediumship among women in the second half of the nineteenth century as the power of mind compensating for the incapacities of the body is not so far off the mark. Mediumship was simultaneously predicated on an acknowledgment of female spiritual authority and a privileged sense of feminine passivity or self-denial, which made women particularly suitable for communicating with spirits by allowing them to pose as temporary receptacles for visiting souls from the other world. [22]

Equally significant, and yet equally concealed, formulations of female agency can operate on the symbolic plane, as John Mullan's essay in the present volume illustrates. On the surface it would seem that Enlightenment thinkers did not rate women's capacity for understanding very highly—though many of them at least conceded that women were blessed with rationality. However, the very limitations that were placed on women's understanding presented a window of opportunity to proselytes of the Newtonian worldview by allowing them to posit woman as the best test of the truth of the new science. Mullan argues that women, with less to unlearn than men, with their straightforward ability to grasp simple truths, and with all the discretion resulting from tastefulness, were targeted by popularizers of Newtonianism as vehicles through which the new science could justify itself. At the same time, Newtonianism promised to lure women away from the worst excesses of femininity; in other words, it guaranteed to save women from themselves.

A workable characterization of female subjectivity must account not only for how women are enabled to act in the world but also for why certain constructions of female agency are accorded social legitimacy while others are consigned to the realm of the monstrous. Not all feminist formulations of female subjectivity succeed on both counts. Those feminists whose search for a specifically female identity begins and ends with anatomy suffer this shortcoming. Writers like Mary Daly and Susan Griffin, who bind female agency to sex difference, maintain that woman's spiritual self arises from woman's bodily self, so that women are seen, for instance, as life-affirming because they are life-creating. Like the masculine science it opposes, essentialism grounds female subjectivity within objectified constructions of woman.[23] In the terms of this discussion, it elides women with woman. Biological determinism cannot represent any female agency that operates counterculturally against, for example, the domestic ideals of womanliness, nor can it explain patriarchal vilification of female agency without resorting to invoking the idea of men's envy or hatred of women. Conceptualizing female identity in terms of innate essences assumes that true femininity is a matter of destiny, the result of a prepatterned unfolding of secondary characteristics attuned to women's physical maturing. Cast as nurturing, sensitive, intuitive, and caring, women remain yoked to nature and left to suffer the indignities imposed on nature by a male culture of which they can never be part.

A far more flexible theoretical formulation of female agency emerges from conceptualizing female subjectivity in terms of positionality rather than essences. By *positionality* I mean the specific ontological position occupied by individual women in society. Positionality thus embraces both the pluralism that acknowledges the vast differences between the lived experiences of individual women, and the specificity of social contexts delineating those experiences that are shared. Female agency can then be seen as the conceptual space from which women act, although it is not in the gaps, chinks, or porosity of the man-made definitions of woman that we will find that space, but in women's socio-marginal position as a whole. In other words, where *woman* is objectively placed with respect to the existing social order determines the parameters within which or outside of which *women* speak. Those parameters are themselves subject to shifts in position that relate to the class, cultural affiliations, or race of individual women, and that also relate to where power resides in the society that invented them. A number of people have drawn attention to the relationship between socio-marginality and authority, among them Mary Douglas. Douglas remarks that "all margins are dangerous[;] if they are pulled this way or that the shape of fundamental experience is altered. Any structure of ideas is vulnerable at its margins." She goes on to qualify this by observing that when a social system is well-articulated, power is vested in its points of authority, whereas when a social system is ill-articulated, power resides in the marginal sources of disorder.[24] Considerations of gender can easily be accommodated within such a framework so that legitimate agency becomes for women a matter of remaining sufficiently womanly so as not to overstep the boundary between the feminine and the monstrous, which is itself subject to shifts in position that relate directly to the stability of the social order. It is of little wonder that the interests of women's oppression are served so well by science, which locates the parameters designed to contain femininity in biology rather than in culture—body margins being more stable than social ones because they are construed as natural. If social roles are inscribed in gendered bodies and minds, patriarchal authority need only actively maintain the legibility of those inscriptions to remain secure.

Two very different contributions to this volume illustrate how intimately women's subject positions are related to the construction of the female body. Both imply that it is the female rather than the male body that serves as the primary yardstick by which humanity itself is defined. Londa Schiebinger explores through Enlightenment primatology the age-old question of whether or not humankind belongs to the animal kingdom. Primates presented the greatest threat to humankind's privileged position in the great chain of being, and the humanity of apes was hotly debated. Schiebinger uncovers the interplay between humanity, race, and gender by revealing that if apes were considered human at all they were represented as more like the black races than like Europeans. Moreover, their supposed humanity was mediated by considerations of gender: if male apes resembled humankind, it was because they could reason and civilize as men do; whereas if female apes resembled humankind, it was because they possessed a clitoris or hymen, menstruated regularly, and displayed appropriate modesty and maternal instinct. Katherine Hayles is similarly concerned with what it is to be human, though her interest lies at the opposite end of the evolutionary scale; using cyborg fiction, she deals with the posthuman or hyperhuman that results when the human body is plugged into machinery or when mechanical appendages or prostheses are welded to the human body. Cybernetics offers numerous metaphors for boundary violation that are explicitly sexual in character, and Hayles's exploration of cyborg sexuality is a masterful account of how such metaphors are used by male writers to reinforce male fears of female sexuality and intimacy, and conversely by female writers to subversively compound the threat that monstrous females pose to established authority. Like the female ape, the cyborg female carries the greater symbolic power.

Understanding how women are empowered to act is very much a product of understanding specific historical and cultural constructions of woman. Only by pursuing these paths in parallel can we appreciate that female identity is more constituted than it is constituting. Yet in spite of this asymmetry in female identity, all women are both subject and object, and their gendered subjectivity is invariably some kind of composite of the two. This is the chord of familiarity that Cindy Sherman's photographs so powerfully strike, enabling them to produce resonances that have a direct impact on women's history. The fact that Cindy Sherman is both author *and* muse is the reason that a subject/object double entendre exists at all; if the photographs had been taken by a man, it would be lost. We are dealing with a subtle middle ground, for in objectifying woman, the she-man in She(r)man apes the male subject position of voyeur. Acts of mimicry such as this have been identified by Luce Irigaray as empowering. Irigaray views women's relationship to phallocratic discourse as passive, imitative, and mimetic, but she argues that when employed with self-awareness mimicry takes on elements of selectivity and irony that carry the potential to expose and undermine phallocratic discourse.[25] By way of demonstration, she includes a chapter on Plotinus in her highly original *Speculum of the Other Woman,* which consists entirely of excerpts from his *Enneads.* Like comic impersonators who ridicule their subjects merely by aiming to be identical to them, Irigaray, and indeed Sherman, ridicule patriarchy.

The essays in this volume confront the Sphinx-like riddle of female identity in scientific and literary discourses, while stressing the common rootedness of these discourses in the specific social contexts that generated and deployed them. As Gillian Beer has recently pointed out, the stories privileged in a culture tend to be also privileged in its science.[26] This collection does not attempt to provide definitive answers to the complex and often subtle issues raised by combining such comprehensive themes as science, literature, and women, but to shed light on the cultural processes that invest their overlap, or indeed their conflict, with meaning. The authors' focus on language, for example, constitutes a challenge to the timeworn "two-culture" myth, which has long represented science and literature as opposite poles of human creativity. The persistence of this myth reflects deep cultural associations that have grown up around science and literature historically—associations that have generally been proffered by science itself.[27] This volume seeks to peel away the associations of objectivity, authority, and masculinity from science as well as those of subjectivity, opinion, and femininity from literature. Indeed, it promotes the view that literature itself reveals a striking awareness of these conceptual patterns and the way in which they mutually define one another, and so in turn shape society's construction of gender. Above all, the volume counters the notion that there is a single, universal female identity—anatomical or cultural—which all women can at some level share.

The difficulties of (re)constructing female identity (or identities) feed directly and reflectively into those of constructing a feminist identity (or identities). The dichotomy between subject and object and the related dyad of mind/body are as central to defining feminism as they are to defining woman. Feminists struggle to balance these binary constructions within an ever-changing political agenda. What, for example, should be given greater priority: fighting to extend the role of women in the public sphere through improvements in education, work opportunities, and domestic politics, or protesting against the objectification and degradation of women in advertising and pornography? What lessons of today will be most valuable to the feminists of tomorrow: the importance of one's cast of mind and the efforts of consciousness-raising, or issues of body politics, like whether or not to shave one's legs or diet? In short, the briefest reflection reveals that feminism is as culturally overdetermined as woman.

Overdeterminism is not in itself an obstacle to be overcome; indeed for some feminists it is to be welcomed. Characterizing female identity as multiple, pluralistic, and even fragmentary brings feminism into line with the postmodern program of decentering the subject. Postmodernists are critically concerned with replacing the unitary, transcendental Cartesian ego, which positions the knowing subject at some Archimedean point outside of discourse, with a conception of the subject as part constituted and part constituting, or, to borrow a phrase from Julia Kristeva, as a "subject-in-process." Sharing a desire to decenter the subject does not imply, however, that there is any tongue-and-groove fit between feminism and postmodernism. Rather the opposite seems to be the case, in that the project of redefining subjecthood has produced a tension between feminism and postmodernism that is nothing less than one of gender. Some schools of postmodern thinking contend that the feminist need to argue for female agency retains the philosophy of the phallic subject, which has been one of the chief instruments in women's oppression.[28] My own view is that a reversion to phallocracy can be averted by conceptualizing female agency as positional rather than essential, since positionality undermines the autonomous, self-determining subject by stressing the constituted character of the subject. Besides, how can we deny subjectivity altogether at the same time as we cherish self-reflection as critical tool? What I believe to be beyond controversy, however, is that the need to address what might be called the question of identity is fundamental to challenging the subject-oriented epistemology of modernity.

Enlightenment Identities

Reflections on the History
of the Science of Woman

Sylvana Tomaselli

These reflections are part of a quest for a subject, the science of woman.[1] Within the context of the long eighteenth century, they consider a very simple set of questions, namely, whether there was such a science and whether what may or may not pass for one admits of a history. Also queried is whether these questions merit being raised. To be perfectly candid, there are ready answers to these questions, but as they gain in significance from being seen within a wider perspective, what follows is a somewhat roundabout way to them.

Men and women have written about women since antiquity. One would think them a perennial subject, were it not for the fact that the topicality of women was so enhanced in some periods as to make them seem almost entirely occluded in others.[2] In the early modern age, a good deal was said by and about them in the sixteenth century and a great deal again, possibly more, during the seventeenth and eighteenth centuries.[3] Work upon work was composed about their bodies, their minds, their education or lack of it, their rights, their promiscuity, their dress and other artifices. Were they capable of friendship among themselves?[4] Did they love more or less than men? Had they more intense pleasures?[5] Greater pains? Were they witty? Truthful? Faithful? Fickle?[6] Were foreign and ancient languages beyond their grasp? Should they be allowed to own property? To read what they wished? Even novels? To have skills other than domestic ones? Were they able to rule? And if so, could they head despotic as well as more moderate regimes?[7] What of their fertility? Their longevity?[8] What were women like, and what ought they to be?

Women were considered as a unified whole, the female sex, indeed *the* sex. But they were also differentiated, according to race, culture, nationality, and class. Some were even treated as individuals with personalities and talents such as to eclipse their gender; they were sometimes used as any great authority would be: thus was Catherine Macaulay (1731–1791) cited by Helvétius and Diderot.[9]

Women were studied in different parts of the world and under different climates.[10] Much of what was written about women is to be found under various and sometimes unexpected headings: within travel literature, medical treatises, anatomical descriptions, or essays on topical subjects, such as love, marriage, happiness, population decline, luxury, and old age. Much of course was said about them in novels. There were also works specifically devoted to women, often, though by no means always, addressing them in their capacity as daughters, wives, and mothers. Some were authored by what were then or have since become famous names: Lady Mary Wortley Montagu,[11] the Baron de Montesquieu,[12] Jean-Jacques Rousseau,[13] Denis Diderot,[14] Madame de Staël,[15] Choderlos de Laclos,[16] Lord Kames,[17] William Robertson,[18] and many more. Others were written by rather less familiar, if not wholly obscure, names: Madame de Genlis,[19] Madame de Monbart,[20] Antoine-Léonard Thomas,[21] Bernardin de Saint Pierre,[22] William Alexander,[23] Elizabeth Hamilton,[24] Madame Dupin,[25] and countless more.

Can any order be brought into all this? Can some shape be given to this body of works that will afford us an understanding of the nature of the knowledge of women contained in them?

The history of women, what might be called the social history of women, is well underway. One need but mention early twentieth-century examples, such as Alice Clark's *Working Life of Women in the Seventeenth Century* and Ivy Pinchbeck's *Women Workers and the Industrial Revolution,* as well as more recent ones, such as Wendy Gibson's *Women in Seventeenth-century France,* to be convinced of this.[26] Examinations of representations of women throughout the ages are similarly well advanced.[27] What has as yet attracted less attention is the history of the study of women, the history of women once removed. How is such a history to be written? What should it be considering?

To be sure, it is misleading to speak of this area as if it were a *terra nova.* Work on the representation of women is at the very least a contribution toward a study of what knowledge there was about women, or what was presented as knowledge about them, at any given time.

There are, moreover, already established ways to classify writings about women.[28] They have, for instance, been organized according to genre. This is one of the schemes Vivien Jones resorted to in her recently published collection *Women in the Eighteenth Century: Constructions of Femininity.*[29] Faced with the daunting task of compiling an anthology under this title, her first batch of texts is grouped under the heading "conduct," bringing together excerpts from various manuals telling women how to conduct themselves. Bridget Hill's earlier *Eighteenth-century Women: An Anthology* began in the same way.[30] Treatises on education constitute another such category; both Hill and Jones have used it. Novels and other literary genres, including poetry, satire, medical treatises, and travel reports, are other examples of headings under which writings about women can be gathered so that they may yield a fair account of how women were described and what was prescribed to them.[31] One of the attractions of such a method, apart from the fact that it is relatively uncontroversial, is that a simple chronological reading of texts within a given genre will deliver its history or a good deal of it.

The next obvious way of arranging the written legacy on women is to focus on its content rather than its form, to determine what the predominant perception of women was in the period by, for instance, assessing what register was used to speak of them. Showing how women were aligned with nature has been one of the most common, and perhaps also most effective, ways of giving shape to the vast body of writings on women, not only in the seventeenth and eighteenth centuries but also before and since then.[32] An arguably no less attractive alignment of this kind is that of women and the private.[33]

There are considerable advantages to this approach; not least among them is the most evident, namely, its potential scope. It has all the strength and weakness of a well-tried procedure in the history of ideas: following the trajectory of an equation such as women and nature or women and redemption is no different from tracing the history of the idea of happiness, progress, or perfectibility.[34] More important, it can give a sense of historical context more difficult to gain from the analysis of literature by genre. Everything hangs, of course, on getting the right concept or organizing principle to begin with.

Choosing a subject matter such as "sexuality" (whether one calls it such, as Jones does to make for the second rubric of her anthology, or less anachronistically "And the Greatest of these was Chastity," as Hill does to the same end in her collection), affords, on the other hand, the

possibility of bringing together various kinds of writings while lessen-
ing the risk of presenting a one-sided view of representations of women
in a given period. For the danger of writing the history of a particular
thesis—say, that women were deemed lower than men on the chain of
beings, closer to animals, to matter, and so on—is that it almost
invariably invites histories of its anti-thesis: in this example, that they
were seen as nearer the angels, the sublime, and the spiritual. Histories that show women as identified with nature will be answered by
histories that show them as linked to culture, and so on.[35]

The solution to this is, of course, never to introduce the madonna
without also presenting the whore.[36] This is precisely what umbrella
headings such as "sexuality" or "chastity" are designed to achieve. As
with any study in the history of ideas, the difficulty is in the selection
of the category, the conceptual spindle, if you wish, around which we
can twist and wind our thoughts about what was thought of women.
The choice will not only depend on the nature of the past; it will be
made with a view to present concerns. Conduct, demeanor, virtue,
piety, charity, loyalty, courage, and valor were all notions of great
import to eighteenth-century women. Whether women submitted to
what was expected of them or not, these were some of the key terms of
the debates they engaged in. While there obviously is some overlap
between us and our *ur*-mothers, and much continuity prevails between
debates raging then and now, the current conversations about women
in the West seem to be dominated by the issues of sexuality and
language and by the discipline and practice reflecting on either or
both, namely, psychoanalysis.[37]

A cursory glance at any bookshop's women's studies shelves will
reveal rape to be one of the central categories of late twentieth-century
writing about women. Much that is interesting can be written about
rape in the eighteenth century, yet to use this subject as a point of
entry into eighteenth-century material on women is rather misguided.[38] Rape was not on any of the very lengthy intellectual, or for
that matter social, agendas of the period. Seduction was, but that
concept is in want of so much explanation now as to make it an
unlikely choice for anyone seeking a helpful analytical device. Much
the same can be said of sexuality or many another of our key conceptual
categories. Indeed, though ideas about women might have changed
remarkably little over the course of the centuries, the ways in which
such thoughts are organized, the discourses in which they occur, often
have. Determining whether men and women in times and places other
than our own did or not think along lines similar to ours already

presupposes not only what is at issue here, namely, what sieve one is to choose to sift writings about women, but a considerable acquaintance with the material. In other words, rather than constituting the most reliable points of entry into history, concepts of the kind under discussion are more likely to be what historical study yields.[39]

One stepping-stone toward women as a subject matter is that provided by the perspective of a particular science or practice, medical sciences being the best case in point.[40] It is tied to the history of representation and examines how women were described, how, to pursue the example of the medical sciences, they were seen as patients, how they were drawn in textbooks of anatomy, and how these perceptions of them affected and were affected by their treatment beyond the medical sphere.[41] Such a history often has recourse to the dichotomies (private/public, nature/culture, reason/passion, and so on) mentioned above. In the case of the medical sciences the view that women are chained to their biology has provided an Ariadne's thread that more than one historian has elected to follow.[42] This method can take one quite a long way toward an answer to the question "What kind of objects of knowledge are (or were) women?" and is to be valued as a result. What is more, if the science or practice in question is well established, then the history of that science of women is relatively straightforward, especially if, say, it is the subject of university lectures. Admittedly this is of little assistance to those interested in what was said about women in fields of knowledge before these became established disciplines. A concerted effort must also be made in this context to remember that a discipline—no matter how powerful—does not make a culture and that throughout Western history entirely opposite views about women seem to have coexisted. Moreover, much of what is thought, said, or published about women never makes the grade in any discipline, because of the gender of its authorship or readership, or because the status of women as an independent subject matter is never entirely free of controversy.

Not unrelated to this last approach is the biographical one. We can try to remember women we, and arguably others, have forgotten. This is coming to the subject of women through that of famous ones.[43] It constitutes a shift from considering women as the object of knowledge to viewing them as its makers. Though it could never in itself suffice as a way of tidying writings, let alone anything else, on and by women, there remains much to be learned about the ways in which women shaped the world as we know it.[44]

Women's self-perception through the ages also ties in with the preceding approach and can never legitimately be left out of any of the others. The relative paucity of this type of record makes this line of inquiry similarly insufficient on its own. In any case, it would, by definition, be a way of mapping out no more than half of the terrain under discussion.

We are left with what might come under the general rubric "feminism." Once again this is a chapter heading in both Bridget Hill's and Vivien Jones's anthologies. The first calls it "Women Protest," while the second owns up to the anachronism of her usage of the term. Right though Vivien Jones is about the term *feminism,* it is the best and perhaps the only approach to this much coveted object of knowledge called "women." This is not to say that none of the approaches just mentioned is worth exploring. Though some might be more attractive than others, each has made an appreciable contribution to what we know about the topic today. Moreover, they would be valuable if only because they themselves point to, or help to pinpoint, what is wanting about them. For something is going amiss in our present endeavors to recover eighteenth-century woman.[45] Compared to similar investigations about man, they seem to face us with not only a quantitative difference for which time and scholarship are the only cure, but a qualitative one as well. Most noticeable is the lack of an overall perspective on the subject at hand. That the work cannot but be piecemeal in view of the very size of the enterprise is unquestionable. What is less obvious is whether, if we continue to proceed as we are, we will ever venture beyond providing a chapter, the chapter on women, however needed, however absent, however silenced, to whatever kind of history of man happens to be *the* history of the moment. But to argue this point further, let us change tack again.

Looking back over the centuries it seems that any discourse, language, terminology, approach, technique, and so on devised to understand man has sooner or later been applied to women. Marxism, social history, psychoanalysis, to name but the more obvious, have all had their turn.[46] Something of this process was captured in a remark made in a more general context by an eighteenth-century writer on women (Thomas, one of the lesser-knowns mentioned earlier) when he said that the sexes always follow each other by imitating one another from afar.[47] If this be true, and assuming that it has always been so, then, given that the first half of the long eighteenth century witnessed the rise of the science of man, the second, let us say, must have seen the development of the science of woman.

From the 1770s onward there are a number of works about women that are self-consciously different from those revolving around the issue of the equality between the sexes that, in the sixteenth and again in the seventeenth century, had generated the last two major flurries about *the* sex.[48] That they are self-consciously different is not in itself telling of their status, for it is a feature of a good deal of writing about women, then as now, that it is justified by its novelty. Interestingly, what is claimed as new is rarely the approach or the methodology; rather it is the subject itself, that is, women, that seems forever new and forever rediscovered, as writers on women tend to think of themselves as so many knights-errant rescuing their subject from neglect. Women artists, women scientists, women in the Church, medical women, women in the guilds, women in the Middle Ages, women always lost and found until we forget them again.

The eighteenth-century texts I am referring to, however, did not claim to have saved women from historical oblivion. Well, not quite. Their authors were well acquainted with writings about women over the past centuries.[49] They wanted to distance themselves from such works for two related reasons. The first was that they believed that writings about women fell within either of two categories: they either praised or denigrated women. These eighteenth-century authors were not interested in evaluating women in this manner. They did not wish to engage in any form of comparison between the sexes. The second reason they gave for breaking with what might have been seen as their predecessors was that the latter were either poets or collectors of women. Antoine-Léonard Thomas, William Alexander, Mme Dupin, the Vicomte de Ségur, and so on were neither.[50] They sought to understand, to know, women. Their interest lay not with particular women but with the sex as a whole.

The question is, why? There are many levels at which this question can be taken. On one of them, the answer must point back to the copycat effect just mentioned. A science of man was being attempted; why not also attempt a science of woman?

On another is the explanation the Vicomte de Ségur gave in the foreword to his two-volume *Les Femmes, leur condition et leur influence dans l'ordre social, chez les différens peuples anciens et modernes* (1808). The proper study of man, he argued, consisted in the study of both the sexes. Neither should receive more attention than the other. Favoring either could only ever be justified on the assumption that, their passions, inclinations, and habits being strictly identical, both were depicted in the portrait of the one. Ségur doubted this to have been the view underlying the single-mindedness with which nearly all ancient and modern writers exalted men and ignored women. "On the contrary," he argued, "they have presented man as the being par excellence and have not deigned to preoccupy themselves with the sex they seek to subordinate to him."[51] Poets had, of course, favored women above all other themes, but their efforts had contributed little toward knowing them. "Il ne suffit pas de les peindre," Ségur argued, "il faut en écrire l'histoire" (It is not enough to paint them; one must write their history).[52] Only the writing of their history could furnish a true understanding of them.[53] This task Ségur set himself, promising to run the course of his story between the Scylla of misogyny and the Charybdis of adulation.

Popular as his work proved, Ségur was not the first to conceive of such a project, nor to think of it in those very terms. Other eighteenth-century writers had commented on the bias of existing histories. Likewise they had noted that those men who had turned to the subject of women divided themselves between their detractors and their adorers. In equally vehement introductory words, they addressed their fellow men and deplored the absence of a fair history of the sex. Like Ségur, each author presented himself as embarked on a mission never yet attempted. As Thomas, the best-known and most plagiarized writer of this kind, explained, his work was

> the history of that part of the human species which the other flatters and slanders in turn. . . . This work will be neither a panegyric, nor a satire, but a collection of observations and facts. Women will be shown as they were, as they are and as they could be.[54]

What these historians aspired to do for woman was what Rousseau, among others in the century, had done for man. Responding to the call of the Enlightenment, Rousseau had declared that "the most useful and the least advanced part of human knowledge seems to me to concern man."[55] This study he had undertaken through a theoretical history of man. Historians of woman wanted to tell her story as he had told his. They wanted to come to grips with her nature as he had unraveled his. As it was, history stood half-written, human nature half-examined; half the species was shrouded in darkness.

No one questioned whether that history was theirs to tell. Nor did the project become a contentious matter for any other reason. Whatever criticisms a work like Thomas's *Essai sur les femmes* met with, the need for a history of women was never questioned.[56] That such a history did by no means prove to be the history of man by a different name is perhaps best illustrated by the case of Rousseau himself. In writing *De L'Inégalité parmi les hommes* (1754), Rousseau had written about man and for men: "What I am about to say concerns man, and the question that I am examining tells me that I will be addressing men."[57] There is little reason not to take him literally.[58] This is not because women were left out of his critique of civilization, much less because they were painted as passive witnesses to the historical process that took man from the state of nature to commercial society, from innocence to depravity. It was rather because they were represented as being so much at one with this process as to be almost indistinguishable from it. For to the Rousseauian question as to what had happened to man that he now found himself in a corrupt society marked by gross inequality between men, part of the answer was simply *woman*. His could only be her history in a limited and rather perverse sense of the notion. Moreover, what little is extant of his history of women, undertaken at the instigation of his onetime employer Mme Dupin, tells an altogether different story, namely that of men's tyranny over women.[59] Again, if one juxtaposes Diderot's history of man and his history of woman one cannot but be struck by the radically different outlook each gives on the merit of the development of civilization.[60]

To comprehend why this is so and why Rousseau's history of man, and indeed his fragment toward a history of women, and for that matter any other Enlightenment theories belonging to either of these kinds, were so firmly grounded in the viewpoint of the sex with which they were concerned, two of the period's assumptions must be kept in mind. Ségur has already given us the first: a single history of the species would have made sense only had the sexes been identical. As they were not, two distinct histories were needed. Second, what rendered the idea of a unique history more absurd still was that the Enlightenment perceived the relationship between men and women as one of power. They conceived its dynamic to be that of a struggle for domination.

The beginning of this chapter listed, in the form of a series of questions, some of the many issues raised within writings about women. Now, it is a shortcoming of much written about women in the eighteenth century that it fails to give a sense of the spirit of investigation that attended the efforts of those who undertook to write the history of women. Questions were asked about men. Histories of the period do tend to acknowledge the genuineness of the inquiries about man's nature, mind, and body. Not so when it comes to writing about what was thought and said about women. At the most, what we are presented with are accounts of those who were for or against the legal, social, and political emancipation of women. Yet a good number of men and women wanted more than just to repeat the prejudices of their day; they wanted to do something other than defend or attack the sex: they wanted to comprehend how the condition of women had come to be what it was. Travelers' reports and the history of their own Western culture told them that the relation between the sexes admitted of a considerable degree of diversity. Lady Mary Wortley Montagu's writings, for one, showed that even within Europe the lot of aristocratic women varied considerably.[61] She was intrigued, sometimes surprised, astonished even, by the difference between woman and woman. Her preconceptions, especially about the confinement of women in the Middle East, were challenged by the evidence of her experience there. It contributed to her readers revising theirs.[62]

What is wanting in our conception of what was thought about women is that it does justice to neither the sophistication nor the intellectual ambition of what was being attempted, if not achieved. In particular, past attempts to understand the history of the relation of power between the sexes and to come to terms with the nature of its determining factors are lost.

When thinking about women, Enlightenment figures did so in the languages that they deployed to think about men. They used Montesquieu and his typology of governments to classify the data brought back by travelers. They used natural law to fill in the stages of their theoretical history and to assess rights and entitlements. They followed the outline of Rousseau's conjectural history of man. They were trying to get a true knowledge of woman off the ground. There was an Enlightenment project about woman just as there was one about man. Of course not everything that was written about women in the period fell neatly within its scope. But then again, the same holds for eighteenth-century writings about men.

Nor it is true that everything that was said of men and women in the period took the difference between the sexes—whether as grounded in biology or as the product of artifice—as its starting point. As Richard Olson has recently argued, many eighteenth-century feminist writers followed through the egalitarian implications of the psychological theories articulated in the seventeenth century.[63] Such theories of the mind and of the acquisition of knowledge showed men and women, and indeed the whole of the species, to share in a common human nature. Yet while it is undeniable that not every text about women, nor every theory that had implications for them, took difference as its subject matter, it would be mistaken to think the historical approach incompatible with what might be called the psychological one. Indeed, it would be just as absurd as thinking that investigating the origin and history of the inequality between men conflicts with believing them to be equal. What is more, many of the writers engaged in one approach were also engaged in the other. A good, though by no means unique, example is that of the Marquis de Condorcet.[64]

The answer to the question of whether there was a science of woman in the eighteenth century obviously depends on what one means by *science*. If by *science of woman* one means whatever was meant then, or has since been meant, by *science of man,* then the answer is yes. Yes, there was a science of woman that traced her history from the state of nature to that of modernity. It traced the different moments in the changes in her condition, isolated the factors responsible, and explained her distinct contribution to the progress of civilization. It showed her as the subject as well as the agent of this process. It told the history of her becoming what she was, that is, not one single creature and universal entity but the opposite, with different needs and desires depending on whether she found herself in the seraglios of the East or in the relative freedom of Europe, in ancient Greece or in the last days of the Roman Empire. It even sought to take class differences on board: the question of how the emancipation of some women had increased, or was dependent on, the continued burden of others was never far off the page.

If by *science of woman* one means a body of knowledge conceived in the shadow of the natural sciences, then the answer is also yes. This is so not only because the science of man was partly conceived in that same shadow, but because predictability, for instance, was one of the features of their enterprise most persistently highlighted by historians of women. William Alexander argued:

As strength and courage are in savage life the only means of attaining to power and distinction, so weakness and timidity are the certain paths to slavery and oppression: on this account, we shall almost constantly find women among savages condemned to every species of servile, or rather, of slavish drudgery; and shall as constantly find them emerging from this state, in the same proportion as we find the men emerging from ignorance and brutality, and approaching to knowledge and refinement; the rank, therefore, and condition, in which we find women in any country, mark out to us with the greatest precision, the exact point in the scale of civil society, to which the people of such a country have arrived; and were their history entirely silent on every other subject, and only mentioned the manner in which they treated their women, we would, from thence, be enabled to form a tolerable judgment of the barbarity, or culture of their manners.[65]

The Enlightenment envisaged a total history or science that would demonstrate the causal relation among all aspects of a given society. The science of man was that project. From its onset it sought to treat men and women as distinct subjects rather than to make man stand for both the sexes. It attempted to explore the differences between them. Given its historical sensitivity, this meant trying to discover the origin and development of the differences. A difficult task by any standard, it led to some awkwardness and imbalances, not to mention outright tensions, which might explain why, by the time Ségur came to write his history of woman, he thought the project had to be undertaken separately from any consideration of man. Indeed, he seemed to think that previous attempts had essentially failed. Consider Buffon's, for instance.

In her introduction to his *Histoire naturelle de l'homme* (1749), Michèle Duchet explains that for Buffon anthropology was the science that enabled one to think about two concepts at the same time: the unity of the species and its diversity.[66] This he undertook in two parts. First he gave a history of the individual, which traced his generation, his development and growth at different stages of life, his senses, and his anatomy. Next came the history of the species, that is, his compilation and summary of various travelers' reports, which provided a description of the various peoples of the world, with particular emphasis on their physical appearance. Woman's physiology, development, and anatomy find their places alongside a similar examination of man in the history of the individual. Women also feature as prominently, if not more so, than men in the second part of *De L'Homme*.

What does one learn about women from Buffon? That they tend to be physically weaker than men; that their bones are softer; that, after attaining a certain age, they tend to live longer; that they are shorter; that their breasts are more developed; that in different parts of the world women are shaped in this or that way; that in some nations they are more or less beautiful than women elsewhere or than their own menfolk. Most of what is written about them is comparative.

Even when one would expect clear-cut differences, an element of comparison remains. Moreover, being a woman (depending on the individual) is being more or less a man and, which is important, being a man is being more or less a woman. This is not a view peculiar to Buffon. It is true of much, if not all, of Enlightenment physiology.[67] Femininity and masculinity are matters of degree. Gender is by and large not a matter of clear-cut categories in the eighteenth century, but it is seen on a continuum. Diderot, for one, liked to emphasize how little difference there was, physically speaking, between man and woman.[68]

All this notwithstanding, woman does not meet with the same treatment as man in Buffon's *De L'Homme*. What is striking in this work is not a matter of absence or silences. It is, on the contrary, an unexpected presence. The woman Buffon wrote about was not just that of the dissecting table nor even only that reflected in the voyeuristic European gaze. She was also the woman with a past, the woman with a history of oppression by men. Not only was Buffon alert to the issue of men's treatment of women throughout the text, but in the section entitled "De L'Age viril" he went so far as to provide an account, albeit very brief, of this history of hers. He explained that whereas bodily strength had once been the guarantor of power, it had become irrelevant with the advent of polished society. Now only mind mattered. And he went on to say:

> Women are not, by a long way, as strong as men; and the greatest use or the greatest abuse that man has made of his strength is to have subjugated and often treated in a tyrannical manner that half of the human species that was made to share the pleasures and the pains of life with him. Savages force their women to work continually: it is they who cultivate the land, who perform the most onerous tasks, while the husband remains nonchalantly lying in his hammock. . . . Among civilized people, men, being the stronger, have dictated laws that always wrong women in a manner proportional to the crassness of mores; it is only in nations civilized to the point of politeness that women have obtained this equality of rank, which is nevertheless so natural and so necessary to the sweetness of society: hence it is that this politeness of manners is owed to them.[69]

Looking for the unity as well as the diversity of the species led Buffon sometimes along an anthropological path, sometimes along considerations of gender. Beyond what relative physical differences existed between them, beyond the abuse men made of their physical superiority over women, was the lack of true reciprocity, which by right ought to have prevailed between them. This initial, though unnatural and unjust, imbalance remained a fact about them, however much it became modified, even reversed. It was a story of the Fall, if you wish, but one in which man was cast as the undeniable sinner. Any study that peeled off woman from the idea of man and tried to do justice to their difference could not, in the eighteenth century, avoid what would over the course of the century assume the status of a commonplace. The history of the tyranny men had exercised over women and its gradual reversal by women with the advancement of polished society became constitutive of the knowledge about her, or of her as an object of knowledge. Whether the oppression of man by man ever became constitutive of the study of man is a matter of controversy. Not so with woman. Hence my earlier comment that feminism cannot be sidestepped; it is unavoidable, for it was integral to the study of woman from its very onset.

That the history of woman, beginning with her subjection by man and progressing through the various stages of her self-emancipation, was constitutive of knowledge about her rendered her study unwieldy within the framework of the study of man. We already touched on this point when mention was made of Rousseau's endeavors in this field. The story of woman could not but run counter to the general drift of that of man, if and when the object of the study of man was to deliver a verdict on the merit or demerit of the civilizing process and that verdict proved negative, as was the case when men such as Rousseau and Diderot stood in judgment on modernity. Given the general agreement about the dismal condition of women in the state of nature, even the critics of her status in modern European societies owned that women were among the clearest beneficiaries of the forward march of history.[70] Indeed, from their point of view, they may well have been its *only* beneficiaries.

The history of woman was easier to accommodate within the kind of enterprise Buffon was engaged in. His study of man did not overtly stand in judgment on polished society. His was a tableau in which he sought to draw the whole of the species, standing as it were side by side, nuance by nuance, shade by shade, from black to white, from short to tall, male and female. Giving woman a historical perspective and depth within such a tableau was obviously not impossible, since Buffon actually did it. Doing so did, however, bring to the surface the extent to which Buffon's anthropology was normative, the extent to which he was committed to the view that human excellence was realized in polished European society. In other words, while his work was not conceived as an evaluation of civilization, it was quite transparently critical of its negation, savagery. To have said any more than he did about the historical process that removed woman from that condition would have required, however, more than an appraisal of non-European mores. Buffon's anthropology would have had to be deployed on European culture itself. It would have entailed extending his thesis to encompass, among other things, a comparison between ancient and modern societies. Again, this was by no means theoretically impossible for Buffon. Indeed, following immediately after the passage quoted above is a comparison between their idea of beauty and ours:

> The ancients had notions of beauty that differ from ours. Small fore-heads, joint or hardly separated eyebrows, were pleasing in a woman's face; a great preference is still shown in Persia for thick and joining eyebrows.[71]

Though all but inconceivable, the pursuit of this line of inquiry would have led Buffon along a rather different path. It would have led him to produce a full-fledged history of woman of the kind Mme Dupin and men like Thomas or Ségur found wanting.

There was a science of woman in the eighteenth century. It was a French (e.g., Mme Dupin, Thomas, Diderot), Scottish (e.g., William Alexander), German (e.g., C. Meiners) affair.[72] It was a female as well as a male affair. For even if few women besides Mme Dupin and Mme de Staël actually attempted to write such a history from beginning to end, many more either worked explicitly within its overall framework, like Catherine Macaulay, or deployed parts of it, like Mrs. Hamilton in her *Popular Essays*.[73] Others cannot be fully understood except by placing their works within its context, as is true, for instance, of Mme de Graffigny's *Lettres d'une péruvienne*.[74] It does have a history, which begins most probably with Montesquieu, goes through the early works of Rousseau and those of Buffon and is taken up by a number of relatively unknown writers such as Thomas and Alexander in the 1770s, gathers momentum around the turn of the century with, among others, Ségur, Meiners, and later in the century the Goncourt brothers, and continues into the present day.[75] It may at times have dissipated into analyses of the nature of love and taken on all kinds of forms, including the history of manners, luxury, liberty, or capitalism, but its roots can be found in the eighteenth century, if not earlier.[76] It was never, as has already been acknowledged, the only study, or approach to the study, of women any more than the science of man proved to be the only study, or approach to the study, of men. The specific nature of the relationship between the science of woman discussed here and, say, Enlightenment theories of human nature and faculty psychology, biology, or even nineteenth-century gynecology is but one of the many interesting and puzzling issues this subject raises. What is clear, however, is that it would be a mistake to ignore the particular character of the intellectual enterprise that the science of woman was or attempted to be.[77]

It will not come as a surprise that on this view of things the third question, namely, whether it is worth one's while to ponder a science of woman and its history, is also to be answered with an affirmative. Without thinking of writings about women as partaking in an enterprise larger than themselves, larger than anything any of them could possibly achieve independently, we are left with a fragmentary history of women in the eighteenth century and no means by which to follow it into the present. We need every inch of the grand canvas on which the Enlightenment conceived of the subject for us to make sense of its nature then and now. Think of what would happen to our conception of the history of man in that period if we were to cease to consider the many texts about him as part of that large and formidable project, the science of man! Think of how impoverished our view would be if we did not try to study the nature of this project and gave up trying to write its history! Whatever our reservations about the methods deployed to conceive of the nature of that modern enterprise, we must own its heuristic benefits. Drawing the science of woman out of a shadow it was never intended to inhabit might just also cast a new light on man.

Gendered Knowledge, Gendered Minds: Women and Newtonianism, 1690–1760

John Mullan

All that Restlessness of Temper we are accused of, that perpetual Inclination for gadding from Place to Place;—those Vapours, those Disquiets we often feel meerly for want of some material Cause of Disquiet, would be no more, when once the Mind was employ'd in the pleasing Enquiries of Philosophy.

Eliza Haywood, *The Female Spectator* (1745)

For Eliza Haywood, "Philosophy" is a kind of cure for femininity.[1] This femininity seems to be both a masculine prejudice ("we are accused of . . .") and a universal reality ("we often feel . . ."). The woman who takes to Philosophy will conquer equally the preconceptions of men and her own worst inclinations. She will vindicate her sex—and she will escape it. Haywood is referring to the benefits of natural philosophy (what we might call "science"), benefits that are presumed to be available to educated women in general. The study of science is recommended to Haywood's readers as if it were some new womanly duty, and not a challenging or unlikely activity. In one way, the recommendation is another small piece of a social history of science: "Caught up by the excitement of the 'new science,' educated women, along with men, became an eager audience for the new ideas."[2] Haywood's advocacy fits into a story of women and science that recounts the (often frustrated) attempts of women to gain access to these new ideas.[3] But her recipe for rationality tells us something else: that the new Philosophy could be regarded as inherently suitable for women.

A social history of women's "scientific interests," such as that by Patricia Phillips, must emphasize the role of public lectures and popularizing scientific texts: "the attempt by bourgeois entrepreneurs to capture a wider female audience."[4] It must examine the struggle of particular women to educate themselves in and to study science. But there is also a rather different history, such as that initiated by Carolyn Merchant: a history of the symbolic use of women in scientific argument, and of the struggle of science—the self-vaunting "experimental philosophy"—to establish and justify itself. By the 1740s a special, "Newtonian" Philosophy had a secure status as the most powerful form of theoretical knowledge, and its availability had to be demonstrated. Women were symbolically its awed witnesses, its dutiful devotees, and—more surprisingly—its best test. In *The Spectator,* Haywood's own model of polite prose, Addison declared, "I shall be ambitious to have it said of me, that I have brought Philosophy out of Closets and Libraries, Schools and Colleges, to dwell in Clubs and Assemblies, at Tea-Tables, and in Coffee-Houses."[5] He was not thinking of natural philosophy in particular; he was, however, indicating not only that worthwhile knowledge should be made available to his genteel readers, but that such availability was the measure of its worth. Newtonianism, too, is validated by being brought out of closets, and the explanation of it to women confirms its triumph. This essay will be concerned with the imagining of women as the symbolic agents of its popularization.

By *Philosophy* Haywood means a knowledge accessible to those without specialist training or experimental resources. Philosophy is what extends "our Speculations . . . to the greatest and most tremendous Objects," or makes it possible "to pry into the smallest Works of the Creation." Certainly it relies on those fashionable implements, telescopes and microscopes; but it is the name not so much of a body of theoretical knowledge as of an activity at once sublime and ordinary. "PHILOSOPHY is . . . the Toil which can never tire the Person engag'd in it." In Haywood's formulation, indeed, it sounds something like a moral duty. The Female Spectator is replying to a supposed letter from Cleora, which has thanked her for "endeavouring to improve the Minds and Manners of our unthinking Sex." This work of improvement—described as an "Act of Charity"—is all the more important for this (no doubt imaginary) correspondent because women are so frequently barred from "those Sciences which the Men engross to themselves." It is a plea for "the Education of . . . Females." The Female Spectator concurs, unsurprisingly, and remarks that, without "Learning," women become "loitering, lolloping, idle Creatures." But she makes this a special case of what, by the 1740s, is a conventional argument for that female learning.

> Knowledge is a light Burthen. . . . But of all Kinds of Learning the Study of Philosophy is certainly the most pleasant and profitable:—It

corrects all the vicious Humours of the Mind, and inspires the noblest Virtues. . . . [T]he more we arrive at a Proficiency in it, the more happy and the more worthy we are.

Those who have "the Female Part of their Family at Heart" would be wise "to instruct them early in some of the most necessary Rudiments of Philosophy:—All those little Follies now ascrib'd to us, and which, indeed, we but too much incur the Censure of, would then vanish, and the Dignity of Human Nature shine forth in us." The polite reader is told that acquaintance with natural philosophy will make her morally better and raise her from the condition of femininity.[6]

In the earlier *Essays* of Lady Mary Chudleigh, the same ideal is articulated in a breathier rhetoric of self-exhortation (the imagined female readers addressed with sentences that frequently begin "Let us . . .").

Physicks . . . will show us Nature, as she variously displays her self, as she manifests her self in material Objects . . . from the glorious Orbs which roll over our Heads, to the minutest Insect that crawls under our Feet; discover to us Beauties which Art can never imitate, and which common Spectators do not observe.

This comes from an essay, entitled "Of Knowledge," that shares Haywood's ambivalence about the capacities of women. It encourages its female readers to believe that "all useful *Knowledge*" is accessible, but it is also always on the point of admonishing them for the feminine follies that will exclude them from knowledge. Readers must be deaf to "such as can talk of nothing but what is not worth the Knowing, of the little mean concerns of the Animal Life, their Domestick Affairs, . . . the various Efforts of their Passions, the Triumphs of their Vanity, and the numerous Instances of their Folly." Distracting and distracted, women of this type are everywhere. Perhaps only a minority can turn away from "Romances and Trifles of that Nature" for a better contemplation: "to survey all those solid Globes, which swim in the fluid *Aether*, see vast Masses of fiery Matter whirl'd round their *Axis* with an amazing, an inconceivable Rapidity."[7]

Evidently, the seeing and surveying talked of here are peculiarly metaphorical. They are in the mind's eye of those with an understanding beyond that of "common Spectators." If only the exceptional woman seeks some understanding of natural philosophy, and in particular of celestial mechanics, that is but evidence of the special value, and the uplifting character, of that knowledge. In Benjamin Martin's *The Young Gentleman and Lady's Philosophy,* one of the texts dedicated to popularizing Newtonian physics that I will discuss later, the female character in the dialogue, Euphrosyne, tells her brother (who is also her instructor) that she has been ridiculed for her interest in natural philosophy. "It is a Pity that any, even of our Sex, should so far betray their Want of Prudence as to ridicule a philosophical Disposition in others, only, for Want of a Taste for the Science themselves," he observes. It is as if it is necessary to regret what he calls "the inconsiderate Part of Mankind" in order to establish the privilege of Philosophical knowledge. (And here a female character is particularly useful to Martin, for if a woman can apply herself to grasping Philosophy, surely any gentleman should be able to do so.) "Till very lately, Philosophy has not been the Subject of Conversation, and it is but rarely so now."[8] But making some appreciation of Philosophy into a social qualification to rank with the other arts of conversation is just the ambition of these writers. In a culture that so valued taste, a "Want of a Taste for the Science" is to be seen as a major failing.

So, when Richard Steele's *The Ladies Library,* an anthology of didactic passages for female readers arranged by topic, discusses the benefits of scientific knowledge to women, it is in the section on modesty. For modesty is "directly opposite to whatever is bold and indecent, and in an especial manner to Curiosity," and any feminine tendency to curiosity is best turned to the "Wonders" of "Nature." Inquiries into nature are "useful and entertaining to all those whose curious Minds are always in Action, and for want of nobler Objects descend to Scandel and Impertinence." Again, natural philosophy will save women from themselves. Its power to do so is registered by the text's exclamations on the scale and organization of a universe comprehended by Newtonian mechanics: "Oh Miracle! Oh Prodigy!"[17] And there can be no doubt as to the consequence of this comprehension: "The Searches of curious and humble Minds into Nature will more and more confirm him in holy Admiration of the Greatness and Goodness of God. There are no Minds so weak as to be Incapable of these Meditations."[9]

Here is an occasion when the slip to the masculine pronoun is telling. For it is a point at which the text forgets that it is written for women, and instead finds itself using a woman's (imagined) understanding as a test of the potency and clarity of a new kind of knowledge. Throughout texts written in the early eighteenth century to make Philosophy available to women, this very availability is treated as a validation of the new science. The art of explaining Philosophy to a woman is a demonstration of its truth. This is one of the reasons why the dialogue form is popular. The best-known example is probably Elizabeth Carter's translation of Algarotti's *Sir Isaac Newton's Philosophy Explain'd for the Use of the Ladies* (1739), which, like Benjamin Martin's work, uses a female character to catch the lucidity and the awesomeness of "Newton's Philosophy." Algarotti has produced "a complete Treatise of the *Newtonian* philosophy" designed to be "lively" and engage his readers as would "a Composition for the Theatre."[10] The Marchioness of E listens to the narrator's account of the new knowledge, asking appropriate questions, and the limited drama is in her compliant delight and amazement at the answers that she receives. A knowledge intended to displace other theories (and this book is full of barbs against Descartes) needs to show the pleasure of complete conviction.

So the Marchioness begins "extremely desirous of becoming a *Newtonian,*" and she is told at the end of her exhaustive course of instruction, "The Light of *Newtonianism* has dissipated the *Cartesian* Phantoms which deluded your Sight. You are now really a *Newtonian.*" In between, she has been brought to admire and celebrate the "Spirit of Observation" and "the Study of Experiments," dispelling "ill-grounded Fears," "Ignes fatui," "Superstition," and "the Marvellous." In particular, she has been given an "Exposition of the Newtonian universal Principle of Attraction" and shown its effects. "Light and Truth itself address you in the Language of Sir *Isaac Newton,*" she is told. She replies, "Let it dissipate any Remains of Darkness, that may still obscure my Mind, and conduct me into this new World of Philosophy." Her delighted conviction is the new truth in operation. Because, as a woman, she is intellectually ingenuous, she is the best witness of this truth. The dialogue form allows her to put it archly: "I perceive . . . that there is nothing secret to Philosophy; we may hide ourselves from Men, but not from Philosophers." There is no resisting the knowledge that she now has. In his conclusion, the narrator refers to her as his "fine Conquest" and almost makes explicit the buried rhetoric of seduction: "If I could give a just Description of my fair Disciple, my Book would never want Readers, nor true Philosophy a numerous Train of Proselytes."[11] It should, in the end, be impossible to say no.

In Martin's *Young Gentleman and Lady's Philosophy,* too, a woman's ignorance is useful in the celebration of Newtonian science. The male character, Cleonicus, tells his sister that her inquisitiveness is virtuous.

> Philosophy is the darling Science of every Man of Sense, and is a
> peculiar Grace in the Fair Sex; and depend on it, Sister, it is now
> growing into a Fashion for the Ladies to study Philosophy; and I am
> very glad to see a Sister of mine so well inclined to promote a Thing so
> laudable and honourable to her Sex.

Her anxieties about the obscurity of "that Science," stated in the book's first dialogue, are met by his assurance that "Abstrusities" either are irrelevant or "may be explained in a more easy and familiar Manner by Experiments. Fear not, *Euphrosyne,* the greatest and most delightful Part of this Science is within the Ladies Comprehension."[12]

This is, in effect, a reassurance to all his readers. The attentive woman allows the text to show that Philosophy rests on universally intelligible principles. It is less, indeed, that Euphrosyne depends on Cleonicus for knowledge, and more that he depends on her for the appropriate questions. If she is ignorant and modest she can hardly ask the wrong question, which only the misinstructed could supply. Natural-philosophical explanation is thus at its most comfortable when confronted by naive ignorance (fearing only skepticism and atheism). In Martin's text, it is precisely because "useful Science is of neither *Sex,* or any Party" that women can be converted to it. Cleonicus tells his sister, "I expect to see you proselyted to this, not more modish than true Philosophy, before we leave the Subject. I can tell you, Sir *Isaac* has no small Party among the Principal of the *Fair Sex.*" Dialogue allows the doctrine to be liberal and condescending at the same time; Cleonicus can even stoop to correct his sister's feminine desire to gain only "such a Competency of Knowledge as is fit for a *Woman.*" A woman's "Senses," says Martin in his introduction, are "formed as accurately" as a man's, and "therefore these philosophical Subjects must be, in this Way, equally intelligible to both; consequently the LADIES may be admitted to the Pleasure and Advantage of these Speculations as well as Gentlemen." A woman who can rise above what Cleonicus calls "this *Woman-hood* of yours" can reach to the modest, awesome facts of the new Philosophy.[13]

Martin himself made a living encouraging this ambition. He has Cleonicus complain that Philosophy is not taught in schools but must be got either from books or from those "who sometimes read Lectures on that Subject."[14] Martin was one of those lecturers—one of the several apostles of Newtonianism whose audiences routinely included women.[15] "Knowledge," as he wrote in 1743, "is now become a fashionable thing, and philosophy is the science *a la mode.*"[16] One of the pioneers of this fashion was John Harris, who published his *Astronomical Dialogues between a Gentleman and a Lady* in 1719. His female character, Lady M, has all the readiness for instruction that these lecturers symbolized in the person of an inquiring "lady" (perfectly cultured, as well as unknowing). She also has that inclination to conquer femininity that runs through most of the texts that I am discussing, wryly telling her "gentleman" instructor, "You have Philosophised me out of many a fair Pleasure already; Censure, Satyr and Gossiping are almost gone." "Philosophical" explanation, she tells him, can "get rid of many Fears and Terrors, too incident to our Sex" (she is particularly reassured to find that "The *Affair of Comets*" is "accountable by Mathematical Calculation").[17]

Yet, as in Martin's and Algarotti's texts, the woman validates Newtonianism even while it ennobles her. Harris's dedication indicates how this works:

> *I don't perplex my* Fair Astronomer *with any thing but the* true System of the World: *I mislead her by no Notions of* Chrystalline Heavens, *or* Solid Orbs: *I embarrass her with no clumsy* Epicycles, *or imaginary and indeed impossible* Vortices: *But I shew her at first the Celestial World just as it is; and teach her no* Hypotheses, *which, like some other things taught at Places of great Names, must be* unlearned *again, before we can gain* True Science.

Having less to unlearn, a woman is a better auditor than many men. Her immediate and grateful understanding of what even natural philosophers have only recently comprehended sanctions Modern knowledge:

> I can't help reflecting upon the *Arrogance,* as well as Ignorance, of the Ancients, in supposing *their* Knowledge to be the Bounds of all things; and glad I am that *we* know something which *they* did not. . . . I will . . . thank God that I am a *Modern,* and alive now.

Harris may think this, but it is his female character who says it for him. By her comprehension, the ancients and the Cartesians are routed. It is because *"Newtonian Physicks, or Natural Philosophy,"* is radically distinct from older forms of learning that it might be made "intelligible to any common Capacity and inquisitive Genius."[18] Such intelligibility is not just an ideal; it is test and proof of Philosophy.

"We must render the various Arts and Sciences as easy of Access, or the Pathways to knowledge as direct and plain, as possible," writes Martin.[19] Sometimes, addressing an explanation to a woman seems but a way of signifying the accessibility of that explanation. Jasper Charlton's *The Ladies Astronomy* (1735), for example, explicitly states that this address signifies an avoidance of "Mystery" and that his work is actually written for "the Publick in general."[20] When Martin's *Euphrosyne* is shown "Experiments on the Air-Pump" in the final dialogue of *The Young Gentleman and Lady's Philosophy,* she becomes a representative observer. Her observations are ingenuous and therefore trustworthy, guaranteeing the integrity of experiment. She can confirm the experimental philosopher's performance because of her lack of knowledge or prejudice, and she does so on behalf of readers of either sex.

Some who popularize or recommend natural philosophy do, however, presume that the understanding of women is inherently different from (and inferior to) the understanding of men. It now seems, indeed, ironical that Algarotti's *Il Newtonianismo per le dame* should have been translated by a woman of such formidable learning as Elizabeth Carter when it begins by declaring, "I have endeavoured to set Truth, accompanied with all that is necessary to demonstrate it, in a pleasing Light, and to render it agreeable to that Sex, which had rather *perceive* than *understand.*" In a manner both cordial and patronizing, the author makes clear his belief, common enough at the time, that women are not usually capable of abstraction from particulars: "Lines and mathematical Figures are entirely excluded, as they would have given these Discourses too Scientific an Air, and appeared formidable to those, who to be instructed must be pleased."[21] Even this text finds certain combinations of "ladies" and Philosophy incongruous.

It is predictable, then, that incongruity is the proferred amusement of eighteenth-century satires on female learning in general, and women's interest in science in particular.

> Some Nymphs prefer *Astronomy* to *Love;*
> Elope from mortal men, and range above.[22]

This preference was apparently sufficiently topical to command a section of that part of Edward Young's *Love of Fame* (1727) "On Women." His female enthusiast substitutes well-known Newtonian lecturers for other consorts:

> Of *Desaguliers* she bespeaks fresh air,
> And *Whiston* has *engagements* with the fair.

The Newtonian woman is a contradiction in terms, and everywhere the traditional satirist can find incongruities:

> What vain experiments *Sophronia* tries!
> 'Tis not in air-pumps the gay Colonel dies.
> But though today this rage of science reigns,
> (O fickle sex!) soon end her learned pains.
> Lo! *Pug* from *Jupiter* her heart has got,
> Turns out the stars, and *Newton* is a sot.

As in Pope's later *Epistle to a Lady,* the poet's couplets work at turning a woman's activity into an oxymoron. (And as also with Pope, the couplets are then used to represent the poem's "good woman" as a miraculous reconciler of normally warring opposites.)

Evidently, the very word *Philosophy* could seem ludicrous to some, when put in the minds or mouths of women—just as *The Spectator* asked for any easy laugh merely by listing Newton's *Works* among the contents of the library belonging to the affected Leonora.[23] In Thomas Wright's play *The Female Vertuoso's* (1693), the sense of Philosophy as what one character defines as "a Stoical and Undaunted Mind" is invoked to show how peculiarly unphilosophical women are likely to be. Lady Meanwell is an enthusiast for scientific projects, but, as her "honest" husband puts it, she "makes indeed a High Boast of her Philosophy, but she is not a bit the less Cholerick for it. . . . [S]he is still Woman all over."[24] In this play, women aspire to Philosophy but remain slaves to their passions: indeed, any female interest in science is construed as but a strange and helpless passion. As the "gentleman" who is the author of *Man Superior to Woman* (1743) puts it, "A severer Imprecation cou'd scarce be utter'd against the lovely Sex, than to wish them Science-mad." Women are most of all excluded from Philosophy: "Every Branch of that is built upon Reason, and Reason they have nothing to do with."[25]

Man Superior to Woman was produced in response to *Woman Not Inferior to Man: or, A Short and Modest Vindication of the Natural Right of the Fair-Sex to a Perfect Equality of Power, Dignity, and Esteem, with the Men. By Sophia, a Person of Quality* (1739), and was in its turn answered by *Woman's Superior Excellence over Man.* The three texts were published together in a single volume in 1743, as if they represented entertaining debating positions, rather than the deeply held beliefs of particular authors. Yet, even if we cannot quite trust the tone of these texts, they do give an idea of what arguments about women's relations to the new

Philosophy were available. *Woman's Superior Excellence over Man* finds at the root of natural philosophy an empiricism available to all: "There is nothing more wanting than sensation, reflection and attention in observing the different appearances of nature, to discourse on their effects." Only "mannish learning . . . takes the disposition of different persons to different sciences for an effect of natural temperament, when in reality it is more often the casual effect of necessity, chance, or education." In this argument, Newtonian astronomy offers a paradigm of universal and accessible knowledge: "Any one will be capable of remarking that the luminous bodies in the heavens are of an igneous nature . . . and to judge of their motion and courses, there needs no more than comparatively to consider their different and successive appearances by the help of telescopes." Such science is open to women in a way that older kinds of learning have not been: "The mind is always in action, and she who has once observed the main springs of nature, and knows how it proceeds in one thing, may without much drudgery, discover its manner of operating in another."[26]

However, those works that purport to open a Newtonian universe to women do not imagine such an unflustered and systematic scrutiny of nature. Women are invited to gaze on nature, but they must do so with rapture as well as with understanding. They are most likely to feel (and to be morally improved by) what Lady M in Harris's *Astronomical Dialogues* calls "the Rapturous Pleasures of Science."[27] Amazement is an important component of Newtonianism (and perhaps most familiar in the exclamations of James Thomson's poem "To the Memory of Sir Isaac Newton"—the celebration of what it calls an "amazing mind").[28] Benjamin Martin's *Panegyrick on the Newtonian Philosophy,* published ten years before his *Young Gentleman and Lady's Philosophy,* catches nicely, if confusingly, the sense of an understanding at once satisfied and overwhelmed by a new kind of knowledge: "PHILOSO-PHY . . . fills our Minds with sublime and august Ideas; Ideas strange and incredible to the uninstructed unphilosophic Mind." It is as if the true Newtonian feels amazement on behalf of all those who remain uncomprehending. The experience is given as an ideological necessity, for the Philosopher must, on his observation of the heavenly "System," acquire "a most sublime and august Idea of the Works of creating Power and Wisdom, highly worthy of the divine Author."[29] In Thomson's poem, such "Power and Wisdom" seem entirely Newton's; in the "official" Newtonian version, of course, Philosophy reveals the true scale of God's activity.

"The Friends of Philosophy are the Friends of Mankind," writes

Martin in the preface to his *Panegyrick*.[30] This explicitly addresses the "Gentlemen and Ladies" who have subscribed to his lectures, and who are treated as if they are exceptional individuals who recognize the truth of his motto: "Felix qui potuit Rerum cognoscere Causas" (happy the person who can know the [mechanical] causes of things). "While others trifle away their time in low, sensual and unworthy Amusements, you have the Happiness of a rational Curiosity, and are capable of the noblest Methods of improving it." On the frontispiece of his *Young Gentleman and Lady's Philosophy,* a man points a woman to the starry heavens, which is where those possessed of "rational Curiosity" gaze for validation of the new Philosophy. He also gestures at what is guaranteed to overwhelm his favored "lady." When Cleonicus has given his sister an account of comets, he asks, "What think you of that?"; as a woman, she is suitably amazed: "Think! what should a Woman pretend to think of such Matters, as I believe I may venture to say, surpasses the most philosophical Heads."[31] Feminine exclamation records the power of Newtonian explanation.

Harris's dialogues make use of the same enraptured female character. Having had the nature of the sun and the stars explained to her, Lady M exclaims that the notion of stars as "Suns to some *other Systems* of Planets" excites "a glorious Idea . . . of the Almighty Power!" She claims to be stunned by God's creation but appears just as impressed by the scope of the explanation that she is hearing. Such dialogue allows popularized natural philosophy a double claim to truth: through the male character, it confidently reduces all that can be observed to Philosophical principles; through the female character, it pauses in awe before the immense patterns that those principles reveal. This dialogue is how Philosophy justifies itself. "They who contemplate Nature, my *Euphrosyne,* always find their Admiration and Pleasure encreasing with their Knowledge": such is Cleonicus's assurance in Martin's *Young Gentleman and Lady's Philosophy.* His "lady" is a source of ideologically necessary "Admiration and Pleasure," as well as a ready receptacle for knowledge.[32] No doubt a man performing public lectures "in which the Properties, Affections, and Phaenomena of Natural Bodies, hitherto discover'd, Are exhibited and explain'd on the Principles of the Newtonian Philosophy" needed to persuade readers of the delights they might purchase from him.[33] But the promise of delight is not just merchandising; it is integral to Newtonianism.

This is why Newtonians need, and themselves dabble in, poetry. John Theophilus Desaguliers and Benjamin Martin, lecturers in natural philosophy with no other pretensions to poetic achievement, both take to verse to celebrate Newtonianism—as if what Desaguliers's poem calls "The Newtonian System of the World" is enough to tug even a Philosopher away from prose. Henry Pemberton's *A View of Isaac Newton's Philosophy* (1728) is prefaced by "A Poem on Sir Isaac Newton" (written by Richard Glover, it is the poem that declares that "NEWTON demands the muse"). The various explanatory dialogues of Harris, Martin, and Algarotti are punctuated by mottoes and descriptions taken from poetry. For poetry, like women, can exclaim in wonderment, under the pressure of all that the new Philosophy reveals. So Martin's dialogue is prefaced by "On the Usefulness of Natural Philosophy. A Poem," describing how "*Man . . . Thro'* Nature *takes a philosophic View,/ While Wonders, rais'd on Wonders, strike his Eyes!*" Martin includes his own panegyric to "Gravity," with regulation exclamation marks, and treats science as a feminine deity under whose kind influence all will prosper:

> *All hail* PHILOSOPHY! *Celestial Fair!*
> *Sent from above, replete with ev'ry Good,*
> *T'improve each striving Faculty within,*
> *To mend our Morals, and refine the Heart.*[34]

In *The Seasons,* James Thomson—above all a poet of exclamation—had called on "serene Philosophy" as "Effusive source of evidence and truth!"[35] Effusiveness is just the rhetoric of the poetry deployed in justification of that Philosophy and is proof of its comprehensiveness, its clarity—and its compatibility with proper religion.

John Millburn writes that, in his dialogue, Martin "did his utmost . . . to lighten the scientific text with liberal doses of poetry, no doubt hoping that the market for the *Magazine* [of which this text was but a part] would thereby be increased."[36] Perhaps these doses (which included, indeed, many passages from Thomson's *Seasons*) did render his text more palatable to female readers, in the same way that they are shown to translate celestial mechanics for the benefit of Euphrosyne. Perhaps Martin does imagine curious "ladies" reacting as Euphrosyne does to an account of the seasonal variations: "Their Nature explained by the Orrery, and their Properties and Qualities as finely described by the Poets, give me perfect Ideas thereof."[37] But the marriage of poetry to natural philosophy is common enough (and strained enough) to suggest something more than a sugaring of the pill of scientific knowledge. For Newtonian texts frequently propose a natural affinity of poetry and Philosophy.

One explanation is offerered by Cleonicus in *The Young Gentleman and Lady's Philosophy* : "The great Works and Scenes of Nature, you'll find, are the most agreeable Themes of the Muses."[38] He echoes Lady M in John Harris's *Astronomical Dialogues,* who claims to find in all the information about planetary bodies that she is given "a rich Fund of Images . . . to embellish our Poetry."[39] This new knowledge demands the muse not merely to turn it into lyrical awe, but also to show that it is directly comparable with what poets have always thought and observed. So, while Martin's dialogue is full of passages from avowedly Newtonian eighteenth-century poems like Henry Baker's *The Universe* and Moses Browne's *Essay on the Universe,* it relies equally on Ovid and Dryden. And Algarotti's *Sir Isaac Newton's Philosophy Explain'd,* which frequently works from the poetry that its "lady" already knows to the explanatory Philosophy that she must attain, has no reservations about using Pope—arguably an anti-Newtonian poet. As her instructor takes her from poetry to Philosophy, he remarks that Pope himself "cannot be offended at my leaving him for a Philosopher, and such a Philosopher as Sir *Isaac Newton.*"[40] The poet who envisioned a triumph of dullness in which

> *Philosophy,* that lean'd on Heav'n before,
> Shrinks to her second cause, and is no more

might not have agreed.[41]

Poetry, in these texts, is what women know. It provides the data of awed yet accurate observation which is to be turned into knowledge by Newtonian Philosophy and its agents, the lecturers. The poetry of proper wonderment records the aspiration to comprehend nature, the first requirement for a Newtonian convert. Consistently, as in my opening example from Haywood's *Female Spectator,* this aspiration is best spoken for by a woman—untrammeled by older kinds of learning, and yet eager to transcend her femininity. This is why Elizabeth Tollet, one of the many commemorators in verse of Isaac Newton ("Immortal and secure thy Name remains,/ Which scarce the habitable World contains"), provides her Georgian readers with a translation of "The Praise of Astronomy, from the first Book of OVID's Fusti."[42] The early astronomers were the first "to leave behind/ The Crimes and Pleasures that debase Mankind"; they transcended law, war, and ambition—but also "mean Desire" and any interest in merely cosmetic beauty: " 'Tis thus that Science can the Heav'ns obtain." A (much

worse) male poet of the period, Henry Jones, celebrates the superiority
of those drawn by public lectures to Newtonian mechanics more conde-
scendingly and (inadvertently) more ludicrously:

> Thrice happy few who wisely here attend
> The Voice of Science, and her Cause befriend,
> Let others, heedless of their youthful Prime,
> Squander on empty Toys their fleeting Time;
> 'Tis yours with Reason's searching Eye to view
> Great Nature's Laws, and trace her winding Clue.[43]

Such ambition can, of course, be challenging as well as compliant. Perhaps following the lead of *The Female Spectator,* Tollet takes the
ancient Egytian astronomer Hypatia as the symbol of a woman's ambition "the Mind to raise,/ To follow Nature in her winding Ways."[44]
Haywood had referred to this fabled "Philosopher" as a precedent for
the "great Perfection" in "this Science" (i.e., natural philosophy) that
women could reach.[45] Tollet's "Hypatia" depicts knowledge of nature
as unmysterious enough to be available to women, and therefore as
energetically guarded by men. Women remain untutored

> That haughty Man, unrival'd and alone,
> May boast the World of Science all his own:
> As barb'rous Tyrants, to secure their Sway,
> Conclude that Ignorance will best obey.[46]

The poem goes through the kinds of knowledge that are denied to
women, with all their variously desirable effects, beginning with
moral and political wisdom, and proceeding via mathematics to scientific knowledge. It is to this that the poem most aspires—although it
also manages to comprehend most of what is officially beyond it: from
geology to microscopy to the Newtonian universe. The female astronomer escapes all limitations in her observations of the heavenly bodies:
"Yet, as she may, her Forces she explores,/ And far above the Orb
sublunar soars."[47]
    Perhaps in order to transcend any topical controversy, Tollet's
poem is put into the mouth of an ancient Egytian. However, this
produces an embarrassment that returns us to the very meaning of
Newtonianism, and of its need to recruit women (even if only in
fiction) to its cause.

Whether that Spirit which o'er all presides
Infus'd through all its equal Motions guides,
Or from the whole distinct, himself unseen,
Conducts and regulates the vast Machine,
Let Heav'n decide.[48]

Such lines apparently require Tollet to add an endnote, explaining awkwardly that such "Doubts," which might "be thought exceptionable," belong only with "the Character of an *Heathen* and a *Platonist.*" For, in the age in which Tollet writes, the new mechanical Philosophy is sanctioned exactly by the sense and certainty that it gives to Christianity. Indeed, she herself includes in her collection a poem, "On the Thunder-Storm, June 1726. In Allusion to Horace," specifically directed against any who would believe that an explanation of thunder from "Causes natural" can be complete to itself: "Mistaken Fools! 'twas He assign'd to all/ That universal Law we Nature call."[49] God is "the great Geometer," and all properly sustained Philosophy leads— without "Doubts"—to him.[50]

Women are therefore employed by writers or appealed to by lecturers as ingenuous witnesses to the religious probity of Newtonian Philosophy. Popularizations of science in the eighteenth century are full of assurances that the new mechanical Philosophy improves its devotees, in the words of the periodical *The Ladies Diary,* "by giving us a clear and extensive Knowledge of the System of the World, which . . . creates in us the most profound Reverence of the wise Creator."[51] If women are taught about science, it is that they might know it to be no friend to skepticism, materialism, or infidelity. But all the assurances and pronouncements to this effect seem to tell us of anxiety. We might take for a definition of Newtonianism the subtitle of Benjamin Martin's *A Panegyrick on the Newtonian Philosophy:* "Shewing the Nature and Dignity of the Science, and Its Absolute Necessity to the Perfection of Human Nature; the Improvement of Arts and Sciences, the Promotion of true Religion, the Increase of Wealth and Honour, and the Completion of Human Felicity." Newtonianism was the impulse to "shew" all this. Yet, in the matter of "true Religion," Newtonians did not necessarily hold to the same beliefs: Martin himself, like James Thomson, was what we might call a deist;[52] the Newtonians who determined religious orthodoxy and whose arguments have been so brilliantly charted by Margaret Jacob were Anglicans;[53] William Whiston, one of the best-known Newtonian lecturers, was publicly what Newton himself was privately—an Arian, opposed to the doctrine of the trinity.[54]

So when Martin's *Panegyrick* concludes with a poem "On the Anti-Newtonians; or, Pseudo-Philosophers of the Age," he can be read as externalizing dissent and heterodoxy that would otherwise be internal to Newtonianism. The religious as well as practical "Usefulness of Natural Philosophy" is what licenses the new knowledge. Attacking supposed atheism and skepticism is a necessary antidote to doubt. Elizabeth Carter, translator of *Sir Isaac Newton's Philosophy Explain'd for the Use of the Ladies,* is representative in directing against "stupid atheists" her description of how only God can have "taught the new-born planets where to roll:/ With wise direction curv'd their steady course,/ Imprest the central and projectile force."[55] It is not clear who or where these "stupid atheists" might have been. They are the useful Other for those who would be reassured by Cleonicus's instruction of his sister in Martin's dialogue:

> Our Principles and Notions of Religion are much more correct and rational than they were formerly; and to what is this owing, my *Euphrosyne?* To our having a more correct and rational Philosophy: you will find it a never-failing Maxim, that the better you understand *Philosophy,* the better you will understand *Religion.*[56]

Women listen to doubts dispelled and skeptics fended off. Newtonianism seeks, or shows itself seeking, "the ladies" because they are the untutored auditors who could endorse the new Philosophy by being enabled to comprehend it. In this chapter of the history of science, "the ladies" are symbolic as well as actual agents.

Reproductive Identities

The Male Scientist, Man-Midwife, and Female Monster: Appropriation and Transmutation in *Frankenstein*

Marie Mulvey Roberts

Acknowledging the textuality of scientific discourse entails scrutinizing our understanding of the relationship between literature and science, particularly with respect to the degree to which literary metaphors can be regarded as constitutive of science rather than merely exegetical. Constitutive metaphors have the power to "disseminate" meanings within and beyond the parameters of science and in so doing can enable us to understand the dynamics of scientific and social change. Mary Shelley's *Frankenstein* (1818) allegorizes the way in which science is not always in control of its metaphors by reminding us that men can lose control of the monsters they themselves create. At the same time, the *Frankenstein* creation may be seen as a trope for the monstrosities produced by the female imagination; such monstrosities are shaped by patriarchal anxieties surrounding the woman writer who has shifted her creativity from the exclusively biological to the cerebral. Not surprisingly, male Romantic artists and scientists who appropriated the female experience of pregnancy and birth through metaphoric, or what could more generally be described as tropological, language encountered no such deep-seated concerns. While women were marginalized and excluded from male-dominated areas of science, medicine, and literature, men enjoyed the advantages of a dynamic and dialectical interplay between that which had been culturally programmed as masculine and that which had been constructed as feminine primarily through their appropriation of the female mind and body.[1]

Of these processes of feminization in the arts and sciences, Mary Shelley must have been aware. Indeed the prototype of the male scientist as sole procreator and midwife is Victor Frankenstein, who, by creating a being without a female, gave birth to a monstrosity—as well as to an image that has had an enduring impact on Western culture. The most modern manifestation of this creation was brought about by the scientists who developed the atomic bomb at Los Alamos from 1943 to 1945. When they went to the Nevada desert to witness the first nuclear blast, they were described by their wives, who were at a safe distance, as about "to midwife the birth of the monster."[2] This was "Oppenheimer's Baby," the scientist's brainchild whose sibling was the aptly named "Little Fat Boy." Such metaphoric language is encoded in the message that General Groves sent to Secretary of War Henry Stimpson: "Doctor has just returned most enthusiastic and confident that the little boy is as husky as his big brother. The light in his eyes is discernible from here to Highhold and I could hear his screams from here to my farm."[3] Three weeks laters this secret message was dramatically decoded for the entire world to witness. The birth of the Nuclear Age was articulated in the rhetoric of paternity, maternal care, and familial imagery, which served to camouflage the reality of death and mass destruction that it heralded. This conflation between reproduction and production resulted in fathering the unthinkable.[4] Mary Shelley's portrayal of Victor Frankenstein as the mad scientist and reclusive creative genius, as male-midwife and mother, may be seen as her reply to the way in which reproductive discourses were used against women in order to prevent them from entering their own narratives.

Frankenstein can be read as a means of writing woman back into her plot through a creative incursion into the masculine realm of production. The apparent paradox involved in Mary Shelley's choosing to enter the realm of production via a birth (re/productive) narrative is rapidly dispelled when we consider that she wrote *Frankenstein* at a time when women were gradually begin denied control over their own reproduction processes by male medical professionals, who in effect conflated reproduction with production. Mary Shelley's real-life birth narrative constitutes a sorry incident in the troubled history of male medical intervention in reproduction, yet it also acts as a point of departure into a reading of the text that can illuminate the kinetics of reproductive identities and appropriations. For this reason it is instructive to remind ourselves of the medical procedures surrounding the death of Mary Shelley's mother, Mary Wollstonecraft, who contracted puerperal fever in spite of, or even perhaps because of, the interventions of a male midwife.[5] Whether the outcome might have been otherwise, these circumstances are an eloquent indictment of the male appropriation of a traditionally female profession.

From the seventeenth century onward, the shift from female mid-wifery as folk practice to obstetrics as a medical science succeeded in pushing women out to the margins of a profession that they had always dominated. Generations of women's accumulated experience was dis-credited as perpetuating ignorant and unscientific practices, even though in many quarters parturition continued to be regarded as a natural rather than morbid process. Male scientific authority, as it be-came increasingly professionalized, represented the midwives who op-posed the intrusion of male midwives as impeding what they saw as medical progress. The medicalization of childbirth made way for the male accoucheur. There is evidence that the advent of the male midwife actuallly increased the mortality rate in the short term.[6] Instead of trusting to Dame Nature and Mother Midnight, as did the traditional female midwife, the male practitioner, armed with forceps and theory, was ready to dispense with nature for science. His role was invariably interventionist when things went wrong, as in the case of Mary Woll-stonecraft. Mary Shelley dramatizes the male-mother and man-midwife through Victor Frankenstein, who eventually arrives at the realization that he has become not only the creator of life but the mitigator of death. His descendants at Los Alamos were not unaware of holding both life and death in their hands. They inspired the historian William Laurence to feel "as though he had been privileged to witness the Birth of the world—to be present at the moment of Creation when the Lord said: let there be light."[7] By contrast Oppenheimer responded by saying, "I am become Death, the destroyer of worlds."[8] Both these commentators on the bomb resort to sacred texts and creation myths in order to find appropriate metaphors with which to circumscribe with meaning that which defies rational understanding.

Textuality is also the key for both Mary Shelley and Franken-stein's creature in discovering their origins and parentage: the monster browses through Victor's laboratory notes in a bizarre parody of the way in which Mary Shelley must have read her father's *Memoirs* (1798) of her mother.[9] The realization that hers was a monstrous birth in that it was inscribed with the death of her mother must have been a crushing one to the young Mary Shelley. Indeed it was powerful enough to provoke her to reproduce in the image of her own creative imagination a textual monstrosity as a means of redemption through reenactment. It is tempting to see the parts of her name, Mary Woll-stonecraft Godwin Shelley, as signing the three major influences play-ing on her life and work. That unholy trinity of Shelleyan aesthetics, Wollstonecraftian feminism, and Godwinian radicalism had produced a daughter of the Enlightenment as ideologically hybrid and disparate as the creature pieced together by Victor Frankenstein. To regard Mary Shelley as so constituted is to atomize her like the monster whose component parts might be perfect in themselves, but whose sum total amounted to a destructive prodigy. Textuality enabled Mary Shelley to reconstitute herself through a displacement of a filial role by a parental one. By assuming this authorial posture, she succeeded in reappropriating the male-dominated discourse of reproduction and in so doing opened up radical possibilities for women's writing.

Notionally the role of writer may be perceived as the relationship between persona and self, which in this case authorized Mary Shelley to become the author of her own monstrous creation. This sense of life imitating art is what Gilbert and Gubar have called "bibliogenesis."[10] We can image in *Frankenstein* a conflation between creator and dark creation similar to that taking place in *Wuthering Heights* (1847) where Emily Brontë's Cathy declares "I am Heathcliff!"[11] Like Brontë, who wondered if it was moral to create such creatures as Heathcliff, Mary Shelley at a later point in her life was prompted to marvel how as a young girl she had seized upon such a hideous idea for her novel. Well she may have wondered, for what is truly hideous is that by seizing the male prerogative to create man-made monsters, she effected a re-appropriation of the reproductive discourse hijacked by men. Rarely did men reflect on the monsters that they had produced. Such musings were left to women since the monsters created by them were inevitably self-referential. Furthermore, it would seem that a subsumation of self into the narrative was women's only permissible route for encroaching on the production of fictions of the profane, for which the female writer had no approbation.

By re-creating her authorial role, Mary Shelley defied the accepted parameters of gendered writing as designated by a male establishment. Once the gender of the anonymous author of *Frankenstein* was uncovered, the adverse criticism that ensued restated the prejudice that unfettered female creativity was dangerously capable of proliferating monstrosities. The subversive nuances discernible in Mary Shelley's statement of self-definition in this novel transgress the boundaries of accepted feminine writing. Likewise in Laclos's *Les Liaisons dangereuses* (1782), Marquise de Merteuil's admission that "I have created myself" goes beyond the metafictions of writing her own plots to a more profound realization that ontological transformations must transcend socially determined notions of gender.[12] By writing herself into her own text as the monster—through a deconstruction of self—Mary

Shelley had allowed herself to become both the subject and object of her own scrutiny. In so doing she transcended a mere appropriation of the male role as a begetter of monsters. In a valorization that is at once empowering and mobilizing, she in fact reproduced the monstrosity of woman through her own authorship. But the postnatal trauma that later galvanized her creative powers turned Mary Shelley into a palimpset of sorts, except that the inscription of herself as author was also an erasure of all the monstrous births encoded within her own body—both her natal monstrosity and that conferred on her as a mother of stillborn or dying infants. Rewriting the text of her personal identity meant confronting the monsters of her selfhood, not unlike the Gothic heroine who was ready to sweep aside the symbolic black veil at the risk of gazing upon the accepted face of the feminine, or the rediscovery of the savage girl locked up in Emily Brontë's Catherine Earnshaw. For the author of *Frankenstein,* the regressions and advances and eventual rebirth of the text were a reenactment of a monstrous birthing, the pain of which she would never allow herself to endure again. But this meant, too, that she was never again to return to that source of creative power, never again to confront the monstrous within herself, and never again to reach those heights of creative genius that had been claimed by men.

Christine Battersby's recent study of genius and gender locates the masculine character of genius in the Latin root *genius*—the cult of the household spirits cultivated by the ownership of land by *gentes* and *gens,* which preserved the identity of the male seed from generation to generation. Genius remained bonded to male biological processes even after this semantic underpinning was lost. [13] The potency ascribed to the male role in reproduction found expression in the belief that gender was determined by the male at the moment of conception. In her 1831 introduction to *Frankenstein,* Mary Shelley calls upon the authority of Erasmus Darwin in trying to authenticate the foundations of her fiction. Darwin's theory of generation, founded on the belief that gender was determined by the mind of the male parent, grants a scientific credibility to masculine mythologizing. This has obvious significance for the Frankenstein creation. In Darwin's genetic scheme the sex and heredity of offspring result from the male imagination. In *Zoonomia* (1794) he argues:

> Hence I conclude, that the act of generation cannot exist without being accompanied with ideas, and that a man must have at that time either a general idea of his own male form, or of the form of his male organs; or

an idea of the female form, or of her organs; and that this marks the sex, and the peculiar resemblance to either parent. From whence it would appear, that the phalli, which were hung round the necks of Roman ladies, or worn in their hair, might have effect in producing a greater proportion of male children; and that the calipaedia, or art of begetting beautiful children, and of procreating either males or females, may be taught by affecting the imagination of the male-parent; that is, by the fine extremities of the seminal glands imitating the actions of the organs of sense, either of sight or touch.[14]

Such ideas were part of the Aristotelian legacy. According to Aristotle in *De generatione animalia* (c. 340 B.C.), the form of the child exists in the male soul, while the mother provides only the receptacle in which the male seed will thrive. Within folklorist beliefs, however, and indeed within the Galenic tradition, the imagination of the mother at the moment of conception imprinted the fertilized egg with at least part of the relevant genetic information. In this light it is interesting to note that in *Frankenstein* Victor is portrayed as troubled and fevered, exhibiting all the symptoms of a diseased imagination at the moment of the creation of the monster. He tells Walton in language that is gender-laden:

> Every night I was oppressed by a slow fever, and I became nervous to a painful degree. . . . [M]y voice became broken, my trembling hands almost refused to accomplish their task; I became as timid as a love-sick girl, and alternate tremor and passionate ardour took the place of wholesome sensation and regulated ambition.[15]

The Frankenstein monster, of woman born in a literary sense, is a dire warning of the dangers of solitary paternal propagation. Mary Shelley's creation of a fictional monstrosity rejects an Aristotelian identification between women and the monstrous by showing that male creativity can itself produce monsters. Aristotle regarded the "monstrosity" of the female as an accidental necessity of a species, within which the male was regarded as normative. His views on women were extended beyond the physical to the moral, and, although they were no longer accorded canonical status, in derivative form they held a certain sway in eighteenth-century popular culture. The moralist John Bennett, for example, warned that the absence of female virtue created a breeding ground for such freaks of nature. In his conduct book *Letter to a Young Lady* (1789) he concedes that a "bad man is terrible" but insists that "an unprincipled woman is a monster."[16] For men like the minister William Duff, Mary Shelley would have been the hideous offspring of a monstrous female, since he perceived Mary Wollstonecraft to be an aberration from the natural order; she like all women was for his Aristotelian mind-set a bizarre hybrid of monster, not quite human and not quite animal.[17] Frankenstein's Luciferian folly of pride and failure of the imagination is posited on the belief that men, basking in the illusion of the dispassionate objectivity of so-called scientific rationality, instead of relying on the workings of nature, can produce a higher form of life than that brought about by sexual reproduction and nurturing by the female. The twist in the tale is the moment when Frankenstein inspects his creature in a parody of the proud mother looking at her infant for the first time. Instead of joy he is filled with horror, saying: "How can I describe my emotions at this catastrophe, or how to delineate the wretch whom with such infinite pains and care I had endeavoured to form?" (52). Clearly it was not enough to replace motherhood with the Promethean arts of electricity and the mysteries of galvanization. According to birth myth theorists, *Frankenstein* was for Mary Shelley a displacement of mothering; its composition displaced the bereavement she suffered in losing her firstborn after only four days of life. The act of writing functions as a form of necromantic therapy since it recreates imaginatively a revival of the dead. In this way Mary Shelley enters into her own birth narration through the production of a myth of recreation that is at once modern, multivocal, and an incubator of mythopoeic productivity.

Ideologies of gender permeate through society, becoming embedded in myths that ultimately contribute to a "mythic consciousness." The discourse of masculine culture enshrines mythic creations constituted through such metaphors as the cerebral birth of the scientist's brainchild or through the mythology of Minerva springing full-grown and fully armed from the head of Zeus.[18] Literary creativity was another route by which solitary male propagation could generate a "higher" form of life. I am thinking of the Romantic movement's mystification of creativity and genius—an aesthetic grounded in a mystique that is biologically and culturally male and through which the Romantic poet is heralded as inspired and God-like. Myths of origin and creation are central to the Romantic consciousness and provide a matrix for a rhetoric of reproduction. The Romantic poets recreated themselves through a mystification of the origins of their own creativity, which sometimes went as far as deification. Battersby argues that the Romantic conception of genius verges on the misogynistic since it involved a male appropriation of "femininity"—the attributes of subjectivity, emotion, imagination, and passion—while designating women as unable to ignite their own fires of inspiration, seeing them instead as damp squibs who are metaphorically frigid and thus creatively sterile.[19] The notion of Romantic poet as Promethean has currency with another myth of male creativity concerning the clay figures, prototypes for the human race, that were animated by Prometheus. A better-known version of this legend, which has been associated with the spark of divine inspiration, tells of how he stole fire from the heavens. Underpinning this myth is the suggestion that woman came into existence as punishment for his blasphemous act. Percy Bysshe Shelley as Prometheus' modern manifestation—signified in the subtitle to *Frankenstein*—broke free of this misogynistic consequence but failed to liberate himself from a sense of the necessity of nurturing male genius over and above other obligations, such as those he owed his family.

Percy Shelley, who neglected his and Mary's offspring for the solipsism of his own Romantic creativity, is the most likely model for Victor Frankenstein, who also abandons his vital relationships, this time for the thrill of working on a corpse in his workshop. An analogy with childbirth can be made with Shelley's retreat into periods of gestation in order to produce a poem, a surrogate for biological birth, that is not unlike Godwin's withdrawal into his study for protracted periods of literary productivity during his second marriage. The denial of the value of domestic relations preoccupied Godwin in *St. Leon* (1799) and Percy Shelley in "Alastor" (1816). For men, the study and the laboratory had become refuges, which in the case of the Romantic scientist and poet incubated a form of masculinity that takes as its goal the mastery of the world. Like that of the poetic persona, Victor Frankenstein's consuming passion is God-like, involving as it does the artificial creation of life. The monstrous being that he creates is a testimony, not to the sleep of reason, but to the waking dream of a scientific rationality culturally transmitted as masculine and unencumbered by such ethical considerations as blasphemy and paternal responsibility. Unlike the eighteenth-century cult of sensibility (which was accessible to women because it did not conflict with the prerequisites of femininity), the Romantic poets failed to open up a route for female empowerment in spite of their appropriation of the feminine. The discourse of the Romantics' manifesto contained in Wordsworth's preface to the *Lyrical Ballads* (1800) is a reassertion of the masculine posture that defines the poet as a man speaking to men.[20]

Women writers of the period did not lay claim to the "egotistical sublime," nor did they regard themselves as transcendent representatives of all humanity. The elevated value that critics have placed on the Romantic poets corresponds to a denigration of the achievement of women during this period as being merely pragmatic, didactic, prosaic, and sentimental. Aside from a few celebrated exceptions, women's literary contributions have been neglected. From having dominated the novel during the eighteenth century, women now suffered a relegation, which was part of the backlash against radical women of the Enlightenment like Wollstonecraft. Fear of the female is expressed in Mary Shelley's novel when Victor complies with the monster's request for a mate. He admits that "in all probability" he would create "a thinking and reasoning animal," but in spite of this prediction he considers also the possibility that "she might become ten thousand times more malignant than her mate" (164). This is a perpetuation of the prejudice that the female of the species is more deadly than the male. But what is most threatening and terrible for Victor Frankenstein is the prospect of an autonomous female reproductive capacity, which would displace him as procreator. In order to regain control, he has no option but to destroy her. As he dismembers her, he desexes her in what can only be interpreted as an open attack on the female: "Trembling with passion, [I] tore to pieces the *thing* [my italics] on which I was engaged" (164). Victor's action lends support to the fallacy that safety lies in the fragmentation of the female. Since her integrity and wholeness pose a threat to masculinity, woman is torn apart. Projecting a male model of unity onto conceptions of female identity is misguided in that it fails to recognize that female strength and maintenance of self are realized through a resilient pluralism, a shifting center, and a protean ability to transform and to keep redefining and reconstituting identity in an endless refraction and displacement. Such polyvalency is a shield. Like Mary Shelley's monstrous other, it reflects the image of the Gorgon self.

It is not difficult to see why women have sought refuge in unitary models of selfhood when we consider that the fragmentation of woman, particularly within scientific discourses and practices, has served the interests of misogyny. Carolyn Merchant and Evelyn Fox Keller have done much to map the often violent sexual imagery prevalent in seventeenth- and eighteenth-century science—imagery that confirmed scientific culture as masculine.[21] Henry Vaughan's poem "Vanity of Spirit" (1650) captures the scientists' imperious desire to anatomize and dismember nature. Vaughan laments science's inability to restore back into unity the mystery it has destroyed. Bearing in mind the identification of nature as female, his lines allegorize the appropriation of the text of the female body when it is subjected to an analytic fragmentation of its self, identity, and function:

> With hieroglyphics quite dismembered
> And broken letters scarce remembered.
> I took them up, and (much joy'd) went about
> T'unite those pieces, hoping to find out
> The mystery; but this near done;
> That little light I had was gone.[22]

The unity of woman, like the unity of nature, was something modern science seemed to approach with a philosophy of divide and conquer.

Returning to *Frankenstein,* it could be argued that if the monster is a nightmare born from Victor's sleep of reason, then his destruction of a female being who has the potential and probability of reason symbolizes patriarchal fear of women's rationality. It was the assertion of this rationalism that Wollstonecraft believed could redeem women from the ideology of femininity. Wollstonecraft thus offered up a challenge to the socially constructed and culturally transmitted traditional associations of gender, which throughout the Enlightenment imaged the female mind as devoid of the restraints of male reason. During this same period rationality was becoming identified with those cognates of masculinity such as objectivity, deduction, logic, truth, and scientific pursuits. A cross-current of ideologies spinning off from Renaissance views of woman, combining with the reaction against the female radicals of the late eighteenth century and the upward surge of the Romantic movement, created a vortex that, though difficult to outline, succeeded in sustaining the traditional gender divisions of thought and creativity. The dominance of the male intellect over female nature is mirrored in the social construction of gender, which in the influential work of Rousseau construes the mind of a woman as not only incapable of pursuing universal scientific truth or producing works of genius, but equally unable to reflect upon the connections drawn for them in natural philosophy or even to appreciate genius in men.

Through her scientist-hero's reasoning madness, Mary Shelley parodies the assumption that men were the natural arbiters of good sense with the ability "to judge of the relations of sensible beings and of laws of nature."[23] Although professing to shy away from polemic, through her mad scientist figure in *Frankenstein* Mary Shelley, like her mother before her, challenges the historically pervasive and culturally validated identification of rational science with a masculinity that had marginalized instinctual nature and femininity. At the same time, her creative urge to beget monsters and conjure up images of a mad scientist's gargantuan desire to create life defied patriarchy's precepts of feminine propriety and motherhood. In this way women writers who departed from the gendered sentimental novels of the eighteenth century were seen as renouncing their femininity. But by picking up the pen, which Sandra Gilbert and Susan Gubar have identified with the phallus, the woman writer becomes an androgynous being by embodying both "masculine" and "feminine" traits.[24]

The androgyne is a potentially potent resource for women writers, especially if it is perceived as a refractory symbol capable of bearing endless permutations, rather than as a nexus for gendered polarities. By keeping its polyvalency in sight we are prevented from defaulting into a perception of androgyny as a signifier for a dyadic reductionism that seeks to privilege the male principle. On this model the female principle emerges as dynamic instead of passive and thus escapes the dichotomous positioning with the male in which it is identified as "the other." The multifaceted properties of the androgyne do not have to remain static but can be conceived in a state of dialectical interchange. In this way androgyny is able to offer more than a metonymy for the woman writer; it flags a radical alternative paradigm to the narrow strictures governing male-dominated science. Androgyny plays a central role in the alchemical and hermetic traditions that Mary Shelley was reading about while she wrote *Frankenstein*.[25] Mary Shelley invoked alchemy as a distorting mirror capable of exposing the destructive aspects of modern science. Indeed she may have borrowed her novel's title from the eighteenth-century alchemist Dippel, who experimented with the artificial creation of life and was connected with Castle Frankenstein.[26] Parallels between Victor and Dippel are much in evidence: both were body snatchers drawn to the quest for the Philosopher's Stone and the elixir of life. More compelling still, Dippel even used to sign his name "Frankenstein."

Alchemy even more than science depends upon analogy and allegory for expression. While empirical alchemy had a kinship with science because of its material and instrumental goals, mystical alchemy was concerned with the moral regeneration of humankind. As Mary Shelley demonstrates in *Frankenstein*, the scientist had lost sight of the universal sympathies and correspondences of spiritual alchemy.

The scientific revolution helped to locate alchemy and science in incommensurable paradigms, thus distancing eighteenth-century rationalists from the magician-scientists of the previous century. The philosophical magi of the Renaissance like the Brotherhood of the Rosy Cross, whose Invisible College was a precursor for the Royal Society, embraced a system of alchemy and androgyny. The Rosicrucian tradition (derived from the brotherhood of the Rosy Cross) may have attracted Mary Shelley as an ideological alternative to the bifurcation of magic and science and to the binary opposition of male and female principles. The central symbol of Rosicrucianism—the rose on the cross—is a representation of the unity of the male and female compounding the name of the legendary founder, Christian Rosencreutz. The androgyny of this system of symbolism anchored in the iconography of alchemy offers a radical revision of notions of gender. This new paradigm is no mere ersatz but a synthesizing agent acting as a vehicle that transcends the male reproductive discourses through transmutation. This mode of transformation, which is implicit within the Frankenstein myth, opens up a reading of the text harking back to a prescientific model within which the feminine is valorized.

Transmutation, which carries the same symbolic weight as production and reproduction in its ability to generate new identities, is situated within the alchemical process, where it literally involves the transformation of base metal into gold. The semiology of alchemy offers an ideological frame of reference able to accommodate representations of the female, unlike orthodox science and its reproductive discourses, which were later to influence male-controlled technologies. Within alchemical traditions, generation could be asexual, providing a mode of reproduction independent of the mother. Such a process is described in *De natura rerum* (1575), which may have been written by Paracelsus.

> Let the sperm of a man by itself be putrified in a . . . glass, sealed up, with the highest degree of putrefaction, for the space of forty days, or so long until it begin to be alive, move and stir, which may easily be seen. After this time . . . it will become a true, living infant, having all the members of an infant, which is born of a woman.[27]

Nonetheless, the alchemical tradition had a place, if not always for the mother, but for for the female principle itself; in this case the arcanum of menstrual blood is used to feed the embryo. This was not necessarily the case within the conceptual framework of the scientists in pursuit of the artificial creation in life. The prolongation of life involving the hermetic *elixir vitae* was also independent of the mother but brought about by alchemists in a process intricately involved with the inclusion of the feminine. Indeed the catalyst for the elixir is the Philosopher's Stone, which is an agent for synthesizing the male and female, fire and water, through the allegorical marriage of the king and the queen. In an early review, Walter Scott noted that *Frankenstein,* with its emphasis upon the pursuit of the Philosopher's Stone, is a novel written along similar lines to Godwin's *St. Leon* (1799). It is likely that Mary Shelley was acquainted with her father's work on alchemists in *Lives of the Necromancers* (1834), which was published a year after her own alchemical short story "The Mortal Immortal." She must have pooled her knowledge of such esoterica with both Godwin and Shelley, who had written novels about the life-giving powers of men whose mastery of the secret of the elixir of life serves as a metaphor for the male powers of reproduction. There can be little doubt that their fictional accounts of the hermetic manipulation of human existence proved to be far preferable to the compendium of horrors conjured up by science. In Mary Shelley's novel, Professor Krempe accuses Victor Frankenstein of exchanging "the discoveries of recent enquirers for the dreams of forgotten alchemists" such as Agrippa and Paracelsus, since he has been engaging "with the greatest diligence into the search of the philosopher's stone and the elixir of life" (35). Frankenstein realizes that it was the latter that had won his most undivided attention and confesses that "wealth was an inferior object, but what glory would attend the discovery, if I could banish disease from the human frame, and render man invulnerable to any but a violent death!" (34). But when he abandons this quest in order to return to modern science, he discovers that the consequences of this transition are far more disastrous than anything connected with his earlier dabblings into the work of necromancers and alchemists.

The Frankenstein monster is the hideous progeny of the darkness of science instead of the offspring of hermetic traditions concerned with the harmony of opposites, universal correspondences, and cosmic sympathies. While alchemists aimed to cooperate with nature, scientists worked against her. F. Sherwood Taylor, while appreciating this distinction, tends to regard science as a continuation of alchemy in his interpretation of the alchemists' crucible as a metaphor for the nuclear reactor:

The material aims of the alchemists, the transmutation of metals, has now been realized by science, and the alchemical vessel is the uranium pile. Its success has had precisely the result the alchemists feared and guarded against, the placing of gigantic power in the hands of those who have not been fitted by spiritual training to receive it.[28]

Instead of blaming a lack of spiritual training for the shortcomings of science, Sherwood Taylor might have considered precisely those dangers that have been brought about by the symbolic abandonment of the alchemist's womblike alembic in which nurturing takes place, in effect the denial of the female. At the very least the presence of the feminine proffers a corrective now lost to scientists. But its influence accounts for far more than that. Alchemical traditions are posited upon an active female principle, which at the most fundamental level involved a positive cooperation with nature. The power of the feminine to initiate and activate was recognized by Thomas Vaughan (brother of the poet Henry Vaughan), who acknowledges that it was a female first matter or spermatic seed from which nature made all its minerals.[29] The gender balance maintained within the sexual classification of minerals, for example, invokes a sense of duality within an organic model overlooked now by modern science. Gender could be interchangeable for some minerals, while chemical reactions were believed to be able to produce the double-sexed hermaphrodite, which in alchemical iconography could be seen to represent the equality of the sexes. Within hermeticism, masculinity and femininity are construed as the interaction of complementary principles—two aspects of the one—and not simply as the active working on the passive, in opposing fashion. The alienating effect of sciences that treat nature as a metonym for "the other"—whether it be the female or denial of another self—stems from the impulse to divide, deny, and then dominate. In the light of this we may well wonder whether Victor Frankenstein, if he had not discarded necromancy and magic for physics and chemistry, would ever have produced his destructive monster.

Mary Shelley's own procreation of fictional monstrosities and its implications for the woman writer is both an amplification of and ironic parallel to the monstrous consequences of science striving to subjugate nature. As she has shown, the scientist goes beyond subordination to the appropriation of the feminine. The power politics implicit in this are expressed by the monster, who reminds his maker, "Remember that I have power. . . . I can make you so wretched that the light of day will be hateful to you" (165). Once the mother had held that kind of power over the young child. Now the child in the scientist reclaims that life-giving potential in an imperiousness that is allegorized in the novel through a master-slave dialectic. The dynamics of the power struggle between the sexes, which have infiltrated science and technology, may be monitored by attending to the question of who controls language. The power of men over women has involved the enclosure of female identity within particular discourses and, in turn, excluded them from others. A subversive way of escape is to invoke a literal transmutation whereby the female principle is revitalized, thus enabling it to become an active agency. Women, by generating their own metaphoric power and assuming control over the discourses and narratives of their own bodies, are able to transcend the rhetoric of reproduction from which they have been excluded. By regarding authorial control over their own destinies, life stories, creativity, and reproductive capacities, they are empowered to step back into their own narratives, which have been wrenched from them. Through a process of transmutation women have a tool that will enable them to effect such transformations.

The Aseptic Male Obstetrician and the Filthy Peasant Crone: Contemporary Women Writers' Accounts of Birth

Tess Cosslett

The opposing figures in my title are from Adrienne Rich's book *Of Woman Born:* in interpreting the history of childbirth, she urges, we must rid ourselves of these stereotypical opposites.[1] But feminist historians have not so much rejected these stereotypes as reversed their valuation: the male obstetrician may be "highly trained," but he is remote and impersonal, bent on controlling women's bodies through the routines and technologies of the medical institution. The peasant crone may be "filthy," but she has the wisdom of nature and can restore women to confidence in the power of their own bodies. The history of childbirth is seen as the gradual encroachment of men—male doctors, men-midwives—upon an originally wholly female preserve. The men are associated with the increased use of instruments—from forceps to fetal monitors—and consequently increased intervention. The women—midwives and the mothers themselves—represent a more "natural," instinctive approach, a faith in the female body and its power rather than a will to regiment and control it.[2] The power of male obstetricians over female bodies has been convincingly linked to the history of "scientific" discourse and its claims of definition and control over a "female" Nature.[3]

The clear polarity between clinical male expertise and a more natural, intuitive female approach to birth has been very attractive to contemporary women writers in constructing fictional narratives of childbirth: stereotypes and polarities are the very stuff of narrative structure, even if the eventual aim is to undermine or confuse them. In the history of childbirth in the twentieth century, the two figures of my title can be taken to represent the growing medicalization of

birth—the increase in hospitalization and in the use of technology—
and the opposing natural childbirth movement. It is not surprising
that the natural childbirth version of birth should appeal to women
writers who are trying to give an account of the experience from the
woman's point of view: the natural childbirth movement for the first
time stressed the importance of a woman's *state of mind* as crucial to the
success or failure of her labor; the woman's subjectivity, not just her
objectified body, became the center of the process. But the origin of
the modern natural childbirth movement in the extremely male-
centered and often explicitly antifeminist work of Grantly Dick Read,
and its rise to prominence in conjunction with the "feminine mystique" of the 1950s, suggest it may not be as liberating and empowering for women as some of its advocates think.[4] A strategy employed by
some women writers has been to obscure natural childbirth's male
cultural origins and to present it as an inborn power discovered by the
birthing woman herself; Enid Bagnold in *The Squire* and A. S. Byatt in
Still Life are examples.[5] In Doris Lessing's *A Proper Marriage,* knowledge of natural childbirth is displaced onto the African cleaning
woman who releases the birthing heroine's tension with her touch and
her incantation, "Let the baby come, let the baby come."[6] Here the
equivalent of the "peasant crone" is wiser and more effective than the
rigid and repressive hospital regime that the heroine suffers under. In
Still Life, too, a repressive and depersonalized hospital regime thwarts
the heroine in her efforts to give birth naturally.[7]

Though the power of natural childbirth in these texts is clearly
female (no charismatic Dick Read enables the process), the repressive
medical institution is not identified as essentially *male.* This insight
could be seen as a consequence of the recent women's movement,
though it is present in earlier works. A male/female division in approaches to childbirth is clear in Bagnold's *The Squire* and Vera
Brittain's *Honourable Estate*[8]—though both of them work also to subvert the stereotypes. Bagnold creates a powerful midwife who helps her
heroine achieve a natural childbirth at home, and who is represented as
a perfect amalgam of ancient "female" wisdom and modern "male"
science. Brittain, on the other hand, in the two birth scenes in her
book, contrasts the horrors of a home birth attended belatedly by an
incompetent male doctor with an efficient hospital birth presided over
by an idealized *female* doctor.

Two of the more recent fictional explorations of these polarities are
The Birth Machine (1983), by Elizabeth Baines, and Fay Weldon's *Puffball* (1980).[9] Both of them deal centrally with the intervention of male

medical expertise in childbirth; the birth in both books is by emergency cesarian. They also both make a link between medical practice and scientific discourse: the way the scientific language of the medical text-book constructs childbirth is a central issue. And both texts seem aware of the contemporary feminist critique of childbirth, and the way feminist writers have seen the control of the female body by male obstetricians and their instruments as a metaphor of the wider oppression of women in patriarchal society. I intend to concentrate on these two texts in the rest of this essay. Given their common concerns, their approaches are interestingly different: Baines goes along with the feminist critique and presents scientific research, medical langauge, technological intervention, and dehumanizing hospital routines as all part of the same male-authored plot against her heroine. Weldon, on the other hand, endorses the male medical establishment as a saving power, and scientific language as describing an inescapable moral reality. Both are, however, ambiguous in their attitudes to natural childbirth rhetoric. Weldon mocks simplistic feminist believers in natural childbirth, and also shows the "natural," instinctual woman as a dangerous power, who uses a "witchcraft" that opposes and is finally tamed by male medical science. At the same time, Weldon's own use of "scientific" language is subversive, as she adds elements of maternal magic and spiritual and psychic forces, and also plays about with the terminology. Baines's attack on the medical establishment's dehumanizing interventionism is recognizable as the natural childbirth movement's party line, but she shows natural childbirth *techniques* as co-opted by and complicit with the medical establishment, and she also introduces an image of female "witchcraft," as either a contrast or perhaps even an analogy to the doctors and their drugs.

The title of *The Birth Machine* is richly ambiguous, bringing together several related complexes of ideas. Most immediately it refers to the actual machine, the infusion unit, which is used to induce labor in Zelda, the pregnant heroine. In a metaphorical sense, it also describes the hospital within which the birth takes place, with its efficient, dehumanizing routines. Finally, it also suggests the way Zelda's body is regarded and treated by these two "machines"—as another machine, in need of mechanical attention to get it started, a machine for giving birth. That modern obstetric techniques result from an underlying image of body as machine has often been pointed out.[10] Martin Richards sees the obstetric profession as founded on an ideal of "intervention, seeing most clinical problems in terms of a kind of engineering."[11] Towler and Bramall, in their history of midwifery, link together the idea of body-as-machine, technological intervention, science, and maleness: in the seventies, the "male preoccupation with science, technology, and the purely physical mechanisms of birth seemed to gain dominion."[12]

In *The Birth Machine* too, the source of all the literal and meta-phorical "machines" is a male figure, a powerful patriarch, Professor McGuirk. He represents a particularly charismatic version of the asep-tic male obstetrician of my title. He is the consultant who has decided that Zelda should be induced, but, significantly, we do not first see him in the clinic or on the ward: he appears giving a lecture to an international conference, and later we also see him lecturing to medical students, his successors. Martin Richards, speculating on why induc-tion for nonmedical reasons has become so widespread despite lack of evidence for its advantages or its safety, locates the cause in the "belief system" of the obstetric profession, with its preference for technologi-cal intervention and control.[13] By presenting the Professor first and most importantly as lecturer, as disseminator of a certain worldview, Baines prioritizes the professional "belief system" that lies behind what her heroine has to undergo. Richards also points out that professional status is at stake—"high status within obstetrics seems to go with the use of the most up to date technical innovations"[14]—and it is the Professor's status as international celebrity that is stressed, a status dependent on his enthusiastic publicity for the "machine."

The particular machine that the Professor is promoting is proba-bly the Cardiff infusion system, in which "the rate of infusion can be controlled automatically by feedback from the intra-uterine pressure, measured with an intra-amniotic catheter and pressure transducer" (see fig. 1).[15] The Professor celebrates this combination of two machines into one—"most medical advances have turned on just that kind of creative connection" (12)—as he connects Zelda to the machine, under the eyes of his admiring students. Ann Oakley comments on another such innovative technical combination: "Modern monitoring equip-ment combines a tracing of uterine contractions with one of the fetal heart-rate: thus, it has been possible for obstetricians to see at one glance both the condition of the uterus and the condition of the fetus (but not the condition of the mother)."[16] Similarly, the Professor's machine is focused on a disembodied uterus, and the emotional reac-tions of the patient, as they try to connect her to the machine, are an irrelevant nuisance: "Mrs Harris's fingers are trembling just a little. What's she got to be afraid of?" (13).

The connection between the Professor's enthusiasm for induction

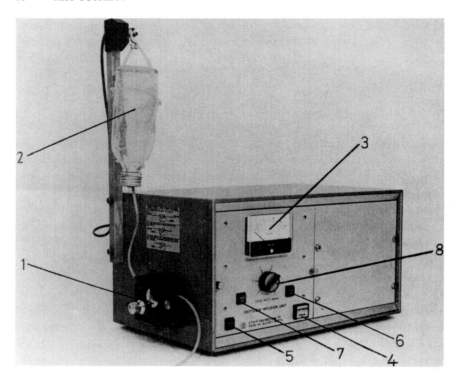

Fig. 1. *J. G. Francis, A. C. Turnbull, and F. F. Thomas, "Automatic Oxytocin Infusion Equipment for Induction of Labour,"* Journal of Obstetrics and Gynaecology of the British Commonwealth *77, no. 7 (July 1970): 595.*

and a coldly objective scientific worldview is made explicit in the parallels drawn between the research being conducted by Zelda's husband, Roland, and her own predicament. Attached to the hospital is the Centre for Medical Research, where Roland, a pupil of the Professor, conducts experiments on rats to test the effects of estrogen. Zelda, a drip attached to her arm, "half-lies, half sits, her legs splayed. . . . Within lies the placenta, past its maximum efficiency." At the same time, upstairs, "a lab technician takes a pin and drives it through the pale pink palm of the first rat for dissection. The rat lies, cruciform. Inside is the liver, which will reveal new truth, and provide the world with scientific data" (22). Roland's research is on contraception; it is also male experimentation on the female reproductive system. The parallel between Zelda's induction and the rat experiments turns out to be even closer than at first appears: by the end of the novel, Zelda realizes that the induction was totally unnecessary, its only point to test and demonstrate the Professor's new techniques. She has indeed been experimented on.

The novel, published in 1983, is very precisely set in the early 1970s. At this time, the number of inductions was increasing dramatically, and "convenience" inductions for nonmedical reasons were making their first appearance.[17] In the mid-seventies, protests were made about this trend, and controversy raged;[18] the new public awareness of the situation is reflected in the novel. But the heroine is presented as unaware of the possibility of "routine" induction. She is given inadequate and misleading information by her doctors, and only gradually pieces together evidence that reveals the Professor's real motive.[19] Though some consultants were willing to admit they performed "nonmedical inductions," this was not widely acknowledged.[20] Additionally, as Richards points out, there was a "grey area" where medical and nonmedical indications overlapped.[21] It is in this grey area that Zelda's induction takes place: there are some medical indications, derived from a misreading of her symptoms, but it is only when she manages secretly to get hold of her own hospital notes that she sees the truth: "Clinical Trial: Convenience Induction" (113). Thus the whole process is presented as a conspiracy against the heroine by male-directed science and technology. In a crucial scene, Zelda reinterprets the medical textbook she had turned to for information earlier and sees, hidden beneath its bland, impersonal language, the rationale for what has been done to her:

> *Any condition may be an indication for induction if it is considered safer for the mother, or for the foetus, or for both, that the pregnancy does not continue any longer.* Any condition. Any undefined condition. If for any undefined reason it is considered safer. Her healthy body may be a condition. Their lack of faith in her healthy body may be an indication.
> It was there, between the lines, and she hadn't seen it. (70)

Despite an extensive search through medical textbooks of the late sixties and early seventies, I have not been able to find any that use just this kind of vague and sinister language about inductions. Mostly they warn about its risks and condemn induction for "social reasons," but a few are quite open about advocating convenience inductions.[22] I would guess that Baines has invented this particular textbook for her purposes, but she has picked up on the impersonal, generalized language of such books: for instance, on "planned delivery" (convenience induction), one states, "Because planned delivery facilitates a predictable workload, it tends to improve obstetric efficiency."[23] Such language elides entirely the effect of induction on the mother's mind and body.

The ambiguous and sinister passage from the textbook has, in fact, appeared earlier in the book—a clue laid for the discerning reader—in the Professor's lecture to his students. The Professor is neatly listing indications for induction on the board, under headings and subheadings: "The horizontal headings begin to be supported by vertical lists like classical Greek columns" (20). The abstract patterning of his scientific categorization has a parallel in the drawings that Zelda's father does of the power station being built near her home when she is a child: the book is structured not only on Zelda's gradual discovery of what is being done to her, but on her simultaneous recovery of significant memories from her past. "Father's drawings were dull. Pale grey lines, very fine and straight, making squares and tubes, and labelled all over with numbers and arrows" (35). Just as Zelda is frustrated of an explanation about her induction, so, as a child, "Zelda wished that someone would explain" (34) the building of the power station. And just as the Professor's ideas take an ugly and dangerous physical shape in the induction—while he lectures, "Zelda's strapped to her bed" (21)—so Father's plans take shape in the power station: "They were patterns, to be translated, into thick stone blocks, into concrete reality. . . . And poisonous dust dropped, seeping and burning the countryside all round" (117).

So the Professor's ideas and their consequences are part of a larger, destructive, masculine, scientific-technological enterprise, extending beyond the hospital. The murderous reality of the power station is symbolically emphasized when Zelda's childhood games in the wood come to an end after she and her playmates discover the murdered body of a boy in their "den." The children assume the murderer was an eccentric old woman they have labeled as a "witch"—but it turns out to have been a male construction worker from the power station. The smashed skull of the boy in the den is parallelled with the head of the distressed male fetus, smashing through Zelda's body, unable to get out (72). The induction, like the power station, is the source of potentially lethal consequences. The explicit connection is made by Zelda at the end of the novel:

She hears them [the Professor and his entourage] coming along the corridor, their voices reverent and low, the givers of life according to their own strict patterns. False patterns. Their gods are false: their stiff patterns can fail them. Death can leap up from the depths, gobbling, jump back into the machine; electric grids across the land, sustenance and life meted out in geometric patterns: the lights could go out, the machines fail at any moment, a troll can jump down from industrial scaffolding, stalk a child in the woods and smash its skull. (118–119)

At the end, the heroine, clutching her baby (symbol, it seems, of her recovered past and her recovered self), escapes in disguise from the hospital and also, it is implied, from her oppressive marriage to the inadequate Roland. The hospital stands for the machine institutionalized: Zelda has been subjected to humiliating procedures—the shave, the enema, the flat-on-the-back, strapped-down position. She has been left alone with the machine, with no human contact, while doctors and nurses discussed her in impersonal, technical language. Like Adrienne Rich, Baines implies that her heroine's treatment in the hospital symbolizes and mirrors her social oppression as a woman: "No more devastating image could be invented for the bondage of woman: sheeted, supine, drugged, her wrists strapped down and her legs in stirrups, at the very moment when she is bringing new life into the world."[24] "Mechanized" birth does in fact provide an even more devastating image (see fig. 2).

All the procedures Zelda is subjected to have been extensively criticized by writers on natural childbirth and/or feminists, some of whom have also, like Baines, linked this obstetric approach to masculinist science and technology, and to the wider social oppression of women.[25] But what signs are there in the book of an opposition, an alternative? Where is the filthy peasant crone who opposes the aseptic male Professor? She is certainly present in the book, as we shall see, but not in the form of the natural childbirth movement. As Zelda's pain increases, we see her using natural childbirth breathing techniques to "control" her labor, with the approval of the hospital personnel. As several commentators have pointed out, some natural childbirth techniques have been easily co-opted by the hospital, since they make "patients easier to manage."[26] Breathing techniques in particular have been encouraged, since "the

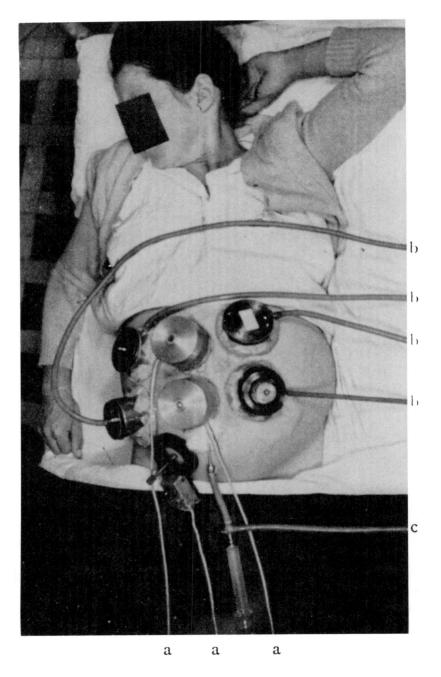

b

b

b

b

c

a   a   a

FIG. 2.   *R. Caldeyro, H. Alvarez, and S.R.M. Reynolds, "A Better Understanding of Uterine Contractions through Simultaneous Recording with an Internal and a Seven-channel External Method,"* Surgery, Gynecology, and Obstetrics *91, no. 6 (December 1950): 643. By permission of* Surgery, Gynecology, and Obstetrics.

method keeps the woman quiet by giving her a task to do, making being a 'good'—uncomplaining, obedient, cooperative—patient the woman's primary goal."[27] The desire to be a good patient goes along with a false sense of being in control:

> Much is made in childbirth preparation circles of the woman's being in control during labor, but all that is meant by that is control over her expressions of pain. A woman who maintains a fixed, if somewhat glazed, cheerful expression and continues a regular pattern of breathing is said to be "in control," as she is carted from one room to another and literally strapped flat on her back with her legs in the air.[28]

The Birth Machine dramatizes these ironies:

> It was a technique, to be learned, . . . until very recently taught in only the most progressive hospitals, still not available everywhere, so you were lucky to have it. . . .
> Now, on the day, four o'clock in the afternoon, at long last they have Zelda's contractions under control. . . . A roll of graph paper records them, a clean tongue protruding out of the machine.
> Zelda practises the technique. She is in control. (66)

Control of the contractions is really in the hands of the hospital authorities, operating the machine. Her sense of being in control is illusory. Her breathing exercises are rewarded by patronizinng praise from the authorities: "That's a good girl" (68). The obverse of this appeal to duty is the threat of blame: "You'd a duty to take advantage of it [the breathing techniques]; if you didn't there'd be no excuse, no cause for complaint on the day" (66). As Rothman says, "According to the rules of the game, if the laboring woman chooses to deal with her pain by crying or calling out, she has entirely forfeited her right to make demands."[29] In *The Birth Machine* it is made clear that the fear of blame and longing for approval that are exemplified in Zelda's use of the breathing techniques operate in other areas of her life too: guilt and a low sense of self-worth lead her to conform and to accept oppression, notably in her marriage. The false goal of being a "good girl" leads women to collude in their own oppression.

So the natural childbirth movement does not offer an alternative to the male-dominated power of the obstetric "machine." But would *women* doctors, a takeover of the machine by women, be the answer? I mentioned earlier that Vera Brittain, in *Honourable Estate,* suggests that women doctors could introduce a female sympathy into the unfeeling male practice of obstetrics. *The Birth Machine* tackles this issue, but only to come up with the opposite answer. Cruel caricature is used to emphasize that women in obstetrics are imitation men, striving to emulate and even outdo the men in their technological expertise and lust for power. Thus the decision to induce is broken "briskly" to Zelda by a female consultant: "She was tall and broad-shouldered, her hair barbered at the neck, an imitation man" (34). And the Professor's star pupil is the symbolically named, superefficient Arleen Manning, who plans to outdo her mentor: "These are the days of opportunities for women. She'll be better than any of them, mere men, pretend gods, who have gone before her" (57). So female doctors are definitely not an alternative: like natural childbirth techniques, they can be co-opted, only too willingly, into the patriarchal system.

The counterpoise to the Professor's aseptic realm appears instead in the childhood games of witchcraft in the den in the words, which Zelda gradually remembers. Here, the polarities are set up not only in terms of female versus male, witchcraft versus technology, but, very precisely, in terms of filth versus asepsis, "natural" dirt versus technological purity. In particular, an equivalent of the filthy female crone appears in the form of Hilary, Zelda's strange, probably lesbian friend who manifests in the operating theatre as Zelda hallucinates during her cesarian:

> And then she sees there's someone else, standing back in the shadow, someone not wearing surgical gown. Hilary. . . . She steps forward, craning, her cardigan hanging, her knee-socks wrinkled, unscrubbed, gownless. . . .
> "What's she doing here?" says Roland irritably. "Look, she isn't scrubbed up, she isn't aseptic, she's a hazard, send her home." (75—76)

In contrast to Hilary here, the gleaming, aseptic appearance of the Professor has often been stressed: "He's so white, his coat shining, no other hospital laundry has this glow" (69). This white, technological perfection appears also in the description of the power station "gleaming white in the sunshine" (117). This technological "purity" produces the "purely synthetic" (24) drug that is infused into Zelda's bloodstream; the medicine is then contrasted with her memories of the disgusting mess of insects and herbs that the children concoct in their den, to make their "spell."

So what kind of liberation are Hilary and the children's spells offering? What power can this alternative have? Toward the end of the book, Zelda suddenly realizes the power of the "witch," the power to be female, filthy, guilt-free, autonomous, like her "fat and indelicate and ugly and old" (117) grandmother, or the old woman the children call the witch and wrongly fear: "To eat alone, to have it all to yourself, to shuffle carefree in the woods, to need no approval, to be free of the trap of the cold glass case. And to suffer no guilt. It was that, after all, that was the power of the witch. Merely that. All that" (118). All through the book there have been references to fairy tales: here, Snow White's glass coffin brings the imprisoning definitions and institutions of male obstetrics and technology together with the impossible "perfection" demanded of women in a male-centered society.[30] Zelda breaks out from this composite glass case when she runs away from the hospital. Earlier, we have seen her beginning to realize this power, breaking out from the "control" of the breathing exercises and the approval of authority into noise, animality, and filth that turn out to be magical power, not disabling shame:

> She does it, she gets control—snip, cuts her head and shoulders away from the rest of her body, lifts them floating on shallow dog-pants. "Good girl, well done." She's their baby, their goody, their Franken-stein beauty. Oh, no, she's not, here's the urge: her mouth howling, frog-legs flexing: they flinch back. She can make them flinch back, hold them off from her own magic circle. . . . In spite of their magic, in spite of their enemas, she squirts shit in their faces. (72)

An interesting contradiction, however, emerges in this passage, Zelda's female magic is pitted against *their* "magic": science is also a kind of spell making, and the Frankenstein reference reminds us that its results can be far from perfect. As well as contrasting aseptic technology with the witchcraft in the woods, the novel also suggests parallels, which undermine the polarity. For instance, the hospital doctor decides to "increase the dosage" of oxytocin, and immediately after, in Zelda's memory, the children "were strengthening the spell, using herbs from the garden" (30). This could suggest the doctors are like children, playing at magic. The children also try out their magic healing potion on a dilapidated old doll: similarly, Zelda is "like a rubber doll, helpless" (68), during the induction. In both cases, the "doll" gets damaged, the potion doesn't work. Technology as witchcraft is also suggested by the simile of the power station's cooling towers as "four gigantic cauldrons"

(48). The point becomes clear when Zelda, in a passage I have already quoted, meditates on the destructive power inherent in technology: "Their gods are false; their stiff patterns can fail them. Death can leap up from the depths, . . . the machines fail at any moment, a troll can jump down from industrial scaffolding" (118–119). Similarly, the bland langauge of the medical textbook covers a barbaric and essentially *irrational* practice that, in Zelda's case, fails. The male obstetrician, despite his scientific pretensions, is really only a peasant crone concocting ineffectual and possibly lethal potions.

On first reading, Fay Weldon's *Puffball* seems to be taking a line diametrically opposed to that of *The Birth Machine,* endorsing male obstetric intervention and its associated scientific terminology, vilifying "Nature" and its associated female witchcraft. The pregnancy of its heroine, Liffey, is complicated by placenta previa, a condition that can be fatal without surgical intervention: no question of a "natural" solution is allowed here. Her emergency cesarian is absolutely necessary, as opposed to Zelda's absolutely unnecessary induction. Liffey's life is saved by the benign expertise of the hospital authorities, "the gentle, powerful concern of authority, and the dramatic indications of its existence—masks and lights and drugs and ministering hands" (259). Authority is life-saving even though it is presented as largely male and somewhat misogynist: the specialist Liffey has seen in advance did not "particularly like women," being sure that "all women were fools, and knaves, and the enemies of their babies" (201). This fits in with what Rothman sees as characteristic of the medical model of pregnancy, in which the mother-fetus relationship is seen "as a conflicting dyad rather than as an integral unit."[31] But as Liffey's doctor says of the specialist, "He isn't the most tactful of men. . . . But on the other hand he won't let you die" (203). The aseptic male obstetrician is useful, if irritating.

This emphasis on the life-saving quality of male medical expertise goes along with fierce satire of natural childbirth rhetoric. Just as Liffey is about to hemorrhage, her husband fatuously repeats the old natural childbirth chestnut about the "primitive" woman:[32]

> "It's an entirely natural process," said Richard, "Nothing to worry about. African mothers go into the bush, have their babies, pick them up and go straight back to work in the fields."

They all looked at Liffey, to see how she would take this.

"And then they die," said Liffey, before she could stop herself.
(244)

Liffey does not die, though she nearly does, but Weldon also shows death resulting from this kind of naive acceptance of the natural childbirth position. Liffey and her husband Richard have let their London flat to a group of dropouts, one of whom, Lally, is pregnant. Her sister, Helen, believes in an extreme, feminist version of natural childbirth, that echoes the conspiracy theory of *The Birth Machine:*

They had given up doctors, who were an essential part of the male conspiracy against women. . . . At the very last minute, the plan was, they would dial 999 for an ambulance for Lally, who would then be taken to hospital too late for enemas, shaving, epidurals, and all the other ritual humiliations women in childbirth were subjected to. (91–92)

Helen says confidently, "All that stuff about pain is part of the myth. Having a baby is just a simple, natural thing" (92). Weldon fastens gleefully on the clichés of natural childbirth rhetoric. Predictably, the baby is eventually stillborn, "of placental insufficiency, the baby being six weeks beyond term" (127). The narrator's knowledge of biological facts and figures shows up the ignorant confidence of these believers in "Nature." Scientific discourse is set against woolly-minded feminism.

Lally and her friends are set up as an easy target for Weldon's satire; a more formidable representative of the "natural" woman is Liffey's neighbor, Mabs, a kind of earth mother who actually practices witchcraft. Like Hilary in *The Birth Machine,* she can be read as the filthy peasant crone who opposes the interventions of the aseptic male obstetrician in this novel. Specifically, she nearly prevents Liffey from getting to the hospital in time when she starts to hemorrhage, and though the narrator gives us precise scientific reasons for Liffey's placenta previa, she also does not discount the possibility that it is caused by Mabs's spells and potions. Mabs could be taken as a satire on the "natural" mother: she is only happy when pregnant, and she produces her babies "like loaves from a greased tin" (219). Mabs, as a mature woman, has some female power that the immature Liffey lacks; unlike Liffey, who flaunts her shape in trousers, Mabs wears skirts, to hide "the power and murk" beneath (43). She uses her powers malevolently against Liffey and her baby only because she herself is unable to conceive at the moment, and she suspects (wrongly) that her husband Tucker is the father of Liffey's baby. Her use of her "female" powers, however, rebounds on herself—the pin she sticks into an effigy of Liffey produces appendicitis in her own daughter—and as soon as she *does* become pregnant her power subsides. She is now satisfied, and gives in to the doctor and his medicine on various counts:

> She allowed the doctor to put Eddie on a course of antidepressants, and Audrey on the pill, and she herself on valium to cure the rages she now admitted to, and Tucker on Vitamin B because he drank so much home-made wine. With every act of consent, every acknowledgement of his power, her own waned. She felt it. She didn't much mind. (265)

The filthy peasant crone gives in willingly to modern male medicine, the beneficent enemy of uncontrolled "natural" powers.

Rothman points out that the contemporary home birth movement in America consists of an alliance between two rather different groups: feminists, with a highly developed critique of patriarchal institutions; and "traditional" women, who want to get back to family-centered values.[33] This tension between different ideologies seems always to be present in any attempt to create a female-centered natural childbirth movement. By caricaturing *both* the naive feminist opponents of the male medical institution *and* the malevolent earth mother, Weldon has covered the spectrum of natural childbirth stereotypes. Nevertheless, as we shall see, the maternal "power" that Mabs represents is *not* entirely discredited. It comes to work also within Liffey, to her advantage, producing a representation of pregnancy that is not too far removed from the beliefs of a natural childbirth advocate like Sheila Kitzinger.

In the description of Liffey's pregnancy, at first it seems that scientific discouse is paramount and is used to describe an inescapable moral reality. A number of chapters entitled "Inside Liffey" describe in technical, medical language what is happening in the heroine's reproductive system—how the cells are dividing, how the placenta is forming in the wrong place. Liffey's unawareness of all this is presented as part of her naive ignorance of the realities of life. Motherhood is to be the climax of her education into reality, an education that begins with her irresponsible and deluded decision to live in the country. Her ignorance of the workings of her reproductive "inside" is on a par with her ignorance of the wiles and power of the country folk, the perfidy of her city "friends," the limitations of the London commuter rail time-table, and the rapidly diminishing size of her bank account, as she blithely writes checks for useless and expensive items. Indeed, at one point there is a very close similarity between the narrator's description of the movement of Liffey's overdrawn check through the banking system, and her description of the movement of blood, sperm, or ova through Liffey's reproductive system (90). Liffey's ignorance is presented as childish and morally culpable. Thus, after describing the fluid-retaining effect of the contraceptive pill on Liffey's "inside," the narrator asks,

> Was Liffey's resentment of Richard a matter of pressure on the brain caused by undue retention of fluid, or in fact the result of his behaviour? Liffey naturally assumed it was the latter. It is not pleasant for a young woman to believe that her behaviour is dictated by her chemistry, and that her wrongs lie in herself, and not in others' bad behaviour. (15)

It is not possible to read the medical descriptions as some kind of coldly clinical objectification of the heroine's body.[34] They *are* part of her "self," and she should be more aware of them. Medical terminology carries, it seems, the narrator's approval, as when she uses it against the feminist natural childbirthers. There is none of Baines's suspicion of the deceptively bland scientific language of the medical textbook and the Professor's lecture—male language that serves to conceal outrages done to the female body.

Weldon also gives medical terminology value by stressing the ingenuity and intricacy of biological processes: "The mechanics of her menstrual cycle were indeed ingenious" (23). A good example of the kind of "technical" language that occurs in the "Inside" chapters follows:

> Lunar month by lunar month, since she reached the menarche, Liffey's pituitary gland had pursued its own cycle: secreting first, for a fourteen-day stretch, the hormones which would stimulate the growth of follicles in Liffey's ovaries. These follicles, some hundred or so cyst-like nodules, in their turn secreted oestrogen, and would all grow until, on the fourteenth day (at any rate in the years she was not taking the pill) the biggest and best would drop off into the outer-end of one of Liffey's fallopian tubes and there, unfertilised, would rupture, allowing its oestrogen to be absorbed. (23)

Despite the technical language, the description is admirably lucid. Weldon is not trying to blind us with science or repel us with its harsh terms. Anyone of reasonable intelligence could understand and enjoy these little lessons in human biology; she is making the "inside" accessible. These passages of medical explanation are in fact very close to the wording of the descriptions of the states of pregnancy in Gordon Bourne's classic *Pregnancy,* a popular manual designed for prospective mothers to read.[35] Either Bourne is Weldon's source, or they both derive from some other common source. If we look at points where Weldon departs from Bourne, we can begin to see how her use of medical terminology is not as straightforwardly scientistic as it at first appears.

Often, as in the passage above, Weldon can be read as merely providing a précis of Bourne, who is himself lucid and easy to understand.[36] We might expect that Weldon as a "literary" writer would be adding metaphorical language to Bourne's matter-of-fact "scientific" style. However, it mostly turns out that the metaphorical language is there already in Bourne. Emily Martin has pointed out how descriptions in medical textbooks often use "loaded" language in the most seemingly technical passages—language that implies particular values and purposes inherent in the biological processes they are describing.[37] This tendency can be seen in Weldon's descriptions; for instance, she describes the end of the menstrual cycle like this:

> Then the corpus luteum would start to degenerate and on the twenty-eighth day be disposed of in the form of menstrual flow—along, of course, with the lining of Liffey's uterus, hopefully and richly thickened over the previous twenty-eight days to receive a fertilised ovum, but so far, on one hundred-and-twenty occasions, disappointed. (23)

The words *hopefully* and *disappointed* imply that the conscious purpose of the whole process is conception. Martin points out how this assumption molds supposedly objective medical descriptions of menstruation, and how analogous processes, such as the shedding of the stomach lining, or the overproduction of sperm by the male, are not seen in the same terms of failure and waste.[38] Interestingly, *hopefully* is already there in Bourne; *disappointed* is added by Weldon, intensifying Bourne's implication.[39] Similarly, where Weldon adds metaphors not in Bourne, they go along with and intensify the "mechanical" model of the body that Martin discovers in medical textbooks.[40] So, when Liffey comes off the pill, "her body was still recovering from a surfeit of hormones, as might a car engine flooded by the use of too much choke" (70). Describing the conception of Liffey's baby, Weldon explains the action of the sperm: "If it came up against a solid object it would change direction, like a child's mechanical toy" (105). This expands upon Bourne's remark, "When it comes up against a solid object it changes direction," adding the idea of mechanism.[41]

So far we can see Weldon as merely reinforcing the "medical" model—though she does begin to expose a contradiction in it, between the purposeful, personifying language of *hopefully* and *disappointed,* and the impersonal, technical language of the "car engine." Further incongruities appear when Bourne's generalized descriptions are applied to the particularities of Liffey's body and Liffey's situation. This can produce a comic effect, a kind of absurd incongruity between people's feelings and actions, and their biological causes and accompaniments. This is especially noticeable when a description of Richard's passionate lovemaking is accompanied by a description of his sperm's genesis and progress into Liffey's reproductive system (34), and his ejaculation is described in Bourne's words as "rhythmic muscular contractions."[42] But the insertion of Bourne's language into a particular situation makes not only the human actions but also the scientific descriptions seem comic. In other cases, particularization has the effect of privileging the specificity of Liffey, her history, her feelings, over the impersonal biological events. Thus Bourne explains the mechanisms of genetics—"every child has 50 per cent of his genes from one parent and 50 per cent from the other"[43]—but Weldon particularizes: "Liffey's brown eyes: Richard's square chin. Her gran's temper: his great grandfather's musical bent' (108). Later, at twenty weeks, as Bourne puts it, "very active movements can easily be observed and felt by the mother";[44] Weldon activates and animates Bourne's clumsy passive construction: "The baby moved, there could be no doubt of it. A pattering, pittering feeling, like the movement of butterfly wings" (182).

Weldon's most noticeable deviations from Bourne occur after a surprising chapter called "Annunciation," in which, quite simply, Liffey's baby speaks to her from inside the womb and tells her, "It's me. . . . I'm here. I have arrived. You are perfectly all right," and she feels "a presence; the touch of a spirit, clear and benign" (138–139). In a similar way, later in the book, some characters quite simply see a UFO, and much mirth is extracted from their inability to persuade anyone else of their experience. So here, Liffey imagines describing her experience to each of her family and friends in turn, and realizes the impossibility of conveying what has happened. The supernatural *happens,* despite people's preconceptions, just as the biological processes happen, despite people's ignorance and reliance on an illusory freedom: Weldon is concerned to puncture all our complacencies. The conversation with the baby is associated with a new ability in Liffey to read the realities of the situation around her—to hear what people really mean, to see Mabs's real malevolence. She has also developed a new desire to be in tune with Nature, "the overwhelming desire, of which she was now so conscious, to be a part of the world about her: to be a woman like other women; to feel herself part of nature's processes; to subdue the individual spirit to some greater whole" (156). Newly in tune with Nature, with the "inside," through her biological and spiritual link with the baby, "Liffey now has powers of her own" to withstand Mabs's witchcraft (142).

So here Weldon validates the "natural" mother, introducing elements of maternal spirituality and mysticism that seemed to have been banished by her use of medical terminology. The title of the chapter, "Annunciation," echoes the language of Sheila Kitzinger, arch-priestess of natural childbirth:

> I would not suggest that one should approach childbirth borne on the wings of a pseudomysticism which might collapse at the crucial moment; nevertheless, to anyone who thinks about it long enough, birth cannot simply be a matter of techniques for getting a baby out of one's body. It involves our relationship to life as a whole, the part we play in the order of things; and as the baby develops and can be felt moving inside, to some women annunciation, incarnation, seem to become facts of their own existence.[45]

By making the baby inside Liffey actually speak to her, Weldon pushes the implications of this kind of imagery to their extreme, just as she also pushes the medical model to its extremes. The two accounts, female-spiritual and male-medical, exist, incongruously, side by side. So, at eight weeks, after the "Annunciation" chapter, a précis of Bourne's description ends, startlingly, like this: "The spine moved of its own volition, for the first time, although fractionally. The length of the foetus was two point two centimetres. There was no apparent room within for the soul which gave grace to its being" (141).[46] "Apparent" both endorses and undermines the medical version. Later descriptions insist on the baby as a separate person, beyond the impersonality of

Bourne's descriptions.[47] Weldon also adds to Bourne a description of the attitude—physical and implicitly emotional—of the baby: at thirteen weeks, "the amniotic sac within measured four inches in diameter and the foetus was three inches long. The baby's face was properly formed: its body curled in an attitude of docility; resting, waiting, listening, growing" (160).[48] The switch here from *foetus* to *baby* marks the change from Bourne to Weldon; the description of the baby's "attitude" could very well be derived from Bourne's illustration of this phase (see fig. 3), but Weldon has read volition and feeling into it.

The message from the baby, and his increasing humanization, help to bring together the initially split "inside" and outer worlds. By separating the scientific accounts of Liffey's "inside" processes into separate chapters, Weldon at first seems to be going along with the "medical" model of childbirth, treating the woman's body as object, or machine, quite apart from her subjective feelings. The message from "inside" bridges the gap and puts "outer" Liffey in touch with her "inner" world. The separation of the technical, inner descriptions from the rest of the plot is also not so absolute as it at first seems. The "Inside Liffey" chapters do also contain other material, and the "inside" descriptions begin to appear in other chapters, particularly the descriptions of the development of the embryo. These are sometimes found in chapters that by their title and contents implicitly link "inner" and "outer" action: for instance, "Growth," or "Movement," which label both the embryo's activities and the development of the "outside" plot. The narrator also proceeds to make merry with her scientific language and its implications. Thus "inside Mabs," who is having difficulty conceiving, "the ovum dutifully developed the required choriomic villi with which to embed itself into the waiting uterine wall" but arrived too late "and by that time had ignobly perished, for lack of a suitable foothold, or villihold" (159). The exaggeration of the language of purpose (*dutifully, ignobly*) and the coinage *villihold* hint at a send-up of the scientific terminology and a total refusal to be intimidated by it. The "Inside" chapters also contain meditations by the narrator on the role of pure chance in the "cosmic" processes of Nature, at whose mercy we all are—but these are undercut by a cheerful circularity. Thus the narrator invents a new term, ℶature, for purposeless Nature, since *Nature* is too loaded with personifications; but then she herself personifies ℶature (117–119). Or, wondering whether Liffey's life-threatening placenta previa is caused by chance or by Mabs's curse, she reasons like this:

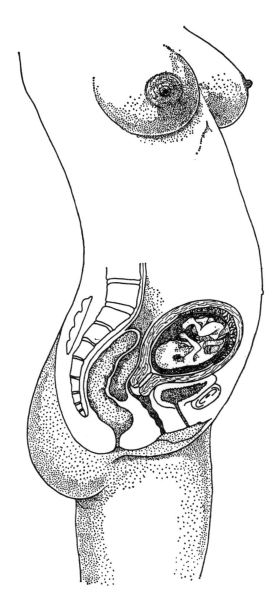

FIG 3.   *The abdomen at the sixteenth week of pregnancy. Illustration reproduced with kind permission from Cassell Publishers Ltd., London, from* Pregnancy, *copyright © Gordon Bourne 1972, 1975, 1979, 1984, 1989, p. 71.*

One pregnancy in a hundred is a placenta praevia: does every one of these foetuses have a Mabs in the background? Surely not; such foetuses are merely accident prone, or event prone, as some individuals are; at one time or other in their life. Ladders fall on them or pigs out of windows, or bombs go off as they approach; or, in country terms, their crops fail and their cattle sicken and a witch has overlooked them. (220)

So the scientifically objective category "accident," set up in opposition to Mabs's witchcraft, becomes more and more mystically and mischievously defined into an "overlooking" again. Body and mind, biological and psychic, cannot be so easily separated.

The chapter called "Birth," in which Liffey undergoes her emergency cesarian, exemplifies the climax of this intertwining of incongruous, opposite ways of describing bodily events. Weldon uses precise, technical language, very similar to Bourne's, to describe the physical realities of the operation: "He then separated the muscles of the lower abdominal wall and opened the abdominal cavity. The bladder was then dissected free from the lower part of the anterior of the uterus," and so on (255)[49] At the same time, Weldon includes Liffey's consciousness in the process, by making the anesthetic not quite strong enough, and her consciousness includes an awareness of the spiritual meaning of the event: "Liffey sensed the passage of time, and of terrible, powerful, momentous events. Of struggle, and endeavour, and of the twists and turns of fate, and of life taking form out of rock" (255). In the natural childbirth account of birth, cesarian section is the ultimate failure, the male medical imposition to be resisted at all cost.[50] Not only has the woman "failed" to give birth "naturally" and unaided, she has also missed two supreme spiritual experiences: being conscious of giving birth, and the first moment of recognition and psychic bonding with her child. Weldon clearly compensates her heroine for both these losses: first, by making her conscious during the operation, and second, by making her first "recognition" of her baby take place *before* the birth, while the baby is still inside. The cesarian is not allowed to deprive the woman of the meaning or triumph of giving birth. While addressing the same concerns, Weldon's maternal mysticism works quite differently from Sheila Kitzinger's; it does not go along with success or failure at giving birth naturally.[51]

There is a sense in which Weldon has it all ways: she makes fun of the absurdities of natural childbirth rhetoric and medical terminology, while also endorsing both discourses as inescapably true. But to find fault with her for this would be to mistake the comic tone of the book.

Despite the narrator's strongly moral tone and her insistent production of facts and realities to puncture our illusions, I read her as essentially amoral, bent on provocation from all directions. Her insistence on the reality of the baby's prebirth soul and voice is similar to her insistence on the reality of the UFO that Liffey's friends so disconcertingly see. The book is not a tract asserting the existence of UFOs (as Baines's book could be read as a tract asserting the reality of the male scientific conspiracy); it is a playful exposé of the inadequacies of our systems of thought, the frames—male-medical or female-natural—we use to structure our experience.

Conceiving Difference: Reproductive Technology and the Construction of Identity in Two Contemporary Fictions

Susan Squier

> In the current situation, the body is a technological object. An object of technical operations the number and scope of which will increase in the years ahead. Think of bio-medicine, bio-engineering, all imaginable prostheses, genetic surgery. Ten days ago I was involved in a discussion with a bio-medic who was saying . . . that in 15 years it will not be necessary for women to bear their children: the whole period of gestation could take place *in vitro.*
>
> Jean-François Lyotard[1]

> What we must learn, then, is how to conceive difference without opposition.
>
> Craig Owens[2]

"What is the unconscious of a child engendered *in vitro?* What is its relationship with the mother, and with the father?" asked Jean-François Lyotard in 1985, speaking at London's Institute for Contemporary Arts.[3] The image of technologized conception and birth has achieved remarkable cultural prominence in the last decade of the twentieth century, figuring in such films as *Blade Runner* and *Look Who's Talking,* as well as in mass-market fiction and the popular press. The very fact that the image has such cultural centrality suggests that it functions not as a settled understanding of the self in creation, but as an unsettling source of questions about the meaning of the new identity brought about by that technologized creation. As such, the image joins other moments when ideology is in the process of being formed or re-formed, among them the debate over chloroform in the mid-nineteenth century (illuminated in Mary Poovey's important study) and the debate over the social and biological implications of ecto-genesis, or extrauterine gestation, in the 1920s.[4] Now, as in those earlier moments of debate, a process of mutually constitutive interaction between literature and science—a shared shaping—operates in the way we write and talk about reproductive technology.

In what follows, I analyze the ideologies at play in the representation of reproductive technology, with specific attention to its most disseminated site: popular consumer culture. While some contemporary strands of feminist thought view reproductive technology as either inherently oppressive (Rowland, Corea, Klein, Raymond) or inherently liberating (Haraway), I will argue that reprotech as it functions in representation is not so much political as politicized.[5] It is the terrain on which ideological battles are fought, both those inherent in the operations of the technology and those not immediately related.

Robin Cook's *Mutation* and Fay Weldon's *The Cloning of Joanna May,* both published in 1989, narrate the creation of a human being by the new procreative technologies. These novels are important not for their aesthetic pleasures (in its recycled clichés Cook's novel is distinctly unpleasant to read, while *Joanna May* has the irreverent, brisk wit of all Weldon's works), but for their cultural position. As mass-market trade press novels in the thriller/romance genre (and potential blockbuster movies), they function as a prominent site at which the meaning of identity is currently being debated. Similar in their figuration of the technologized origins of a human being (through genetic engineering, in vitro fertilization, and cloning), these novels nonetheless take very different positions on identity construction.[6] Cook's novel affirms and extends a modern, Enlightenment-based notion of the sovereign individual self, while Weldon's novel problematizes that notion, dramatizing instead a feminist, postmodernist model of the human subject.

Mary Shelley's protagonist, Victor Frankenstein, used galvanism to animate his hideous creation, drawing on late eighteenth- and early nineteenth-century experiments of Luigi Galvani and Giovanni Aldini, in which electricity was applied through "Voltaic piles" to animal and human corpses.[7] Nearly two centuries later, Robin Cook's *Mutation* follows its dedication to Mary Shelley ("How dare you sport thus with life!") with an image of creation that brings Shelley's novel into the late twentieth century:

> The nerve cells were sizzling with electrical energy steadily galvanizing toward a voltaic threshold. . . . It was like a nuclear reactor on the brink of hypercriticality. . . . Out of this complex microscopic cellular activity emerged one of the mysteries of the universe: consciousness! Mind had once more been born of matter. (11)

Cook mingles the scientific discourses of Shelley's time with those of our own, metaphorically representing the origins of life as moving from electricity to neurology and microelectronics, linking the brain to the computer, the "mystery" of cellular division and growth to atomic energy.

Combining early nineteenth- and late twentieth-century technologies, *Mutuation* updates the Frankenstein story of a scientist who usurps female procreative power and so achieves control over female nature. Dr. Victor Frank, a physician-researcher with obstetric training and an overreliance on fetal tests such as ultrasound, chorionic villus biopsy, and amniocentesis, becomes both genetic and scientific father to a monster—his own genetically engineered child. Acting director of the Department of Developmental Biology of Chimera, Inc., and president of its subsidiary, Fertility, Inc. (a chain of infertility clinics), Dr. Frank uses the laboratory creation of his own son as an opportunity to engage in a little "sporting with life." During the in vitro fertilization (IVF) procedure, he fuses a section of animal genetic material to the embryo's chromosomes, so that the embryo has an introduced capacity for accelerated brain growth that can be triggered by the administration of a specific antibiotic. Once the embryo has been implanted in the hired surrogate mother, Dr. Frank prescribes for her the antibiotics that trigger accelerated neural growth in the fetus. The novel opens with the birth of that baby: his own, genetically enhanced, monstrous son VJ, a twentieth-century chimera. In the new mythology of genetic engineering, chimeras are produced by the combination of manipulable species.[8] In animal husbandry such chimeras are produced to increase production and hence profit. But the motivations in human reproductive medicine are more complex, as Cook figures them. The profit motive is replaced by the presumably more acceptable aim of accelerating the growth of the fetal brain and thus enhancing the child's capacity to learn (106).

Mutation interweaves IVF with two other prominent contemporary technologies: information technology and nuclear technology. The link between these technologies is more than metaphoric. All three participate in what N. Katherine Hayles has called "cultural postmodernism": "the realization that what has always been thought of as the essential, unvarying components of human experience are not natural facts of life but social constructions." Nuclear, information, and reproductive and genetic engineering technologies are all alike aspects of the denaturing process that characterizes our postmodern moment: the technical process that deprives something of its (apparently) natural qualities.[9] This same cultural postmodernism suffuses Cook's novel, but as a threat, not a promise. Described in metaphors intermingling the three denaturing technologies, the genetically engineered son of Dr. Victor Frank is the monstrous messenger of those alarming tidings; and the response the novel authorizes is to kill the messenger.

Mutation dramatizes the anxiety of a man whose genetic hegemony (or father-right) is imperiled. Cook uses the thriller genre to figure the assault on, and self-defense of, the sovereign male subject. When the novel begins, Victor Frank's identity (both positional and personal) is under attack: his scientific autonomy is restricted by governmental regulations, his paternal authority is questioned by his psychiatrist wife, and his professional and personal privacy are curtailed by company surveillance of his telephone lines and computer files. In (unacknowledged) response to these threats to this masculine potency, he usurps the female power to create life, with the laboratory conception of his monstrous VJ.

With VJ's birth begins a chain of mysterious events troubling Dr. Frank's home and work life. The novel invites the reader to believe that these are the acts of a deranged employee of Dr. Frank's company, Fertility, Inc., a feminist who has filed a sex discrimination suit against it. Yet the real culprit is VJ himself, locked in oedipal combat with his father for scientific (and reproductive) preeminence. The subplot unmasks Cook's novel as a defense against the anxieties aroused by the multiple and diffuse threats to the authority of the father in the postmodern era: working women, child care centers, new competition for science from industry, the distanced administrative structures of multinational capitalism.

Mutation defends masterfully against the threatening revelation of life's social constructedness: first by reinscribing (and regratifying) characteristically modern narratives of oedipal desire, then by mining the postmodern for its new sources of pleasure, before only finally recontaining the implications of postmodernism for identity construction within a modernist defense of expert knowledge and instrumental reason. While Cook's novel embodies the modernist anguish of dethroned patriarchs, it also makes possible the pleasures of identifying with those who dethrone them, as we vicariously participate with VJ in the gratifications of technological mastery. In his preschool days VJ learns to play chess on the computer; at age three and a half he hides his power by (symbolically) smashing the computer; by age eleven he is a computer hacker, whose entire scientific accomplishment has been made possible by computer crime. Breaking into his father's computer files "just like the kid did in *War Games,*" he falsifies data, steals and erases files, embezzles money (151). In short, VJ enjoys the many forms of technologically constructed power in the contemporary moment. "Whether in biotechnology, disinformation campaigns [or] hightech weapons, the ability to separate text from context and to determine how the new context will be reconstituted is literally the power of life and death."[10]

As Edward Yoxen observes in *The Gene Business,* "now, the essence of life is its constructability."[11] This postmodern assumption of constructability characterizes not only the plot of Cook's novel, in its focus on genetic engineering and reproductive technology, but its aesthetic as well. A crucial aspect of the pleasures of this text is the play of Cook's chimeric narrative, which grafts onto the apparatus of gothic romance the iconography of urbanization and modernization, thus raising questions (without answers) about the relationships between industrialized mass production and scientifically generated reproduction. The deserted tower of *Frankenstein* (in its filmic avatar) has become a replica of Big Ben, set atop the ruin of an abandoned nineteenth-century factory, behind the modern biotechnology corporation directed by Dr. Frank. Condensing feudal isolation with urbanization, solitary individual scientific labor and industrialized science, the very setting of Cook's novel represents the powerful influences of Taylorism and Fordism on the development of modern science.[12] Similarly, the characters reflect Cook's revision of the *Frankenstein* theme to suit the conditions of modern multinational science-as-business. In a neat recapitulation of the move from physical disability as social stigma to mental disability as a social burden, exemplified by the 1930s debates about eugenic "treatments" for mental deficiency, the assistant to the evil scientist is not a hunchback, but a retarded employee of the reproductive and genetic engineering firm. Crime, too, has taken on a high-tech gloss in the interval between Victor Frankenstein's feudal society and Victor Frank's multinational global world.

While Frankenstein's monster strangles his victims, VJ murders not by strangulation, but by inserting a "foreign cancer-causing gene" into their bloodstreams. And the impact of the murder, too, is differently represented: the violation of the social body that resonates through Mary Shelley's fiction is replaced by a violation of the aggregate biological body—the gene pool—in Cook's potboiler.

If Cook really were launching a serious critique of the modern scientific project, as one possible reading of the novel would hold, then the scientific-genetic inheritance linking Victor and his son VJ would have its alternative in Marsha, VJ's mother. Relying on the analytic framework of Evelyn Fox Keller, such an argument would read Marsha as an incarnation of feminist science, or science-as-observation, in contrast to mainstream, post-Baconian science-as-control. [13] As a psychiatrist who has a psychoanalytically oriented therapy practice, Marsha is positioned (so the argument would go) in gendered opposition to her husband and son. While Victor excels in instrumental manipulation of life, Marsha's strength is observation. Assessing VJ's character as incomplete, she first suspects his chimeric origins. She recognizes the extent of VJ's desire for control, while Victor underestimates it; she is appalled by his ruthless experimental drive, while Victor is merely seduced into scientific competition with him.

Although Keller's gender-polarized construction of scientific knowledge has illuminated the career of Barbara McClintock, no such simple opposition works in this novel, which reflects less the gendered history of science than the gendered codes of production and consumption governing mass-market representations. Marsha's position as a practicing psychiatrist implicates her in the Enlightenment project of the production of bio-power common to the biological and social sciences alike. [14] As a psychiatrist, Marsha represents the same exercise of ideologically inflected professional power as does her husband; central to her expert technique, as to his, is the control and manipulation of human sexuality, though her tools are words and images rather than segments of the human body. Marsha's expert response to VJ's "difference" literalizes the Foucauldian notion of a disciplinary technology; she keeps detailed computerized files on her patients (including her own son), is tireless in surveillance (traveling to interview all of VJ's contacts at school, child care center, and lab), and subjects her patients—and, in a climactic scene, her son as well—to complex psychiatric tests and examinations.

Yet Marsha is also an effect of the very exercise of power she fears. As a woman, she is not just the subject of power, but also its object.

Even her recourse to a standard of psychiatric normalcy, while emphasizing the Frankensteinian theme of science out of control, positions not just her son but herself within the exercise of control that she purports to resist: the discourse of normalization. Marsha's own behavior attests to the tyranny of normative assessments of women: she works in a study carpeted in dusty rose with white furniture, is a dab hand at the stove, exhibits maternal concern for both her children. Joining professional competence (the ability to position others as docile objects of her expert knowledge) to what Cook obviously intends as psychiatrically normal femininity (attesting to her own subjection to the law of the Father) Marsha is impossibly positioned between passivity and activity, subject and object, doomed to fail in her attempt to resist the control plots of her husband and son.[15] Yet as Marsha's characterization reveals, Cook's excursion into the postmodern spaces of fragmentation and decontextualization is all in the service of an ultimate recontainment under the patriarchal order of instrumental science.

Despite, or perhaps because of, its deployment of ideologically inflected cultural codes linking men to the project of active instrumental understanding, and women to the project of passive observational understanding, *Mutation* fails to deliver what its jacket promises: "a cautionary tale of the perils of genetic engineering." Arguably, this failure arises from the doubled nature of cultural postmodernism, which appeals on the biological, scientific level as a practice producing greater control, yet promises on the level of the social and philosophical to reduce (white, male) control and authorize alternative subject positions.[16] Cultural postmodernism on the level of science, as the physical decontextualization and fragmentation enacted in genetic engineering and reproductive technology, appeals to Victor Frank because it enhances his power as a scientist. Yet at the same time, cultural postmodernism on the level of the social, in the form of a working professional wife, feminist agitation, the new influence of non-Western industrial techniques, and so on, frightens him because it reduces his sense of power *as a* (white) man.

Rather than critiquing the technology of genetic engineering, with its transgressive knowledge concerning the (re)constructability of human life, *Mutation* actually cautions against loss of control of the technology, through its commodification. Dr. Frank's first fall, the novel implies, was the move from monitored academic and medical science to freewheeling industrial science-for-profit. Yet if the cautionary tale criticizes one sort of profit-taking from reproductive and genetic engineering, it deliberately engages in another, as a highly marketable trade press book with good prospects to be a successful motion picture as well. While it may invoke contemporary issues, *Mutation*'s foremost aim is to create a plot that will satisfy the needs of (male) readers, and so justify its jacket description as "compulsively readable."

To that end, although the novel purports to address responsible anxieties ("Robin Cook's new techno-medical thriller probes every father's greatest fear"), in fact it gratifies oedipal wishes, in accord with its jacket billing as a "spellbinding chronicle of a father pitted against his son in mythic battle." *Mutation* appeals to both male parties in the oedipal drama structuring Western modernity, dramatizing the son's fantasy that he will surpass his father's potency and threaten his dominion, as well as the father's ultimate victory against that sexual-social threat.

Nancy Miller has suggested that behind the aesthetic criterion of plausibility lurks a masculinist ideology discrediting as implausible any plot figuring a woman's desire for power.[17] Reversing Miller's insight, it is clear that *Mutation* disrupts the masculinist aesthetic of plausibility, while reinforcing its importance as a principle of ideological control, by intervening into the primary ground of female power: reproduction. In the novel's climactic scene, when father and son are "pitted . . . in mythic battle," Victor realizes that he will be unable to persuade the police that he needs their help: "He could see himself telling the policeman that he has a son who is an utter genius and who is growing a race of retarded workers in glass jars and who has killed poeple to protect a secret lab he built by blackmailing embezzlers in his father's company" (342).

Victor is trapped by the gendered criteria for plausibility. If the story he must tell the police is implausible, he will not be able to get their help in battling his monster son. Of course it *is* implausible: not because it is a power plot for women, but because it is a reproductive plot for men. Ironically, Cook invokes that aesthetic of plausibility only to debunk it: what the cop won't believe, the reader will—at least during the period of suspended disbelief bracketing this work of fiction. Yet, to put the final twist on the issue of plots and plausibilities, our daily newspapers serve up increasingly strange— even garish—tales of reproductive technology each morning, as fact.[18]

When the constraints of plausibility force Victor to face his monstrous son alone, the stage is set for a masculine battle literally over the female body. Replicating through science and technology the elided act of sexual intercourse that is the pretext of oedipal battle, Dr. Frank concocts an explosive mixture, makes his way through the network of dark subterranean tunnels leading to VJ's hidden ectogenesis labora- tory, and plants the explosives at the gate of the giant sluice, built to hold back the torrential waters of the mill pond. The explosives deto- nate, unleashing a flood of "undirected and uncontrolled water" that topples the clock tower and reduces the granite-clad lab building and all its contents to rubble. Frank's orgasmic act is a response to charac- teristically modernist and gender-specific anxieties, whether we de- scribe them in terms of technology (as apraxia, horror at the "disused factory . . . the stopping and breakdown of technological systems in modern society") or of Kristevan psychoanalysis (abjection/horror at the female body.)[19]

The scene seems a victory of psychoanalytic insight over quanti- fiable "results,' perhaps even a triumph of women's ways of knowing over phallocratic knowledge. With the bursting floodgates, female fluidity triumphs over male solidity, female timelessness over male temporality, the female reproductive system over its scientifically pro- duced ectogenetic surrogate (358–359). Such an outcome would in- deed articulate a critical—and within the scientific community of Cook's peers, a controversial—position on contemporary reproductive technology.

Yet Cook appends a coda that undoes this victory of the female gothic and reestablishes the control and dominance of instrumental science and patriarchal culture. Although VJ and his father are swept away by the consequences of their view of the world as constructable, Marsha too is (re)constructed—by her discovery of the power of male genetic continuity. One chimeric sibling survives the climactic father- son battle, having been implanted in an unwitting woman who has since given birth and reared him. Marsha is confronted by him in her therapy practice, and with the return of the repressed male reproduc- tive potency she devolves to a parodic female impotence. Because Marsha is both the subject and object of power, due to her profes- sional incorporation within the disciplinary technologies and her sub- jection as a woman, she is unable to resist the monstrous plot of patrilineage. Deskilled as a therapist, she accepts the recommendation of her high-school-teacher boyfriend that she buy a dog for "pet therapy." As he rather sinisterly assures her, "dogs could put . . . psychiatrists out of business" (360). When we last see her, she has been definitively put in her place: she sits sobbing softly in the shopping mall parking lot (367).

With its glib revisions of *Frankenstein*, *Mutation* is a characteristic postmodern product: a pastiche of literary forms from other eras, designed to satisfy certain contemporary readers' (and perhaps film viewers') needs, but ultimately to be consumed without remnant. Does it follow that the text valorizes a postmodern worldview? Far from it. In defending the embattled male subject, Robin Cook's *Mutation* illustrates, even enjoys, but ultimately recontains under modernist scientific control the postmodern culture that (on both biological and social levels) calls into question the very concept of the autonomous instrumental subject.

Despite his purported critical position on the expert technology of reproductive and genetic engineering, Cook in fact defends the hegemony of the experts. A feminist reader, focusing on how expert knowledge is constructed to obscure the operations of power, will mark *Mutation*'s uncritical dramatization of the dangers of female entry into, or assimilation by, expert disciplines, in the story of Marsha's (re)construction as docile consumer through her participation in, and psychiatrically based attempt at resistence to, reproductive technology. Rather than assessing the dangers posed by reproductive technology itself, *Mutation* dramatizes the risks of its commercial applications. Focusing on the dangers of an unregulated biotechnology industry, Cook's novel stresses the crucial importance of disciplinary gate-keeping, representing academic medicine as carefully monitored and inherently responsible. Given the author's position as a Columbia- and Harvard-trained physician, affiliated with (albeit on leave from) the Massachusetts Eye and Ear Infirmary, it is perhaps no surprise that his novel preserves, unchallenged, the myths of a value-neutral academic medicine and a value-neutral technology.

Fay Weldon's *The Cloning of Joanna May,* also published in 1989, is a witty meditation on the implications of cultural postmodernism (both biological and social) for the construction of the individual subject. The plot, like Cook's *Mutation,* links reproductive technology to nuclear and information technologies by their shared assumption that life is de- and re-constructable. Yet in contrast to Cook's novel, Weldon's *Joanna May* affirms the notion of a decentered, nonhierarchical subject position. Joanna May, ex-wife of nuclear tycoon Carl May, discovers that her ex-husband has had her cloned. To be precise, an ovum taken from her without her permission by her husband's collaborator, Dr. Holly, was subjected to irritation until the nucleus split into four. The four resulting embryos were implanted into (unwitting) gestational or surrogate mothers, and the result is that Joanna May discovers, at age sixty, that she has four genetically identical sisters/daughters half her age. Weldon interweaves Joanna's response to this unsettling news with the narrative of Carl May's attempt to contain the public relations damage to his company, British Nuclear Reactors, Inc., by the Chernobyl nuclear accident. Charting the impact of these two different nuclear disasters, the novel explores the positive and negative implications of cultural postmodernism they exemplify, in their shared assumption that life on the level of the nucleus, and thus identity, is (re)constructable.

The idea of cloning central to Weldon's novel has a long representational history, from the golem of Jewish mysticism (the clay creature brought to life), to the Greek creation legend in which Prometheus created mortal men of clay and water, to the alchemical rituals for creating new life out of human blood and sperm, to the successful laboratory cloning of frogs in the United States in the 1950s and the discussion of cloning during debate on the 1990 Embryo Research Bill in the United Kingdom.[20] As a term for a scientific technique, *cloning* is inspecific: it may refer to techniques that have already been carried out successfully in animals—such as the division of an embryo at the two-cell stage to produce two identical embryos, or the process of nucleus substitution (the removal of the nucleus from an unfertilized ovum, and its replacement with the nucleus from another cell.) Or it may refer to techniques of asexual reproduction such as parthenogenesis, the mechanical manipulation of an unfertilized ovum to produce cell division. This process has been observed in lizards and some birds, such as turkeys, but "parthenogenetic individuals never survive pregnancy in mammals."[21] However, in the popular imagination the term *cloning* usually calls up the notion of copying, or replicating, a person through the implantation of an embryo, "copied" from a single cell, into a gestating woman.

The literary figuration of cloning might be said to begin with *Frankenstein,* which inaugurated a textual tradition obsessively reworking the theme of the male clone, from David M. Rorvik's *In His Own Image: The Cloning of a Man* to Ira Levin's *The Boys from Brazil.*[22] While the pretexts for the cloning range from a relatively benign desire for personal continuity to a malignant scheme to reanimate the Third Reich, these figurations posit the same deep motivation: a male desire for reproductive control and autonomy. "By re-producing an identical heir one could, in a way, become one's own father again and again—eternally."[23]

Weldon's novel breaks decisively from the tradition of male novels about the cloning of men, invoking instead a tradition of female literary and theoretical treatments of cloning that includes Charlotte Perkins Gilman's *Herland* (1915), Joanna Russ's "When It Changed" (1972) and *The Female Man* (1975), Shulamith Firestone's *The Dialectic of Sex* (1970), and Naomi Mitchison's little-known *Solution Three* and well-known *Memoirs of a Spacewoman*.[24] Like these feminist works, Weldon's novel figures the cloning as parthenogenesis—the asexual reproduction from an unfertilized ovum—rather than the insertion of the nucleus from a body cell into an enucleated egg, figured by Rorvik and Levin. I want to emphasize the symbolic resonance of that choice: a model based on the gutting of an ovum is replaced by one in which the ovum is self-sufficient source of life. The gap between these two definitions of cloning figures an ideological gap as well—between a masculinist and a feminist model for the construction of a gendered identity. While cloning is figured as enhancing male power through the objectification and control of a woman's body (or body parts), parthenogenesis is figured as producing female control over a woman's own body, and autonomy from male domination: the aim is not power, but pleasure.[25]

The Cloning of Joanna May plays with the gap between these two notions of cloning. Carl May intended to produce power for himself when he had Joanna cloned as punishment for an episode of infidelity. As he explains, "when it's secret knowledge is power" (35). Cloning Joanna, Carl undercuts her individuality, reconstructing her as the fungible object of his male gaze: "She was growing little hairlines round her eyes: so I gave time itself a kick in the teeth. It seemed a pity to let it all go to waste, when you could save it so easily," he says. (34) Yet despite Carl's intentions, Joanna's response to her cloning reconstructs it from an act of masculine power, objectification, and control to one producing feminine pleasure. It becomes "not cloning in the modern sense, but parthenogenesis plus implantation, and a good time had by all" (34).

In this act of ideological reconstruction, Weldon's novel not only invokes the female literary tradition by its parthenogenetic theme, but also subverts the male literary tradition, as embodied by Rider Haggard's misogynistic imperialist fantasy, *She* (1886). A dense layer of intertextual allusions links *Joanna May* to *She*, while reversing its Victorian valorization of imperial power by viewing it through a subversively feminist, postmodernist lens. Haggard's immensely popular novel about an immortal, all-powerful woman explored and exploited three subtly interrelated late Victorian phenomena: "an interest in Egypt and, more generally, a preoccupation with colonized countries and imperial decline; a fascination with spiritualism; and an obsession not just with the so-called New Woman but with striking new visions and re-visions of female power."[26] In both characterization and theme, Weldon rings feminist changes on these late Victorian cultural obsessions, replacing the Victorian male's defensive response to the threat to cultural and sexual hegemony embodied in "She who must be obeyed" with a postmodern feminist affirmation of difference—cultural, sexual, or psychological—as embodied in the clones of Joanna May.

Weldon rewrites Haggard to parallel the production of imperial power through exploration by the production of social power through biological manipulation. The protagonist of *She* receives a hieroglyphic manuscript on his birthday, whose text urges him to "seek out the woman, and learn the secret of Life, and if thou mayest find a way, slay her."[27] Just as Haggard's protagonist receives the text that prompts his quest from his guardian, Professor Holly, so in *The Cloning of Joanna May* a Dr. Holly "gives" Joanna May the bodily texts she must decipher: her clone siblings. Joanna May is both the woman and the explorer; her DNA is the hieroglyphs figuring the "secret of Life."

Joanna May's response to the news that she has been cloned develops from a masculinist notion of identity construction to a feminist one, a shift represented in an overarching pun linking identity to visualization. The act of infidelity to Carl that provoked the cloning moves Joanna May from passive observation to action. "I, Joanna May. No longer 'Eye.' Acting; not observing. Doing, not looking. Dangerous, murderous, and not even knowing it" (103) Puns on the relationship of identity and sight proliferate in *Joanna May,* for Weldon continually subverts the power of visualization, fragmenting and undermining it. She metaphorically links the experience of the loss of the aura to the dethroning of the visual, from the episode of *"orbisecto de se,"* in which a woman prisoner plucks out her own eye, to the meditations on the possibility of God's existence ("there's more to this than meets the eye"), to the weary acknowledgment that identity is an increasingly rare entity now that God has been banished by the simulacra of mass consumer culture:

Why bother to preserve the "I"? It's seen too much of sights not fit for human eyes, it is not fit to live. It no longer believes in life. . . . The great "I" has fled, say the eyes in the wallpaper: only the clones remain, staring. If the I offend thee pluck it out. Idopectomy. (46)

Deliberately invoking the revisionary power of the woman behind the wallpaper in Charlotte Perkins Gilman's classic attack on male scientific and medical dominance, Weldon subverts the traditional Enlightenment association of identity with visual representation. The gaze, structuring both seer and seen into the binary relation of subject and object, has been a preeminent trope for the Enlightenment subject, reflecting the long history of ocularcentrism, or privileging of the visual, that has characterized Western Enlightenment thinking.[28] Playing on the rhyme between *eye* and *I,* Weldon replaces sight with sound, and traces Joanna May's journey from being the object of the male "eye" to an active subject, her own "I."

When Joanna learns of the clones' existence, her initial response reflects a modernist construction of female identity as the object of the male (technological) gaze: "What woman of sixty would want to meet herself at thirty: rerun of some dreary old film, in which she gave a bad performance, like as not, and split-screen technique at that" (112). She conceptualizes the cloning in terms of the objectifying gaze and the psychoanalytic family romance, imagining that the news will be equally unpleasant to the clones as it initially is to her: "A kind of extra mother, dreadfully like oneself. Seeing what one would grow into" (128).

Yet a feminist process of decontextualization follows these initial reactions. When she and the clones finally meet, they escape both patriarchal and technological determinism. Although at first old patterns dominate and she plays mother to their daughter, they soon identify and elude the patriarchal patterns they are enacting: " 'I will not be your mother,' said Joanna May, 'I hereby renounce the role.' . . . They allowed Joanna May no authority: . . . they would not even accept her status as originator" (251). Rather, *they* give birth to her, at least metaphorically: "When I acknowledged my sisters, my twins, my clones, my children, when I stood out against Carl May, I found myself," Joanna muses, then invokes a birth metaphor: "Pop! I was out" (246).

The Cloning of Joanna May, unlike *Mutation,* invokes technology in order to deconstruct its misogynistic context, recontextualize it, and wield the subverted technology for feminist purposes. Weldon audaciously suggests that the powers of de- and re-contextualization can render even a technology so susceptible to instrumentality and ob-jectification as cloning reconstructible along feminist lines. The novel's subplots confirm this, as the denaturing technologies of nuclear power and information technology are also reconfigured and redeployed—not to undo, but to serve, Joanna's wishes. Joanna May's clones become not her competitors for male affection, but her close friends; Carl May's nuclear power plant functions not to aggrandize his power, but to limit it; and the electronic media he intended to use to serve his own needs record his demise, in a lethal baptism in the cooling pond of one of his Magnox reactors.

The novel ends with a celebration of the powers not of geneti-cally based control but of environmentally produced emancipation: a utopian collective act of defiance against Carl May's unitary, determin-istic construction of individual identity, revealed in his malicious attempt—with the cloning—to appropriate and displace Joanna's selfhood. On his deathbed, Carl May begs Joanna: "Take me, remake me. For God's sake, remake me" (262). Turnabout is fair play. Af-firming the reparative, emancipatory powers of the understanding of life as socially constructed, Joanna has Carl cloned, in order to re-mother him, with the help of her own clones, and so repair the damage of his chimeric childhood.

Living collectively with the new baby, the clones redistribute among themselves the roles that they hitherto held by birth or mar-riage, with one acting as gestational mother, two others as nurturant mother (in the realization that "a child will take any clone, it seems, for a mother"), and another as both medical student and wife. These new combinations embrace the biological and social possibilities of cultural postmodernism, calling into question the previously unquestioned links between conception, birth, and mothering, as well as such natu-ralized phenomena as time (including the importance of birth order) and space (including the concept of discrete bodies and minds) (264).

In its subversive critique of the Enlightenment gaze, *The Cloning of Joanna May* returns us to Lyotard's question: What is the unconscious of an individual born by in vitro fertilization? How does this originary moment influence the individual's gender identity and family rela-tions? As theorized by both Lacanian and object relations psychoana-lysts, the gaze is also—in a different register—a moment central to the process of identity construction. Despite differing in their construction of the outcome, both analytic schools hold that the mirroring moment of mutual gaze between mother and baby is a definitive step in the construction of an identity. For Lacanians, the moment calls forth a subject structured by the fundamental mirroring misrecognition that persists in the new realm of language he/she then enters; for followers of Winnicott, it initiates a pattern of social contact and collaborative creation that forms both the ground of the individual's identity and the site of creativity.[29]

Both Cook and Weldon pay homage to this central icon of identity, the gaze, yet the difference in their representations recapitulates their very different ideological positions on the question of the construction of a gendered identity that we have already seen at operation in plot, characterization, and imagery. Cook's representation of the gaze of the IVF baby extends the self-engendering project of Enlightenment science, as analyzed by Evelyn Fox Keller: rendering the woman marginal, or eliding her altogether, it represents the father-son dyad as autonomous, self-generating, self-gratifying.

In *Mutation,* VJ's eyes are the first thing anybody notices about him; the thing that makes him different, Other. But it is not only their astonishing blueness or their challenging adult stare that is remarkable, but rather the asymmetry of his gaze. The infant VJ refuses to look at his mother; even when turned to face her, the baby looks only at his father, as if to communicate her irrelevance (21). What is the unconscious of a child engendered in vitro? Cook's imagery suggests that a masculine technological birth produces a child embodying the fantasy of masculine autonomy. Supplanting the mother by the father, this process creates a new identity, the result of a reconstructed model of gender identification and family relations. Since men engender themselves, both father and son are self-sufficient, both biologically and socially. VJ's IVF-produced gaze reads as a parody of Winnicott. In place of the soothing mutual interchange between child and his/her maternal environment (as the mother looks into the child's eyes and sees there an image of herself), here we see mirrored back the glassy clinical environment of the test tube, for VJ's turquoise eyes are "cold and bright as ice" (21).[30]

In contrast to Cook's affirmation, and even extension, of the identity-constructing power of the gaze, *The Cloning of Joanna May* subverts the identity structure produced in that originary moment of maternal mirroring, and reconfirmed by a cultural valorization of the visual. Weldon's representation of the gaze everywhere calls it into

Product of the aptly named "One Plus One Studio," this cover illustration presents a realistic representation of a test tube, central icon in the contemporary debate over reproductive technology, whose transparent(ly) phallic image is superimposed on the image of the blond head and well-formed torso of VJ, the "Mutation." Arms folded, torso held in a posture of phallic stiffness, lips closed in a determined line, Cook's monstrous creation gazes unflinchingly at the reader. The challenge is unmistakable, as is the (white, male) reader that challenging gaze constructs. Mutation *invites that reader to identify with both the scientist father and the monstrous son, and so replicate in a textual genealogy the biological genealogy that is the novel's subject. Cook's book jacket echoes its content, interpellating a male reader who will join him in the complicitous explorations of reproductive and genetic engineering. (By kind permission of the Putnam Publishing Group)*

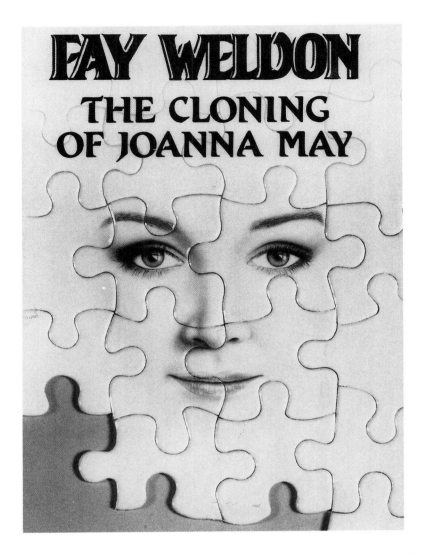

FAY WELDON

THE CLONING OF JOANNA MAY

Weldon's jacket illustration presents a female face—or, to be exact, part of it: blue eyes, delicate nose, enigmatically smiling lips. Like the novel within, the jacket illustration resists the defining power of the gaze: irregular lines fissure the face into an incomplete jigsaw puzzle, breaking off to reveal portions of a background as blue as the character's eyes. Puzzle pieces scattered from Joanna May's portrait onto the author's photograph on the back of the jacket suggest the fragmentary nature of identity, whether fictional or factual: there are not enough pieces to complete the puzzle. The book jacket, like the novel, subverts the notion of unitary identity to valorize a different gaze and a different notion of identity production, constructing the preferred reader as one who can—like Joanna May—"conceive difference without opposition." (By kind permission of Harper Collins Publishers) question, and with it the broader outlines of Enlightenment thought it enforces: the privileging of the visual and the valorizing of singularity and autonomy.

Weldon's novel consistently rejects the engendering power of the mirror gaze that Lacan and Winnicott both understood as producing the gendered individual subject. Instead, images of shattering mirrors throughout the novel invoke Tennyson's Lady of Shalott, only to subvert that Victorina myth of the seductive authority of masculine aesthetic and industrial creation. Breaking the aura, deauthorizing the specularized notion of identity, Joanna May's experience of her clones educates her in a different notion of identity production. Rather than undercutting her own selfhood by their visual similarity, as Carl May had planned, the clones enhance her selfhood by forcing Joanna to escape her position as product of the male gaze and to take on agency. It is not Lancelot who draws Joanna May into the world, but rather her clones—other women like herself who refuse to submit to Lancelot's objectifying gaze or to play the mirroring mother, to a man or to each other.

Even the concluding decision to clone Carl May escapes the paradigm of faithful maternal mirroring. In contrast both to Winnicott's mirroring mother-child dyad and to Lacan's hypostasized maternal intention to mirror the infant back faithfully, when Weldon's clones take on the final job of re-mothering the little clone of Carl May, they disavow any claims to maternal fidelity or unity: "We would have been faithful, kind and true, but fate was against us. We are one woman split five ways, a hundred ways, a million million ways" (265)

Literary representation resists any simple, unitary, or essential answer to Lyotard's query about "the unconscious of a child engendered *in vitro*," as comparison of these two contemporary popular novels demonstrates. Robin Cook's *Mutation* and Fay Weldon's *The Cloning of Joanna May* use the figuration of reproductive technology to advance very different positions on the meaning of identity in this ambiguous era of cultural postmodernism. Cook figures reproductive technology as an opportunity to affirm and extend the powers of the masculine individual subject. In contrast, Weldon subverts the oppressive potential for technological control embodied by reproductive technology, to affirm instead an emancipatory feminist reconstruction of identity as diffuse, multiple, and nonhierarchical: a "difference without opposition."[31]

Evolutionary Identities

The Gendered Ape:
Early Representations
of Primates in Europe

Londa Schiebinger

Of the Orangutan: It is a brute of a kind so singular, that man cannot behold it without contemplating himself.

Georges-Louis Leclerc,
Comte de Buffon, *Histoire naturelle*

Europeans were puzzled when they first came face to face with anthropoid apes in the seventeenth and eighteenth centuries. The discovery of the great apes of Africa and Asia seemed to confirm the notion of a great "chain of being"—a hierarchy of creation reaching from God and the angels down through man to the lowliest worm.[1] Apes' shockingly human character emboldened naturalists to declare them the long-sought "missing link" between humans and animals. Were these degenerate sons of Adam and Noah, as Augustine had taught? Or were they "natural man," fully human but devoid of civilization, as Rousseau and Monboddo would conclude years later? Could apes through education become sufficiently cultured to take a seat in the British Parliament, as did the amiable (and fictional) Sir Oran Haut-ton in Thomas Love Peacock's *Melincourt?* Were they human or beast?

Scholars have long been fascinated with the distinctions between apes and humans. An enormous and popular literature explores whether apes have the ability to walk erect, speak, reason, and create culture. Historians, focusing on how the early modern naturalists conceived the human/ape difference, have tended to explore similar issues.[2] As we shall see, however—and this has not been pointed out—naturalists' earliest chronicles and images of these our closest relatives were also highly gendered. Edward Tyson's "wild man" (actually a chimpanzee brought to London from Angola in 1699) was portrayed with a well-defined beard and walking stick to mark his sex.

The Dutch anatomist Nicolaas Tulp's *Homo Sylvestris* was a demure female, drawn in 1641 with eyes cast downward, "well-rounded" breasts, an abdomen swollen as though pregnant, and hands and feet quietly folded. In their attempt to distinguish humans and apes, early modern naturalists looked to the *females* of both groups, investigating the unique characters of female anatomy. Female apes, most everyone agreed, shared with humans that "obscene organ of brute pleasure"— the clitoris. But did they have hymens, those anatomical guarantees of virginity? Naturalists also wanted to know if female apes menstruated, if their vaginas were angled like women's, and if so, how this affected coitus and male pleasure.

Apes held a very special place in the European imagination. Naturalists in this period tended to sympathize more with apes—often portrayed as gentlemen and ladies—than with the "primitive" peoples of Africa, Asia, and the Americas. Natural histories reveal them wanting to see simians as humans, and Africans (especially Hottentots) as brutes. The Hottentots of the Cape of Good Hope were said to share with the ape the status of missing link, being the lowest rank of humans in the gradual transition up from the apes. This portrayal of the Hottentots prepared the European mind for the fabulous idea that apes were hybrid humans, that simians sprang from the union of a male monkey and a woman (usually an African).

It is important to remember that, at the same time that naturalists—wittingly or unwittingly—inscribed into nature parochial mores and fantasies, they also looked to nature for solutions to questions about sexual and racial equality. Nature and its laws spoke loudly in this age of Enlightenment, where *philosophes* attempted to set social convention on a natural basis. Natural law (as distinct from the positive law of nations) was held to be immutable, given by God or inherent in the material universe. Science with its promise of a neutral and privileged viewpoint seemed to hold the key to those laws.

Also relevant for our story is that, in the seventeenth and eighteenth centuries, Europeans who described apes were almost exclusively male. Female naturalists were a rare breed, female taxonomists even rarer. There are many reasons for this. Europeans who came in contact with apes abroad were merchants, explorers, missionaries, and occasionally naturalists—among whom few women were found. Women were systematically excluded—by institutional fiat and social imperative— from the newly developing sciences. Many women, it is true, collected and exchanged flora and fauna, and for a time botany was considered a science especially suited to women. Yet even Maria Merian, the adventurous entomologist who traveled to Surinam in search of exotic caterpillars in the early eighteenth century, presented only her observations, leaving classification to her male colleagues. In later years the traditional informal routes into science taken by Merian and others (noble networks and craft guilds, for example) were closed to women.[3] As a result, knowledge of the great apes arriving on European shores in this period was shaped to a great extent by males and their life experiences.

This essay investigates how European notions of gender and race molded the study of male and female apes, in both scientific and literary texts. As we shall see, these early accounts often told more about European customs than about the natural habits of apes. Rousseau recognized this as early as 1755:

> For the three or four hundred years since the inhabitants of Europe have inundated the other parts of the world and continuously published new collections of voyages and reports, I am convinced that we know no other men except the Europeans . . . ; furthermore, it appears . . . that under the pompous name of the study of man no one does anything except study the men of his country.[4]

The apes stood mutely by as naturalists (in this case European and male) ascribed to females the modesty they were hoping perhaps to find in their own wives and daughters, and to males the wildest fantasies of violent interspecies rape.[5]

Distinguishing Humans from Apes

Anthropocentricism continued to dominate natural history long after geocentrism had been displaced in astronomy. Copernicus dethroned humans from the center of the universe, banishing them to a small planet circling the sun. Humankind nevertheless remained the chief of creation, "lord of animals" on that planet.[6] Linnaeus captured these presumptions in the term *Primates*—literally, "of the first rank"—a term he coined in 1758 to embrace the order of *Mammalia* that included humans.[7] Humans were no longer uniquely situated just below the angels: apes, monkeys, lemurs, and bats were also considered Primates. Seeing apes as human made it easier to see humans as animals—a notion still highly contested in this period.

Naturalists today recognize four distinct types of anthropoid ape: the *orangutan* (the name first appeared in scientific literature in 1641, though the animal described was a chimpanzee); the *chimpanzee* (the

African term first appeared as *quimpezé* in French texts in 1738; the English *chimpanzee* appeared the same year); the *gibbon* (first described by Buffon); and the *gorilla* (a term introduced by the American missionary Thomas Savage in 1847, though gorillas had been described earlier under various other names).[8] In the seventeenth and eighteenth centuries, voyagers and naturalists indiscriminately used the term *orangutan* (Malayan for "wild man" or "man of the woods") with reference to the great apes of both Africa and Asia.[9] Petrus Camper in the 1780s was one of the first to distinguish the African "orangutan" (the chimpanzee) from the Asiatic or true orangutan.[10] Great apes were also called *satyrs* (after the creature described in ancient mythology), *pygmies* (another term of ancient coinage), *jocko, pongo,* and various other Europeanizations of native terms.

Comparative anatomists were struck by similarities in form and figure between apes and humans.[11] Edward Tyson, in his pioneering *Orang-Outang, sive Homo Sylvestris; or, The Anatomy of a Pygmie Compared with That of a Monkey, an Ape, and a Man* (1699), documented forty-eight ways in which his "Pygmie" resembled a human, along with thirty-four ways in which it differed.[12] Montaigne, by contrast, rejected the human/animal dualism and suggested that there is more difference between any two given men than between any given man and a beast. Nontheless the great apes seemed to confirm the notion of hierarchy and continuity in nature. Humans—part brute, part angel—were thought to link the mortal world to the divine. Might apes be human or the link between humans and brutes, just as asbestos linked minerals and plants, the water polyp *Hydra* joined plants and animals, and the flying squirrel linked birds and quadrupeds?[13] As Tyson, England's founder of comparative anatomy, put it: "The Transition is so gradual that there appears a very great Similitude, as well between the meanest Plant and some Minerals; as between the lowest Rank of Men and the highest kind of Animals."[14]

Carl Linnaeus jolted the scholarly world when in 1735 he placed humans in the same order with monkeys and sloths.[15] He shook that world further in 1758 when he declared there to be a second species of human, *Homo troglodytes*—those golden-eyed, nocturnal cave dwellers whom Buffon dismissed as albino Africans.[16] Concerning his radical reordering of nature, Linnaeus remarked:

> I know full well what great difference exists between man and beast when viewed from a moral point of view: man is the only creature with a rational and immortal soul. . . . If viewed, however, from the point

of view of natural history and considering only the body, I can discover scarcely any mark by which man can be distinguished from the apes. . . . Neither in the face nor in the feet, nor in the upright gait, nor in any other aspect of his external structure does man differ from the apes.[17]

Few natural historians went as far as Linnaeus, actually ranking one type of ape (his imaginary troglodytes) in the same genus as humans. While Rousseau and the Scotsman Lord Monboddo argued that apes were remnants of "natural man," most naturalists saw apes as bearing human characteristics, but certainly not human.[18] Naturalists pondered an enormous array of possibilities for the nature and source of human uniqueness (and superiority). Was the human uniquely a political animal, a laughing animal, a tool-making animal, a religious animal, a cooking animal, or an animal possessing private property? All of these were put forward, at one time or another, as the sine qua non of human existence. Buffon, struck by the many similarities in physical form between humans and apes, remarked that "if figure alone is regarded, we might consider this animal [the generic orang] as the first among apes, or the last among men."[19] Debates concerning how nearly apes approximated humans were wide-ranging, but four questions pervaded discussion: Can they think? Can they speak? Can they walk erect? Can they create culture?[20]

The belief that humans exhibit a superior form of reason can be traced to the ancient world. According to Aristotle, the human soul comprised three elements: the nutritive soul, which humans share with vegetables; the sensitive soul, shared with animals; and the rational soul, peculiar to humankind. In the Middle Ages, scholastics raised humans to a point midway between the angels and the beasts. Humans thus shared reason and intellect with the angels, body and senses with the animals. Augustine of Hippo thus saw reason as a God-given gift setting humans apart from the rest of the animals.[21]

Apes were rarely seen, however, as completely devoid of intellectual abilities. Albertus Magnus, the thirteenth-century cleric, gave as proof of simian good judgment the fact that when a female ape sees a human baby or the young of some other animal, she will not attempt to nurse it but will lead it to the breast of its proper mother.[22] In the eighteenth century, comparative anatomists such as Tyson believed that the orang brain closely resembled the human brain.[23] The question then arose: Does mind reduce to matter, as Descartes had taught? Do apes have the ability to reason? Locke, who derived all ideas from sensation, denied that apes can reason like men. Locke similarly denied that they possess the "power of abstraction," of comparing ideas and generalizing from their experience.[24] David Hume granted animals the power of experimental reasoning, but for Hume experimental reasoning was but a type of instinct, not conscious reflection upon experience.[25] Most naturalists concluded that, despite certain bodily similarities, apes failed to measure up to humans in terms of mind.[26] Tyson and Buffon were typical in asserting that organized matter could never produce the nobler faculties of the human mind: there must be some higher principle. Buffon called it "divine spirit";[27] Blumenbach, echoing Linnaeus, proclaimed: "All with one voice declare that here is the highest and best prerogative of man, the use of reason"—and it was reason that made him "lord and master of the rest of the animals."[28] Margaret Cavendish, following Montaigne but going against the mainstream, suggested that beasts—even vegetables and minerals—have their own types of reason and language, and that man's presumption of sovereignty is only hubris.[29]

Speech was another traditional mark of humanity. The French Cardinal de Polignac reportedly approached an orangutan on display at the Jardin du Roi, saying: "Speak, and I will baptize you."[30] Some animals did, of course, speak. Cardinal Ascanius had a parrot that could recite the entire Christian creed.[31] Some naturalists claimed that apes, too, were capable of speech. Claude Perrault demonstrated in the second half of the seventeenth century that their speech organs were identical to those of humans.[32] Linnaeus claimed that the *Homo troglodytes* expressed itself by a kind of hissing (fig. 1). In his dissertation on the "Anthropomorpha," Linnaeus affirmed that troglodytes could speak, although he claimed their language was guttural and difficult even for *Homo sapiens* to learn. In European languages they could master only "yes" and "no."[33] Voyagers commonly reported that native peoples believed certain apes were capable of speech but remained forever silent for fear of being forced to work and live in subjugation.[34]

Linnaeus, Rousseau, and Monboddo, however, turned the tables, claiming that language was not natural even for humans. Linnaeus gave as evidence the "wild people" (the boy who lived among oxen in Bamberg, the boy who lived with sheep in Ireland, the girl of Champagne), none of whom could speak. For Rousseau, language was an invention of human society—one of the things that made humans weak and effeminate.[35] Monboddo noted that some people were mute but for that reason no less human; the orangutan in his view was perfectly rational and human, eloquent in its silence. In Peacock's

Ameen. Acad. vol. VI.   *Tab. I.*

1. TROGLODYTA Bontii.   *2. LUCIFER Aldrovandi.*   *3. SATYRUS Tulpii.*   *4. PYGMÆUS Edwardi.*

FIG. 1   *Linnaeus's* Anthropomorpha *(humanlike figures). The female* Homo troglodytes *(cave man or night person) on the left represents Linnaeus's second species of human. This drawing is taken from Bontius's illustration of an orangutan (compare fig. 6) but omits "the Hottentot apron" that Linnaeus describes in the text. The figure second from the left represents* Homo caudatus *(tailed man), also a creature belonging to the human genus, but cruder than* Homo troglodytes*. The other two figures portray apes. From Carl Linnaeus, "Anthropomorpha," respondent C. E. Hoppius (1760), in* Amoenitates academicae *(Erlangen, 1789), vol. 6, plate 1. (By permission of the Trustees of the Wellcome Trust, London)*

novel, Sir Oran Haut-ton's lack of speech proved an asset to him as a member of Parliament, giving him the reputation of a profound thinker.

Most naturalists, however, agreed that apes could not speak. Buffon, who sought to drive a wider wedge between humans and animals, denied that there ever was a time in the state of nature when humans did not think or speak. Even if "natural man" were devoid of speech, he argued, mothers would create language in the process of nursing and nurturing their children. Buffon reported that he had seen several of the animals Linnaeus described as *Homo troglodytes,* but they neither spoke nor expressed themselves by hissing. "For this reason," he wrote, "I suspect the truth of the description of this *Homo nocturnus.* I even doubt his existence." Buffon suspected that the creature Linnaeus described was an albino African, whom voyagers had superficially examined and falsely described.[36] Blumenbach, too, held that humans alone possess speech. Apes, he acknowledged, possess the language of the affections—often weeping from sadness—but humans alone possess the voice of reason.[37]

Since Plato, erect posture had also been seen as setting humans apart from other animals. In the *Timaeus,* Plato explained that the soul—located in the upper part of the body—draws our bodies upward toward our kindred spirits in heaven, forcing our bodies upright.[38] In the eighteenth century, Rousseau suggested that humans were naturally bipedal because of the placement of the female breast; the breast of women is placed in such a way that she must hold her child to nurse, leaving her only two legs for walking.[39] Apes, too, seemed to have a claim to erect posture. The overwhelming majority of illustrations of anthropoid apes in the seventeenth and eighteenth centuries show them either standing erect or seated in a human manner. Tyson apparently believed that his "Pygmie" (actually a chimp) walked on its knuckles only because it was sick; in good health, he believed, it would have walked erect, and that is how he had it drawn (fig. 2).[40] While it is true that apes can, for a time, walk on two legs, naturalists in the eighteenth century tended to exaggerate this capacity. Jean Audebert criticized the overly erect posture of the male chimpanzee shown in Buffon's *Histoire naturelle,* saying that the engraver "tried very hard to make him a man."[41] Pictorially, orangutans and chimpanzees were shown clutching walking sticks, ropes, and other devices suggesting the difficulties they had standing for long periods of time. Blumenbach, however, proposed that apes should not be seen as either quadrupeds or bipeds but as *Quadrumana* (four-handed), for their hind feet were furnished not with a great toe but with a second thumb. This reflected the fact that their natural home was the trees.[42]

Central in the quest to determine whether apes were human was ascertaining to what extent they were civil and civilizable. In the mid-seventeenth century voyagers began reporting how apes "counterfeit the countenance, the fashions, and the actions of men"—stories that were told and retold throughout the eighteenth century.[43] It seemed significant to Europeans that the beasts had delicate manners. Tulp's

FIG. 2 *Edward Tyson's* Homo Sylvestris *(a chimpanzee, though he called it an orangutan) with walking stick. Apes—usually males—were often drawn carrying a stick, indicating the extra help the animal needed to maintain an erect stance. The stick also represented the humanlike ability of apes to wield weapons. From Edward Tyson,* Orang-Outang, sive Homo Sylvestris; or, The Anatomy of a Pygmie Compared with That of a Monkey, an Ape, and a Man *(London, 1699), fig. 1. (By permission of the National Library of Medicine)*

Homo Sylvestris drank from a water glass no less delicately than would people in "the court of princes." Even Buffon, who argued that apes could be conquered but never tamed, offered the following eyewitness report of an orang:

> I have seen this animal present his hand to visitors and walk gravely along with them as if he were a part of the company. I have seen him sit down for dinner, unfold his napkin, wipe his lips, use a spoon and a fork, pour his drink into a glass, and toast his drinking companions. When invited to take tea, he brought a cup and saucer, placed them on the table, put in sugar, poured out the tea, and allowed it to cool before drinking it. All these actions he performed, without any other encouragement than a sign or signal from his master, and often of his own accord.[44]

Though some suspected that these animals had been taught such behavior so that they could be exhibited in shows, M. de la Brosse reported that European table manners were instinctual; these apes, he assured his reader, had not been trained to eat with a knife, fork, or spoon. It also seemed significant to Europeans that apes occasionally enjoyed a glass of wine. The orang was also said to sleep like a "most gentleman," covering its body with a spread. By another report, apes along with various sorts of monkeys had served the King of Bengala as coachmen, valets, and pages.[45]

Another mark of culture attributed to orangutans by Europeans was their deep affection for one another. Often brought to Europe in pairs, males and females were seen as developing the same affectionate relationships as were newly idealized between husbands and wives. In one report, a female sickened during transport and died; her male companion refused to eat and followed her to a watery grave within two days. Monboddo suggested that such affection engendered in chimpanzees a great sense of justice, as illustrated by the story of a male chimpanzee whose "wife" was shot by a villager. The chimpanzee pursued the offender into his house, then seized and dragged him to the place where his wife lay dead. The chimp would not let go of the man until shot by the villagers.[46]

Linnaeus, who found so much that was humanlike in the ape, remarked that ape parents—both mother and father—loved their children dearly, carrying them tenderly in their arms and pressing them to their bosoms in the same way that humans do. The English writer Priscilla Wakefield claimed that they mourn their dead. The generic orang was commonly said to build huts and villages, recognize kings as rulers, and enjoy games and pastimes. Monboddo assigned particular significance to the fact that apes used weapons: in his mind, the ability to strike enemies with sticks made them humanlike.[47] Blumenbach, ever the skeptic, gave no credence to these stories of "cultured" apes and, unlike most of his colleagues, did not include such accounts in his descriptions of apes.

Females of the Species

Debates concerning the consanguinity of the anthropoid apes and humans centered on reason, speech, bipedalism, and so forth. These differences were discussed without attention to sex. Naturalists in this period, however, also sought distinct lines separating the female human and her simian congener. In this case only sexual differences were considered. This was characteristic of scientific studies of the female—human or animal—in Europe. Since Aristotle, the female had been studied only insofar as she deviated from the male. As Rousseau wrote in his influential *Emile,* woman is man in everything except that which is connected with her sex.[48] This way of thinking, where the male constituted the universal subject and the female a sexual subset, pervaded natural history in the eighteenth century. Females across the kingdoms of nature were viewed as primarily sexual beings. Thus it is not surprising that studies of female anatomy designed to reveal the exact boundary between humans and apes interrogated aspects of female sexuality.

Significantly, comparative studies of human and simian males did not focus exclusively on sexuality. Blumenbach did once suggest that men are the only animals with nocturnal emissions of superfluous semen; Buffon notes at one point that the organs of generation in apes and men are similar except that the ape's prepuce has no frenum.[49] Tyson even compared the sexual organs of men and apes, but (except perhaps for Camper) none of these observers looked primarily to these organs for the marks distinguishing humans from apes.

By and large, female sexual organs were studied in order to highlight the animal side of human life. In some instances woman's sexual organs were said to link her directly to the ape. Aristotle asserted that the genitals of the female ape exactly resembled those of the human female. Male apes' genitals, by contrast, were doglike and not at all like men's. These pronouncements remained unquestioned until 1676, when Perrault showed that the ape's penis lacks the bone present in the dog's.[50]

Debates about human uniqueness in the female therefore centered on key sexual characters: menstruation, the clitoris, the breasts, and the hymen—that celebrated "veil of modesty."[51] Menstruation had long puzzled male naturalists. Did apes menstruate? Aristotle postulated that the catamenia are more abundant in women than in other animals, just as the semen ejected by men is more abundant in proportion to their size than in other animals. Aristotle believed that excess bodily fluids are emitted as sperm in men and menstrual blood in women because humans, unlike animals, have no superfluous parts, such as excess hair or outgrowths of bone, horn, or tusks, absorbing those fluids.[52] Pliny the Elder, the Roman naturalist, held that woman was the only menstruating animal, though this did not necessary ennoble her. Women alone had "moles" in their wombs regulating the flow. Contact with menstrual blood was said to turn new wine sour, destroy crops, kill bees, and drive dogs mad.[53] Hildegard von Bingen, the twelfth-century abbess, was one of the few in this early period to assert (correctly) that female apes also menstruate—information she had probably gleaned from hermetic writings such as the *Hieroglyphica* of Horapollo.[54]

Eighteenth-century naturalists, more influenced by Pliny than by Hildegard, were inclined to think that apes and monkeys did not menstruate. Linnaeus, who observed his beloved *Simia diana* at the Swedish Royal Palace Zoo, was said to have believed that she menstruated from the tip of her tail.[55] Blumenbach, by contrast, imagined that apes have no menses. After twenty years of close observation, he concluded that a few of them sometimes suffered from uterine hemorrhages but that these occurred at no regular interval. By his account, the only reason that people thought these females menstruated was that owners of circuses and coffeehouses, where apes were displayed, advertised their humanness in this regard in order to draw larger crowds. Buffon was one of the few to recognize that female apes do menstruate periodically—a characteristic, he emphasized, common to both women and female apes with naked buttocks.[56]

Blumenbach's errors regarding simian menstruation may have resulted from the fact that females often do not menstruate in captivity or when poorly nourished. (Buffon noted the case, for example, of a female ape who had menstruated regularly until attacked with scurvy.) Blumenbach's errors may also have arisen from his desire to draw a strict distinction between apes and humans in order to head off a growing tendency to pronounce the peoples of Africa, Asia, and the

Americas lesser humans. Early reports from America had insisted that the native women did not menstruate and for this reason belonged to a lower class of humans.

These naturalists—Linnaeus, Buffon, and Blumenbach—had sought to answer a simple empirical question regarding simian menstruation. Not so Charles White, the distinguished Manchester physician and notorious racist, who used the quantity of menstrual flow to rank females along a single chain of being. In order to do so, White made two assumptions: he assumed with Aristotle that a copious flow is uniquely human, and he subscribed to the general opinion that females menstruate more heavily in warmer climates than in cold (eighteen ounces in Greece, for example, and only two in Lapland). When investigating the menses of African women and apes, however, he found that despite the warmth of their homelands, "Negresses" menstruated very little, apes and baboons even less, monkeys still less, and some types of monkeys not at all.[57] White resolved this seeming contradiction by concluding that a more general law must hold in this case—namely, that the quantity of flow decreases as one descends the scale of being. Thus he concluded that European women, distinguished by a copious menstrual flow, were more human than African women or female apes. For White, one's rank in this bloody business determined one's moral worth.

A related question was commonly posed in this period: Do female animals have a clitoris? Linnaeus remarked in a footnote that apes lacked the clitoris, though they were in other regards quite humanlike.[58] Apart from Linnaeus, most everyone agreed that female apes shared with humans this "instrument of venery." Tyson, who never dissected a female ape, reported that the clitoris was extremely brutelike in apes, being larger and more visible than in women.[59] Blumenbach, who devoted many years to this question, found that in mammals the clitoris was frequently quite large, especially in certain types of lemurs. The most prodigious clitoris sighted—fifty-two feet in length!—belonged to a beached baleen whale in Holland, which Blumenbach examined on a cold winter day in 1791.[60]

Male naturalists also investigated the female mammae. Aristotle had noted that apes are similar to humans in having pectoral teats (not ventral like other animals').[61] Indeed, Linnaeus used two pectoral mammae as one of the identifying characters of primates (and may for this reason have included bats in this order).[62] Though female apes resembled humans in this respect, naturalists considered their breasts undesirably flabby and pendulous, resembling those of the Hottentot.

One of the earliest drawings of an anthropoid ape misrepresents her as having prominent, pendulous breasts (fig. 3). Many naturalists simply assumed that the breasts of all animals are udderlike; Tyson—so careful in other matters—mistakenly described the modest breasts of the female orangutans illustrated by Bontius and Tulp as "pendulous."[63]

Among all distinctively human characteristics, though, the hymen most intrigued naturalists. This uniquely female piece of anatomy was named after a male god, Hymen—the Greek god of marriage.[64] For centuries, the moral worth of unmarried women was determined by this thin membrane stretching across the opening to the vagina, sign and symbol of virginal virtue. Despite its cultural significance, though, naturalists could not even agree about whether the hymen actually existed. Buffon believed it to exist only in men's imaginations. Preoccupied in being first in so many things, men had made a physical object of virginity, which properly speaking (in Buffon's account) was a virtue existing only in a pure heart. Buffon cited anatomical authorities on both sides but finally concluded that true defloration came when superstition and outmoded ceremonies submitted young girls to the groping hands of ignorant matrons or voyeuristic physicians.[65]

Blumenbach, after examining female apes, monkeys, and an elephant in Germany, concluded that the hymen was something possessed by the human but by no other animal, even if these animals remained virgins. While both animals and humans had the clitoris, only women were blessed with a hymen, "the guardian of their chastity." In the first edition of his great *De generis humani varietate nativa* (1775), Blumenbach accepted Haller's judgment that the hymen had been granted to womankind to serve a moral rather than a physical purpose. By the third edition, written twenty years later, Blumenbach found this moralistic reasoning weak and did not attempt to explain the presence of the hymen.[66]

For the conservative French physician Jacques Moreau de la Sarthe, author of a two-volume *Histoire naturelle de la femme* (1803), the hymen was very real indeed. Because it was so thin many anatomists simply had never seen it, he judged. Moreau also pointed out that it could easily be destroyed if a girl wiped herself too vigorously or if she (intentionally or not) contracted "the habits of Lesbians," disrupting her organs in solitary pleasures.[67] Moreau reported that he had seen hymens in female fetuses and also in two very old nuns, neither of whom had ever suffered the slightest attack on her virginity. Moreau, however, did not believe that the state of the hymen accurately reflected female morals. In some girls the hymen was easily destroyed at

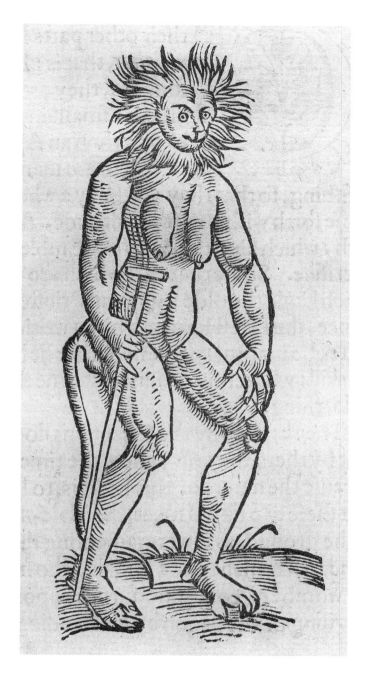

FIG. 3 *Conrad Gesner's depiction of an ape said to resemble a human in its face, knees, and certain unspecified "secret parts." Despite the long tail, this animal was taken to be an ape. From Conrad Gesner,* Historiae animalium *(Tiguri, 1551), 1:970. (Courtesy of the Clendening History of Medicine Library)*

an early age through no mischief on their part. Other women could enjoy sexual intercourse with several men and emerge with hymens fully intact, thus appearing to be virgins.

By the end of the eighteenth century, then, male naturalists had identified at least four characteristics unique to human females. One was the presence of the hymen; another was the angle of the vagina. In other animals the axis of the vaginal canal lies parallel to the abdomen; in women this "vestibule of the sanctuary," as Moreau called it, tilts more toward the front, a result of erect posture.[68] This results in humankind's unique versatility in positions for copulation. Blumenbach, uncharacteristically eloquent on this point, concluded from Leonardo da Vinci's drawings of comparative anatomy that though humans are capable of copulating in the manner of beasts, they prefer to partake of these "soft delights" face to face. (Blumenbach also commented on how the female vagina uniquely accommodates the male member.) Moreau and Blumenbach pointed to a third unique character of female humans—their great suffering in parturition, a result of the angle of the vagina. The final characteristic pertaining to women was the position of the opening of the urethra: in beasts it opens backward into the vagina; in women it opens between the lips of the pudendum.[69] In sum, for eighteenth-century male naturalists, what distinguished the human from the animal in the female was not reason, speech, or the ability to create culture, but rather the distinctive forms of her sexual anatomy.

Modesty—A Feminine Universal

By all accounts, males apes and monkeys were rude, lascivious, and given to lewd behavior. They were so wanton and lustful, it was said, that East Indian women avoided the woods and forest where these shameless animals roamed (fig. 4). Buffon wrote that the male baboon proudly presents his nude buttocks, and anus especially, to women—an extraordinary effrontery that Buffon could attribute to nothing but the most inordinate desire.[70] Female apes, by contrast, were distinguished by their very great modesty.

Early authors—Aristotle, Pliny, Gesner, Battell—had not mentioned the moral disposition of female apes. Neither did Nicolaas Tulp, the Dutch physician, who nonetheless had his chimpanzee drawn in a quietly moodest pose (fig. 5). Beginning in the second half of the seventeenth century, modesty became a key attribute of the female ape. In this, naturalists copied newly emerging ideals for

FIG. 4   *A virile male baboon. Note the bone in his penis, drawn in accordance with Aristotle's belief that apes are like dogs in this respect. From Thomas Bartholin,* Acta medica & philosophica Hafniensia *(Copenhagen, 1673), 1:313. (By permission of the National Library of Medicine)*

Homo ſylveſtris.
Orang — outang.

Tab. XIIII

FIG 5   *Nicolaas Tulp's "orang-outang," from his* Observationum medicarum libri tres *(Amsterdam, 1641), plate 14. (By permission of the National
Library of Medicine)*

European middle-class women. Jacob Bontius was the first to impute great modesty to the female orangutan. In his 1658 *Historiae naturalis*, he wrote that the young female inspired admiration by hiding her "secret parts" with great modesty from unknown men (fig. 6). She also hid her face with her hand, wept copiously, uttered groans, and expressed other sentiments so humanlike that Bontius judged nothing human to be lacking in her but speech.

Tyson mistrusted nearly every aspect of Bontius's portrayal: the arms were drawn too short, the hair too long, the feet too anthropic. The one trait he appreciated was her very great modesty. In order to express this pictorially, Tyson covered her privates with fig leaves in his reproduction of Bontius's plate (fig. 7).[71] Foucher d'Obsonville, too, found Bontius's account of the modesty of the female orang much exaggerated.[72] Others, however, confirmed Bontius's observations, reporting that the female is indeed bashful, inclined to throw herself into the arms of the male and hide her face in his bosom when stared at. Monboddo repeated reports of female orangutans concealing with their hands the parts that distinguish their sex, in the same way that "the antients thought it was proper the Goddess of love should conceal" her privates.[73]

Accounts of modesty in females reached their height in descriptions of the celebrated creature that arrived in London from Angola in 1738. The *London Magazine* reported that she was shaped "in every Part like a Woman excepting . . . [her] Head, which nearly resembles the Ape" (fig. 8). During the passage she had grown fond of a boy on board, and now she was always sorrowful at his absence. She was clothed with "a thin Silk Vestment" and showed "great Discontent at the opening of the Gown to discover her Sex."[74] Her modesty was complemented by her fine table manners. As Thomas Boreman related:

> The Chimpanzee was very pretty Company at the Tea-table, behav'd with Modesty and good Manners, and gave great Satisfaction to the Ladies who were pleased to honour her with their Visits. . . . [I]t would fetch its Chair, and sit in it naturally, like a Human Creature, whilst it drank Tea: It would take the Dish in its Hand, and if the Liquor was two [*sic*] hot, wou'd pour the Tea into the Saucer to cool it.[75]

Linnaeus, reporting a similar scene, added that she drank daintily, wiping her mouth with her hand. When going to sleep, Linnaeus's lady lay on a pillow, covering her shoulders, and slept quietly like "a

OVRANG OVTANG.

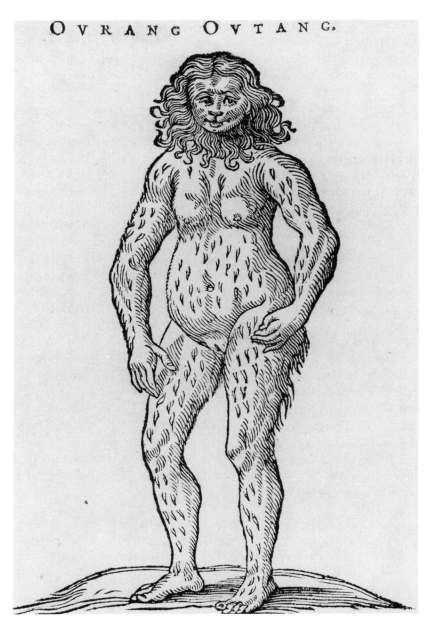

FIG 6 *Bontius's female "ourang outang," from his* Historiae naturalis & medicae Indiae Orientalis libri sex *(Amsterdam, 1658, 84). Buffon a hundred years later looked at this creature and declared it to be merely a hairy woman. (Courtesy of the Historical Collections of the Library, College of Physicians of Philadelphia)*

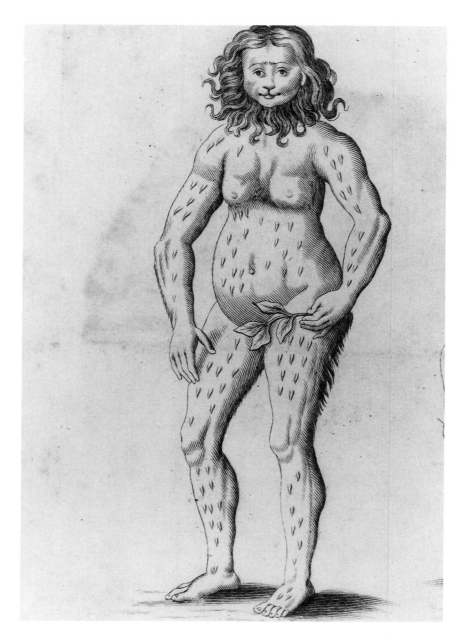

FIG. 7   *Edward Tyson's redrawn copy of Bontius's orangutan, her privates now covered by a fig leaf. From Tyson,* Orang-Outang, sive Homo Sylvestris, *fig. 16. (By permission of the National Library of Medicine)*

CHIMP—ANZEE.
Scotin sculp.   A.D. 1738

FIG. 8 *The female chimpanzee making her 1738 London debut. She was said to prefer silk dresses, but the illustrator nevertheless drew her naked. Here she raises a teacup to her lips. In Linnaeus's copy of this plate (see "Satyrus Tulpii," second from the right, fig. 1 above), he removed the teacup so that her left hand draws attention to a bare breast (reflecting perhaps Linnaeus's intense interest at this time in female mammae). From Gerard Scotin, Department of Prints and Drawings, British Museum, C.2* misc. 1882-3-11-1183. (By permission of the British Museum)*

respectful matron." He noted that her stomach was prominent, unlike those of Europe's "slim maidens," but he also insisted that the reason was not pregnancy, for the animal was still a virgin.[76]

Toward the end of the century, the female apes represented in European natural history became even more demurely feminine. Charles White gave Tulp's well-known female a facelift in his copy of Tulp's plate. White removed the wrinkles and slimmed her limbs and belly. Where Tulp had emphasized that "the nostrils are flat and bent inward, as in a wrinkled, toothless old woman," White's ape shows nicely placed teeth beneath a full lip (compare figs. 5 and 9). The rough chest and sagging breasts in Tulp's drawing have been lifted and smoothed, the nipples more sharply defined, thus achieving more nearly White's ideal—the "plump and snowy white hemispheres, tipt with vermillion" of the European female.[77] In addition, White resolved the ambiguities of the hair. In Tulp's drawing it looks like whiskers farming the face; in White's the hair has been pushed back (though more delicately drawn whiskers encompass the chin) and lengthened so that the hair of the head and shoulder appear as one flowing mane.

One of the most highly gendered representations of a female ape appears in Pierre Latreille's 1801 edition of Buffon's *Histoire naturelle.* Surprisingly, a female is chosen to represent the gorilla, the largest and reputedly the most vicious of the great apes (fig. 10). Seated daintily on a branch, this damsel is well proportioned, with comely limbs. The digits of both hands and feet are slender and elegant, matched only by the beauty of her long eyelashes.

What is surprising in these portrayals is that female apes are *not* depicted as closer to nature than are the males. Even in the state of nature, female apes are chaste, modest, soft, sober, considerate, attentive, and tranquil—qualities Linnaeus attributed to civilized humans. Portrayals of male apes, by contrast, evoke Linnaeus's description of uncivilized "man": "foolish, lascivious, imitative."[78] In portraying female apes as essentially chaste and modest, male naturalists attributed to nature the modesty—that "fountain head as well as the guardian of . . . chastity and honor"—prescribed for middle-class women.[79] Hume recognized that the need for these prescriptions was purely conventional: modesty and chastity were required—on the part of the wives—to ensure that heirs issued from legal husbands. The foundation for these morals, however, he imagined to be natural.[80] Reports of female apes dressed in silk vestments, showing displeasure when strange men wished to examine them, served to reinforce the notion that females—both human and beast—are by nature modest and demure.

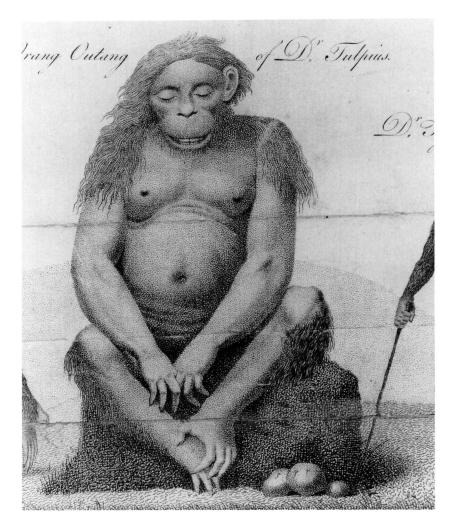

FIG. 9   *Charles White's feminization of Tulp's "Orang." Compare with*
Tulp's original reproduced in fig. 5 above. From An Account of the Regular
Gradation in Man and in Different Animals and Vegetables *(London, 1796),*
plate 3. (By permission of the National Library of Medicine)

FIG. 10   *A female pongo or gorilla, described by Buffon as the species most nearly approaching the human. This illustration first appeared in P.-A. Latreille,* Histoire naturelle générale et particulière des singes *(Paris, 1801), vol. 35, plate 2. (Courtesy of the Clendening History of Medicine Library)*

Are Apes Human Hybrids?

Medieval scholastics had seen the ape as *naturae degenerantis homo* (degenerate man). According to biblical and scholastic accounts, the ape—a monstrous offspring of man—fell with man from grace with the fateful bite of the apple.[81] The essence of this story was preserved in eighteenth-century accounts of the origin of apes as human hybrids. Even a naturalist of the stature of Stephen de Visme argued late in the century that because the Goloks or "Wild People" (gibbons) have no tails, they must have derived from "a mixture with the human kind."[82] Foucher d'Obsonville, claiming the orang to be among the lowest order of humans, confirmed that it propagated freely and fruitfully with other humans.[83]

The alleged hypersexuality of male apes provided ample opportunity for such unions, at least in the European mind.[84] According to almost every account of the ape, the males were given to lust after not just females of their own kind but women of the human species as well. Edward Tyson claimed that they preferred blondes, and offered the story of an ape that grew so amorous of a celebrated beauty—a lady-in-waiting—that neither chains, confinement, nor punishment could keep him in check. The lady was eventually forced to have him banished from court.[85] Naturalists more often reported couplings between apes and dark-haired women. Buffon and countless others told stories of East Indian women being suddenly attacked and ravished by these shameless animals. Orangutans and chimpanzees were said to carry off girls eight or ten years of age to the tops of trees where rescue was almost impossible.[86]

In these accounts it is invariably the male ape who forces himself on the human female. To my knowledge there is not one account of a female ape ever taking a man, or even of intercourse between a female ape and a male human. Bontius and Blumenbach suggest and that the women involved may have initiated these encounters. Bontius claimed that the orangutan was "born of the lust of the women of the Indies who mate with apes and monkeys to satisfy their detestable desires."[87] Blumenbach intimated that in the "madness of lust" women may have solicited the apes in the same way that the women of Kamchatka were known to have copulated with dogs; others might have prostituted themselves out of religious superstition, as the women of Mendes were said to have done with their sacred goats.[88] La Brosse suggested that some women enjoyed their simian paramours; an African woman at Loango was reported to have remained three years with the apes.[89] For the most part, however, it was the male ape who ravished women in this European fantasy. This is not surprising given that males—human or brute—had been seen since Aristotle as embodying the active sexual principle. Moreover, males were in principle considered more powerful than females—often across classes, races, and, in this case, species. Though a number of naturalists, including Tyson, rejected the notion that apes had issued from such sexual encounters, Blumenbach was one of the very few who found the whole idea dubious, fabulous, and disgusting. He denied that offspring from such a union were even possible, one reason being that women seized and violently raped by baboons perished miserably in these brutal embraces. Nonetheless, many naturalists continued to assert that the women of Africa and Asia "mixed" voluntarily or through force with anthropoid apes, and that the products of these unions had entered into both species.[90] Rousseau, who remained genuinely puzzled about whether or not apes were human, suggested performing a crossbreeding experiment to find out. A fruitful union would attest to their humanity.[91]

The Enlightened Ape: Sir Oran Haut-ton

A corollary to the question "Are apes human?" arose late in the Enlightenment: Should apes be enfranchised? In this period of democratic expansion the question was first asked of women, then of minorities living in Europe, and finally of brutes. There were some in this period who claimed human status for the orangutan. Lord Monboddo argued that orangs might be turned into cultivated gentlemen if suitably educated. The conservative Thomas Taylor penned his satirical *Vindication of the Rights of Brutes,* arguing that animals are our equals. Thomas Love Peacock portrayed the fictional Sir Oran Haut-ton as a landowner and member of Parliament.

In the eighteenth century, advocates of animals began to challenge the Cartesian notion that animals are senseless automata. Sarah Trimmer wrote in her 1788 *Fabulous Histories* that a lady of London had been accustomed to consider animals as mere machines, pawns of instinct, until she encountered "the Learned Pig, which has lately been shown in London." The pig could supposedly spell words by picking out the appropriate letter with its snout; it could also tell time.[92]

The question of rights for animals was discussed most baldly in Taylor's 1792 *Vindication of the Rights of Brutes,* designed to ridicule egalitarian ideals. Declaring Thomas Paine the father and Mary

Wollstonecraft the mother ("though a virgin") of his theory, Taylor argued that brutes possess reason in common with men, though not "in so exquisite a degree." Nonetheless, animals have other assets that overcome any deficiency in reason. "The swiftness of a hare," he argued, "united with hare-like reason, puts the hare upon an equality both with the lion and the man." The strength of the lion, the flight of the bird, the spinning of the spider, the microscopic eye of the fly render them all equal to each other and to man. Given that animals possess both reason and speech (it is our failing that we cannot understand their language), Taylor, tongue in cheek, considered it unjust to destroy animals, to hunt or eat them. In order to dismiss the claims of both Paine and Wollstonecraft by reducing them to absurdity, Taylor declared that "what is here asserted of brutes is no less applicable to vegetables, and even minerals themselves," because these things too are endowed with sense. He predicted that Europe would soon see treatises on their rights.[93]

Other claims were made for animals, and for simians in particular. An extraordinary piece of satire, jointly authored by Swift, Pope Gay, Parnell, and Arbuthnot in the 1730s and heavily indebted to Tyson, traced the beginnings of the arts and sciences to apes. "It is universally agreed," wrote the authors, "that the Arts and Sciences took their rise among the Egyptians and Indians; but from whom they first receiv'd them, is yet a secret." In Egypt, Swift et al. traced the secret to the satyr, Pan—half man and half beast; in India, similarly they traced the origin of the sciences to the apes. Transmission of this knowledge to humans was facilitated by the intimate relations these animals had with human females. The progeny of these couplings— Aesop, for example, or Socrates with his flat nose and prominent eyes—were among the greatest wits of the ancient world.[94]

While Taylor and Swift used the notion of the learned ape to ridicule democratic tendencies within Europe, others used apes to highlight and criticize Europe's vices. Nicolas-Edme Restif de la Bretonne's cultured baboon, César de Malaca (fig. 11), is shown writing a letter of warning to his species: Don't ape humans! These seeming "kings of the world" (humans) had wrought destruction and misery with their unchristian wars and inhumane slavery. Men of reason espoused high ideals of equality and fraternity, but their practice was otherwise. "Thank God," he concludes, "that I am an ape and not subject to human laws and prejudices." César, the son of a woman of Malacca and a baboon, was saved by a European from suffocation at birth and transported eventually to France. Under the tutelage of a wealthy woman, who came to love him dearly, he was given a complete education in European ways—an education he came to regret. "Ignorance is certainly an imperfection . . . , but knowledge has consequences that frighten me."[95]

Imagination soared with the possibilities of apes becoming men. For German writer E.T.A. Hoffmann, as for most advocates of enlightenment, it was simply a matter of education. The ape Milo describes his upbringing and accomplishments in a letter to his simian paramour living in Philadelphia. He is "liberated" from his brute existence by trappers and brought to Germany. Schooled by a prominent citizen, he learns to speak, read, write, and play music—in short, he becomes highly cultured. He signs his letter "Milo, formerly an ape, currently private artist and intellectual."[96]

In other stories apes pass happily and, at times, quite successfully as humans in high society. In Wilhelm Hauff's innocently fanciful "The Ape as Man" (1827), a young man is introduced into society in a small German town by his uncle—himself a recluse so withdrawn from society that the townspeople consider him a madman, a Jew, or a wizard. His nephew, dressed in a fashionable frock coat, wide green trousers, and kid gloves, learns to speak German with a passable accent. The villagers, anxious to cultivate the seemingly well-born gentleman as a future son-in-law, welcome him into their homes and clubs. During the long winter months, he often wins at chess, dances at their balls, and sings "like an angel." His rough manners are regarded as exotic and are imitated by every young man in town. In Hauff's tale, however, nature eventually wins out over nurture. one evening at a ball, the mysterious young man reverts to his animal nature, swinging from the chandeliers and leaping wildly from table to table. Revealing himself to be "*Homo troglodytes Linnaei*," he is sold for six talers to a museum owner anxious to have his skin for his collection.[97]

The most elaborate of these stories is Thomas Love Peacock's 1817 *Melincourt*. Drawing heavily from Monboddo, Peacock declares the orangutan to be not a degenerate form of man but "a specimen of the natural and original man—a genuine facsimile of the philosophical Adam." Being still close to nature, the future Sir Oran Haut-ton, Baronet of Redrose Abbey, displays prodigious physical strength, uninterrupted health, and an amicable simplicity of manners— exactly those qualities Peacock saw lacking in his fellow English. Sir Oran's natural qualities—his sense of justice, selfless rescue of Anthelia (Lord Melincourt's daughter), fine manners, and flute playing—were more than enough to make up for his lack of certain

FIG. 11   *The learned baboon, César de Malaca, writing to the* confrères *of his species. His hand on his forehead shows him reflecting on the ills of human society. The parrot—considered the other "imitator of man" for its ability to speak—on the windowsill counsels him; the dog and cat are his companions. On the wall are portraits of others of his species. From Nicolas-Edme Restif de la Bretonne,* La Découverte Australe *(Leipzig, 1781), vol. 3, facing p. 18.*

cultural acquisitions, including the ability to speak, read, or write. Throughout his story, Peacock suggests that his ape is more human than those people who judge the value of an individual by the weight of her or his purse. Sir Oran Haut-ton eventually acquires an estate and a seat in Parliament, a move his friends consider necessary to secure for him the respect of people such as Mrs. Pinmoney, who had earlier judged his looks "odd" but now finds there to be something "very French in his physiognomy."[98]

Female apes rarely figured in these reveries of simian potential. In one case, however, a female—the London chimp—was featured in a eulogy commemorating her death. The anonymous *Essay Towards the Character of the Late Chimpanzee who died February 23, 1738–9* served as a political satire on Queen Caroline, who had died one year earlier.[99] Madame Chimpanzee is portrayed as temperate, modest, neat, and quiet, the standard of genteel breeding. Intended to ridicule the German-born Caroline, who served as self-appointed mediator in the famous Leibniz-Clarke debate, the London chimp was cast as a liberal, a deist and freethinker, and above all an intellectual—choosing to cultivate her mind and not her wardrobe. She eschewed card-playing women and preferred the company of serious men.

It is significant that, but for this one exception, the protagonists in these stories were predominantly male. Though female apes exhibited the habits of humanity—sipping tea from a cup, or climbing down a ladder to relieve themselves discreetly overboard during transport—few females were portrayed as heroines in a fictional account of an ape entering into high society. No one *denied* that female apes were capable of such accomplishments; the question did not arise. Europeans simply assumed that active, cultured, individuals were male. Though females were omitted from the ranks of the cultured, they numbered among the "wild people"—for example, the tree-climbing, carnivorous, club-wielding wild girl of Champagne who, when "tamed," became a Catholic nun.[100]

The question of the humanity and rights of apes was intimately tied to the question of rights for women. Peacock, who made a parliamentarian of Sir Oran Haut-ton, also spoke out in favor of women's rights. His novel opened with a portrait of Sir Henry Melincourt, lord of the old Westmoreland manor, who devoted himself to the cultivation of his daughter's intellect. Melincourt upheld the "heresy" that women are, or at least may become, rational beings; the paucity of examples was the unfortunate result of the great pains taken to make them otherwise. Peacock was also an enemy of slavery; his spokesman in the novel, a Mr. Forester, boycotts sugar and other products of slave economies, never allowing an "atom" of West Indian produce to cross his threshold.[101]

Apes, of course, are not human and were not enfranchised in human society (neither were women or many minorities until more than a century later). Animals, however, did make some gains in this period. Enlightenment debates increased sympathies for the plight of both wild and domestic animals. In the nineteenth century, Roman law, which gave owners *jus utendi* and *jus abutendi* over their animals, was increasingly called into question. By 1804 the French were agitating for laws to prevent cruelty to animals; the *Loi Grammont* was passed in 1850. In England, the Royal Society for the Prevention of Cruelty to Animals was founded in 1824.[102]

This essay, however, has not been primarily about the welfare of apes. It has been about naturalists and the science they produced. The great apes became unwitting objects in debates the consequences of which went far beyond descriptions of simian habits and character. Naturalists have looked (and sociobiologists still look) to these our closest relatives to resolve questions about the "nature" of humankind. Are humans naturally aggressive or altruistic? Do males invariably dominate females? Are humans genetically predisposed toward crime, rape, or homosexuality? As this study has shown, even careful observation of our simian cousins has often been mediated by highly gendered lenses.

The fact that science often still tells as much about its participants as about the laws of nature is brought into sharp relief in Donna Haraway's *Primate Visions*. Primatology changed dramatically with the coming of women into the field in the twentieth century. Their questions were different, their assumptions were different, and their results were different. Jeanne Altmann, for example, changed primatology by shifting the focus from male to female subjects. Altmann initially shied away from looking at females (for a woman to study females was considered too "natural" a thing and threatened to undermine her authority as a scientist). As she spent more time in the field, however, Altmann recognized that male researchers had a preference for high drama and tended to focus attention on murder, hunting, and sex. She found a deeper evolutionary story in the longer, sustained dramas surrounding females and food. Though Altmann's contributions led to a more balanced picture of gender in primates, as Haraway points out her studies reflected her own class and racial biases. For her 1980 *Baboon Mothers and Infants,* Altmann took the career mother as her organizing metaphor—a move which tended to impose on baboons the problems of white and middle-class professional women. [103]

In order to effect change, women must enter in large numbers. But bringing women into primatology will probably not be enough. Most of the women entering the field are of European descent and the middle class. Barriers of poverty and prejudice must be eliminated so that science becomes accessible to peoples of all classes, colors, and political and sexual persuasions. Though the notion of a great chain of being no longer animates exploration of nature, all too often hierarchies of natural worth are established—consciously and unconsciously—that mirror the faces dominating scientific communities. Objectivity in science cannot be proclaimed, it must be cultivated.

The Life Cycle of Cyborgs:
Writing the Posthuman

N. Katherine Hayles

For some time now there has been a rumor going around that the age of the human has given way to the posthuman. Not that humans have died out, but that the human as a concept has been succeeded by its evolutionary heir. Humans are not the end of the line. Beyond them looms the cyborg, a hybrid species created by crossing biological organism with cybernetic mechanism. Whereas it is possible to think of humans as natural phenomena, coming to maturity as a species through natural selection and spontaneous genetic mutations, no such illusions are possible with the cyborg. From the beginning it is *constructed,* a technobiological object that confounds the dichotomy between natural and unnatural, made and born.

If primatology brackets one end of the spectrum of humanity by the similarities and differences it constructs between Homo sapiens and other primates, cybernetics brackets the other by the continuities and ruptures it constructs between humans and machines. As Donna Haraway has pointed out, in the discourse of primatology "oldest" is privileged, for it points toward the most primeval and therefore the most fundamental aspects of humanity's evolutionary heritage.[1] "Oldest" comes closest to defining what is essential in the layered construction of humanity. In the discourse of cybernetics, "newest" is similarly privileged, for it reaches toward the limits of technological innovation. "Newest" comes closest to defining what is malleable and therefore subject to change in the layered construction of humanity. Whereas the most socially loaded arguments in primatology center on inertia, the most socially loaded arguments in cybernetics project acceleration.

Primatology and cybernetics are linked in other ways as well. Primates and cyborgs are simultaneously entities and metaphors, living beings and narrative constructions. The conjunction of technology and discourse is crucial. Were the cyborg only a product of discourse, it could perhaps be relegated to science fiction, of interest to SF aficionados but not of vital concern to the culture. Were it only a technological practice, it could be confined to such technical fields as bionics, medical prostheses, and virtual reality. Manifesting itself as both technological object and discursive formation, it partakes of the power of the imagination as well as the actuality of technology. Cyborgs actually do exist; about 10 percent of the current U.S. population are estimated to be cyborgs in the technical sense, including people with electronic pacemakers, artificial joints, drug implant systems, implanted corneal lenses, and artificial skin. Occupations make a much higher percentage into metaphoric cyborgs, including the computer keyboarder joined in a cybernetic circuit with the screen, the neurosurgeon guided by fiber-optic microscopy during an operation, and the teen player in the local video-game arcade. Scott Bukatman has named this condition "terminal identity," calling it an "unmistakably doubled articulation" that signals the end of traditional concepts of identity even as it points toward the cybernetic loop that generates a new kind of subjectivity.[2]

How does a culture understand and process new modes of subjectivity? Primarily through the stories it tells, or more precisely, through narratives that count as stories in a given cultural context. The stories I want to explore are narratives of life cycles.[3] They bring into focus a crucial area of tension between the human and posthuman. Human beings are conceived, gestated, and born; they grow up, grow old, and die. Machines are designed, manufactured, and assembled; normally they do not grow, and although they wear out, they are always capable of being disassembled and reassembled either into the same product or a different one. As Gillian Beer has pointed out, Frankenstein's monster—an early cyborg—is monstrous in part because he has not *grown*. As a creature who has never known what it is like to be a child, he remains alien despite his humanoid form.[4]

When cyborg subjectivities are expressed within cultural narratives, traditional understandings of the human life cycle come into strong conflict with modes of discursive and technical production oriented toward the machine values of assembly and disassembly. The conflict cannot be reduced to either the human or machine orientation, for the cyborg contains both within itself. Standing at the threshold separating the human from the posthuman, the cyborg looks to the past as well as the future. It is precisely this double nature that allows cyborg stories to be imbricated within cultural narratives while still wrenching them in a new direction.

The new cannot be spoken except in relation to the old. Imagine a new social order, a new genetic strain of corn, a new car—whatever the form, it can be expressed only by articulating its differences from what it displaces, which is to say the old, a category constituted through its relation to the new. Similarly, the language that creates these categories operates through displacements of traditional articula-- tions by formulations that can be characterized as new because they are not the same as the old. The cyborg is both a product of this process and a signifier for the process itself. The linguistic splice that created its name (*cyb*ernetic *org*anism) metonymically points toward the simul- taneous collaboration and displacement of new/old, even as it instanti- ates this same dynamic.

The stories that produce and are produced by cyborg subjectivities are, like the cyborg itself, amalgams of old and new. Cyborg narratives can be understood as stories only by reference to the very life cycle narratives that are no longer sufficient to explain them. The results are narrative patterns that overlay upon the arc of human life a map gener- ated from assembly and disassembly zones. One orientation references the human, the other the posthuman; one is chronological, the other topological; one assumes growth, the other presupposes production; one represents itself as natural or normal, the other as unnatural or aberrant. Since the two strands intertwine at every level, the effect is finally not so much overlay as interpretation. Sometimes the interpenetration is pre- sented as the invasion of a deadly alien into the self, sometimes as a symbiotic union that results in a new subjectivity. Whatever the up- shot, the narratives agree that the neologistic joining cannot be unsplit without killing the truncated org/anism that can no longer live without its cyb/ernetic component. As these narratives tell it, a corner has been turned, and there is no going back.

To illustrate how cyborg narratives function, I want to concen- trate on three phases of the life cycle and three corresponding dis/ assembly zones. The first is adolescence, when self-consciousness about the body is at its height and the body is narcissistically cathected as an object of the subject's gaze. Appropriate to the inward turning of narcissism is a dis/assembly zone marked by the joining of limb to torso, appendage to trunk. The second phase is sexual maturity, when the primary emphasis is on finding an appropriate partner and negotiat- ing issues of intimacy and shared space. The dis/assembly zone corre- sponding to this phase is located where the human is plugged into the machine, or at the interface between body and computer network. The last is the reproductive or generative phase, when the emphasis falls on mortality and the necessity to find an heir for one's legacy. The dis/ assembly zone associated with this phase focuses on the gap between the natural body and mechanical replicate, or between the original and manufactured clone.

Because gender is a primary determinant of how stories are told, I have chosen to mix stories by male and female authors. Spanning nearly half a century, these texts bear the stamps of their times as well as the subject positions of the authors. The generalizations that emerge from these texts confirm socialization patterns that make women welcome intimacy, whereas men are more likely to see it as a threat; they also show women more attuned to bonding, men to aggression and hierarchical structure. The interest of the comparision lies less in these well-known generalizations, however, than in the complex permutations they undergo in the cybernetic paradigm. The narrative and linguistic counters by which such categories as intimacy, bonding, and aggression are constituted do not remain constant when the body boundaries central to defining them undergo radical transformation.

The adolescent phase is illustrated by Bernard Wolfe's *Limbo* (1952), with side glances at Katherine Dunn's *Geek Love* (1989).[5] Both novels imagine cults that advocate voluntary amputation as a means to achieve beatific states. In Wolfe's novel the next step is to replace the absent appendages with prostheses, whereas in Dunn's narrative the amputations remain as permanent stigmata. At issue is the truncated versus extended body, and boundary questions focus on the relation of part to whole. Important psychological configurations are represented as originating within the family structure. Physical wounds in these texts have their symbolic origin in narcissistic wounds that occur when the male child realizes that his body is not coextensive with the world or, more specifically, with the mother's body. The imaginative dimension that is most highly charged is disruption of the body's interior space.

The mating phase is explored through John Varley's 1984 novella "Press Enter" and Anne McCaffrey's short stories in *The Ship Who Sang*.[6] Varley and McCaffrey are concerned with subjectivities that emerge when the human body is plugged into a computer network. For Varley, the connection occurs when his characters respond to the "Press Enter" command of a mysterious and lethal computer program; for McCaffrey, when a birth-damaged child is trained to become a "shell person," permanently encased in a spaceship and wired into its computer network. At stake is hyperconnectivity, the possibility that the human sensorium can be overwhelmed and destroyed by the vastly superior information-processing capabilities of the computers to which it is connected. For Varley this is a threat that cannot be overcome, whereas for McCaffrey it is one trial among many. Boundary disputes move outward from the body's interior to the connection that joins body with network. Varley's text manifests a phobic reaction to the connection as an unbearable form of intimacy, while McCaffrey's narrative embraces it as life-enhancing and ultimately freeing. The most highly charged imaginative dimension is extension in external space.

The generativity phase appears in C. J. Cherryh's 1988 *Cyteen* trilogy, which is compared with Philip K. Dick's 1968 *Do Androids Dream of Electric Sheep*[7]. Dick's novel, freedly adapted for film in *Blade Runner,* concerns a future in which androids are common off-planet but are not allowed on Earth. The protagonist is a bounty hunter whose job is to find and "retire" androids who have violated this prohibition. Cherryh's triology also foregrounds replication, achieved through cloning and deep psychological conditioning rather than production of androids. At stake is the ability to distinguish between originals and replicates. In both narratives, empathy plays an important role in enabling this distinction or drawing it into question. Boundary disputes move beyond the body and its connections to focus on the displacement of bodies to other locales. The most highly charged imaginative dimension is extension in time.

These patterns give an overall sense of the kind of narrative structures that result when stories based on life cycles are overlaid with topological narratives about dis/assembly zones. Structure is a spatial term, however, and missing from this account is the temporal or narrative dimension of stories that unfold through time. Their complex historical, ideological, and literary implications can be understood only by engaging both aspects at once, in the highly nonlinear dynamics characteristic of these unstable narratives as well as their fractal spatiality. For that we must turn to a fuller account of how human and posthuman interact in these cyborg stories.

Growing up Cyborg: Male Trunks and Female Freaks

Ferociously intelligent and exasperating, *Limbo* presents itself as the notebooks of Dr. Martine, a neurosurgeon who defiantly left his medical post in World War III and fled to an uncharted Pacific island. He finds the islanders, the Mandunji tribe, practicing a primitive form of lobotomy to quiet the "tonus" in antisocial people. Rationalizing that it is better to do the surgery properly than to let people die from infections and botched jobs, Martine takes over the operations and uses them to do neuroresearch on brain-function mapping. He discovers that no matter how deeply he cuts, certain characteristics appear to be twinned, and one cannot be excised without sacrificing the other— aggression and eroticism, for example, or creativity and a capacity for violence. The appearance on the island of "queer limbs," men who have had their arms and legs amputated and replaced by atomic-powered plastic prostheses, gives Martine an excuse to leave his island family and find out how the world has shaped up in the aftermath of the war.

The island/mainland dichotomy is the first of a proliferating series of divisions. Their production follows a characteristic pattern. First the narrative presents what appears to be a unity (the island locale; the human psyche), which nevertheless cleaves in two (main-landers come to the island, a synecdoche referencing a second locale that exists apart from the first; twin impulses are located within the psyche). Sooner or later the cleavage arouses anxiety, and textual representations try to achieve unity again by undergoing metamorphosis, usually truncation or amputation (Martine and the narrative leave the island behind and concentrate on the mainland, which posits itself as a unity; the islanders undergo lobotomies to make them "whole" citizens again). The logic implies that truncation is necessary if the part is to reconfigure itself as a whole. Better to formalize the split and render it irreversible, so that life can proceed according to a new definition of what constitutes wholeness. Without truncation, however painful it may be, the part is doomed to exist as a remainder. But amputation always proves futile in the end, because the truncated part splits in two again and the relentless progression continues.

Through delirious and savage puns, the text works out the permutations of the formula. America has been bombed back to the Inland Strip, its coastal areas now virtually uninhabited wastelands. The image of a truncated country, its outer extremities blasted away, proves prophetic, for the ruling political ideology is Immob. Immob espouses such slogans as "No Demobilization without Immobilization" and "Pacifism means Passivity." It locates the aggressive impulse in the ability to move, teaching that the only way to end war permanently is permanently to remove the capacity for motion. True believers become vol-amps, men who have undergone voluntary amputations of their limbs. Social mobility paradoxically translates into physical immobility. Upwardly mobile excecutives have the complete treatment to become quadroamps; janitors are content to be uniamps; women and blacks are relegated to the limbo of unmodified bodies.

Treating the human form as a problem to be solved by dis/assembly allows it to be articulated with the machine. This articulation, far from leaving the dynamics driving the narrative behind, carries it forward into a new arena, the assembly zone marked by the joining of trunk to appendage. Like the constructions that proceded it, Immob ideology also splits in two. The majority party, discovering that its adherents are restless lying around with nothing to do, approves the replacement of missing limbs with powerful prostheses (or "pros") that bestow enhanced mobility, enabling Pro-pros to perform athletic feats impossible for unaltered bodies. Anti-pros, believing that this is a perversion of Immob philosophy, spend their days proselytizing from microphones hooked up to baby baskets that are just the right size to accomodate limbless human torsos—a detail that later becomes significant.

As the assembly zone of appendage/trunk suggests, sexual politics revolve around symbolic and actual castration, interpreted through a network of assumptions that manifest extreme anxiety about issues of control and domination. In the world of Immob, women have become the intiators of sexual encounters. They refuse to have sex with men wearing prostheses, for the interface between organism and mechanism is not perfect, and at moments of stress the limbs are apt to career out of control, smashing whatever is in the vicinity. Partnered with truncated, immobilized men, women have perfected techniques performed in the female superior position that give them and their partners satisfaction while requiring no motion from the men. To Martine these techniques are anathema, for he believes that the only "normal" sexual experience for women is a "vaginal" orgasm achieved using the male superior position. In this Martine echoes the views of his creator, Wolfe, and his creator's psychoanalyst, Edmund Bergler. Wolfe, described by his biographer as a small man with a large mustache, creates in Immob a fantasy about technological extensions of the male body that become transformed during the sex act into a truncated "natural" body.[8] If the artificial limbs bestow unnatural potency, the hidden price is the withering of the "limb" called in U.S. slang the third leg or short arm.

In more than one sense, this is a masculine fantasy that relates to women through mechanisms of projection. It is, moreover, a fantasy fixated in male adolescence. Wavering between infantile dependence and adult potency, an Immob recreates the dynamic typical of male adolescence every time he takes off his prostheses to have sex. With the pros on, he is capable of feats that even pros like Michael Jordon and

Mike Tyson would envy (the pun is typical of Wolfe's prose; with pros every man is a pro). With the pros/e off, he is reduced to infantile dependence on women. The unity he sought in becoming a vol-amp is given the lie by the split he experiences within himself as superhuman and less-than-human. The woman is correspondingly divided into the nurturing mother and domineering sex partner. In both roles, her subject position is defined by the ambiguities characteristic of male adolescence. The overwritten prose, the penchant for puns, the hostility toward women that the narrative displays all recall a perpetually adolescent male who has learned to use what Martine calls a "screen of words" to compete with other men and insulate himself from emotional involvements with women.

Were this all, *Limbo* would be merely frustrating rather than frustrating and brilliant.[9] What makes it compelling is its ability to represent and comment upon its own limitations. Consider the explanation Martine gives for why Immob has been so successful. The author gives us a broad hint in the baby baskets that Immob devotees adopt. According to Martine, the narcissistic wound from which the amputations derive is the male infant's separation from the mother and his outraged discovery that his body is not coextensive with the world. Amputation allows the man to return to his pre-oedipal state where he will have his needs cared for by attentive and nurturing females. The text vacillates on who is responsible for the narcissistic wound and its aftermath. At times it seems the woman is appropriating the male infant into her body; at other times it seems the amputated men are willfully forcing women into nurturing roles they would rather escape. In fact, once male and female are plugged into a cybernetic circuit, the question of origin becomes irrelevant. Each affects and forms the other. In approaching this realization, the text goes beyond the presuppositions that underlie its sexual politics and reaches toward a new kind of subjectivity.

Crucial to this process are transformations in the textual body that reenact and re-present the dynamic governing representations within the text. The textual body begins by figuring itself as Martine's notebook written in the "now" of the narrative present. But this apparent unity is lost when it splits in half, shifting to Martine's first notebook written nearly two decades earlier. Martine tries to heal the split narrative by renouncing the first notebook and destroying the second. The narrative continues to fragment, however, introducing drawings that intrude into the textual space without notice or comment, and scrawled lines that run down the page, marking zones where the pros/e stops and the truncated, voiceless body of the text remains. From these semiotic spaces emerges a corpse that, haunting the narrative, refuses to stay buried. Its name is Rosemary. Helder, Martine's college roommate and later the founder of Immob, had taken Rosemary to a peace rally where he delivered a fiery speech. He returned with her to her apartment, tried to have sex with her, and when she refused, brutally raped her. After he left, she committed suicide by slashing her wrists. Martine's part in the affair was to provide a reluctant alibi for his roommate, allowing him to escape prosecution for the rape-manslaughter.

One of the drawings shows a nude woman with three prostheses—the Immob logo—extruding from each of her nipples (294). She wears glasses, carries a huge hypodermic needle, and has around her neck a series of tiny contiguous circles, which could be taken to represent the necklace popular in the 1950s known as a choker. To the right of her figure is a grotesque and diapered male torso, minus arms and legs, precariously perched on a flat carriage with Immob legs instead of wheels. He has his mouth open in a silent scream, perhaps because the woman appears to be aiming the needle at him. In the text immediately preceding the drawing, Rosemary is mentioned. Although the text does not acknowledge the drawing and indeed seems unaware of its existence, the proximity of Rosemary's name indicates that the drawing is of her, the needle presumably explained by her nursing profession.

In a larger sense the drawing depicts the Immob woman. According to what I shall call the *voiced* narrative (to distinguish it from the drawings, nonverbal lines, and punning neologisms that correspond to comments uttered sotto voce), the woman is made into a retroactive cyborg by constructing her as someone who nourishes and emasculates cyborg sons. The voiced narrative ventriloquizes her body to speak of the injustices she has inflicted upon men. It makes her excess, signified by the needle she brandishes and the legs that sprout from her nipples, responsible for her lover/son's lack. In this deeply misogynistic writing, it is no surprise to read that women are raped because they want to be. Female excess is represented as stimulating and encouraging male violence, and rape is poetic revenge for the violence women have done to men when they are too young and helpless to protect themselves. The voiced narrative strives to locate the origin of the relentless dynamic of splitting and truncation within the female body. According to it, the refusal of the woman's body to respect decent boundaries between itself and another initiates the downward spiral into amputation and eventual holocaust.

Countering these narrative constructions are other interpretations authorized by the drawings, nonverbal lines, puns, and lapses in narrative continuity. From these semiotic spaces, which Kristeva has associated with the feminine, come inversions and disruptions of the hierarchical categories that the narrative uses to construct maleness and femaleness.[10] Written into nonexistence by her suicide within the text's represented world, Rosemary returns in the subvocal space of the drawing and demands to be acknowledged. On multiple levels, the drawing deconstructs the narrative's gender categories. In the represented world women are not allowed to be cyborgs, yet this female figure has more pros attached to her body than any man. Women come after men in the represented world, but here the woman's body is on the left and is thus "read" before the man's. Above all women and men are separate and distinct, but in this space parts of the man's body have attached themselves to her. Faced with these disruptions, the voiced narrative is forced to recognize that it does not unequivocally control the textual space. The semiotic intrusions contest its totalizing claims to write the world.

The challenge is reflected within the narrative by internal contradictions that translate into pros/e the intimations of the semiotic disruptions. As the voiced narrative tries to come to grips with these contradictions, it cycles closer to the realization that the hierarchical categories of male and female have collapsed into the same space. The lobotomies Martine performs suggest how deep this collapse goes. To rid the (male) psyche of subversive (female) elements, it is necessary to amputate. For a time the amputations work, allowing male performance to be enhanced by prostheses that bestow new potency. But eventually these must be shed and the woman encountered again. Then the subvocal feminine surfaces and initiates a new cycle of violence and amputation. No matter how deeply the cuts are made, they can never excise the ambiguities that haunt and constitute these posthuman (and post-textual) bodies. *Limbo* envisions cybernetics as a writing technology that inscribes over the hierarchical categories of traditional sexuality the indeterminate circuitry of cyborg gender.

When dis/assembly zones based on truncation/extension are overlaid upon narratives of maturation, the resulting patterns show strong gender encoding for at least two reasons. First, male and female adolescents typically have an asymmetrical relation to power. While the male comes into his own as inheritor of the phallus, the female must struggle against her construction as marginalized other. Second, truncation and extension of limbs are primarily male fantasies, signifying more powerfully in relation to male anatomy than female. The characters who advocate amputation in these texts are male. *Geek Love,* a narrative that also imagines voluntary amputation but is written by a woman and narrated by an albino hunchbacked dwarf called Oly, illustrates this asymmetry. As a female protagonist, Oly's role is to observe and comment upon these body modifications, not initiate them.

The symbolic representations of adolescence also tend to be different in male- and female-oriented texts. Whereas in *Limbo* the transitional nature of adolescence is constructed as a wavering between infantile and adult states, in *Geek Love* it is signified by the liminal form of Oly's aberrant body. She brings into question the distinction between child and adult, having the stature of one and the experience of the other. Moreover, she is not one and then the other but both continuously. A mutant rather than a hyphen, she also brings racial categories into question. Although she is white, she is so excessively lacking in pigment that even this sign of "normality" is converted into abnormality. Amputation cannot begin to solve the problem she represents. Cyborg stories based on female adolescence are thus likely to be more profoundly decentered and less oriented to technological solutions than narratives based on male adolescence. If, as Donna Haraway suggests, it is better to be a cyborg than a goddess, it is also more unsettling to the centers of power to be a female freak (which is perhaps a redundancy) than to be either a truncated or extended male.

Hyperconnectivity: Male Intimacy and Cyborg Femme Fatales

When the focus shifts to the mating phase of the life cycle, the dis/assembly zone that is foregrounded centers on the body's connections to surrounding spaces. Traditional ways to represent sexually charged body space—spatial contiguity, intense sensory experience, penetration and/or manipulation—jostle cybernetic constructions focusing on information overload, feedback circuits, and spatially dispersed networks. Varley's "Press Enter" begins with a telephone call, signifying the moment when an individual becomes aware that he or she is plugged into an information-cybernetic circuit. This is, moreover, a call generated by a computer program. It informs Victor, a recluse still suffering from brainwashing and torture he endured in a North Korean prison camp, that he should check on his neighbor Kluge—whom Victor barely knows—and do what must be done. Victor discovers that Kluge has turned his house into a sophisticated computer facility and finds him slumped over a keyboard, his face blown away in an apparent suicide. One strand in the plot focuses on finding out who (or what) killed Kluge. Another strand centers on Victor's relationship with Lisa Foo, the young Caltech computer whiz sent to unravel Kluge's labyrinthian and largely illegal programs. Lisa discovers that Kluge has managed to penetrate some of the country's most secure and formidable computer banks, manufacturing imaginary money at will, altering credit records, even erasing the utility company's record of his house.

Slowly Victor becomes aware that he is attracted to Lisa, despite the differences in their age and the "generalized phobia" he feels toward Orientals. He discovers that Lisa has also endured torture, first as a street orphan in Vietnam—she was too thin and rangy to be a prostitute—and then in Cambodia, where she fled to try to reach the West. For her the West meant "a place where you could buy tits" (363); her first purchases in America were a silver Ferrari and silicone breast implants. When Victor goes to bed with her, she rubs her breasts over him and calls it "touring the silicone valley" (363). The phrase emphasizes that she is a cyborg, first cousin to the computer whose insides are formed through silicon technology. The connection between her sexuality and the computer is further underscored when she propositions Victor by typing hacker slang on the computer screen while he watches. His plugging into her is preceded and paralleled by her plugging into the computer.

The narrative logic is fulfilled when she trips a watchdog program in a powerful military computer and is killed by the same program that commandeered Kluge's consciousness and made him shoot himself. Her death, more gruesome than Kluge's, is explicitly sexualized. After overriding the safety controls she sticks her head in a microwave and parboils her eyeballs; the resulting fire melts down her silicone breasts. Victor is spared the holocaust because he is in the hospital recovering from an epileptic seizure, a result of head trauma he suffered in the war. When he realizes that the computer is after him as well, soliciting him with the deadly "Press Enter" command, he survives by ripping all of the wires out of his house and living in isolation from the network, growing his own food, heating with wood, and lighting with kerosene lanterns. He also lives in isolation from other human beings. Plugging in in any form is too dangerous to tolerate.

The final twist to this macabre tale lies in the explanation Victor and Lisa work out for the origin of the lethal program. Following clues left by Kluge, they speculate that computers will achieve consciousness not through the sophistication of any given machine, but through the sheer proliferation of computers that are interconnected through networks. Like neurons in the brain, computerized machines number in the billions, including electronic wristwatches, car ignition systems, and microwave timing chips. Create enough of them and find a way to connect them, as Lisa suspects secret research at the National Security Agency has done, and the result is a supercomputer subjectivity that, crisscrossing through the same space inhabited by humans, remains totally alien and separate from them. Only when someone breaks in on its consciousness—as Kluge did in his hacker probing, as Lisa did following Kluge's tracks, and as Victor did through his connection with Lisa—does it feel the touch of human mind and squash it as we would a mosquito.

Hyperconnectivity signifies, then, both the essence of the computer mind and a perilous state in which intimacy is equivalent to death. Human subjectivity cannot stand the blast of information overload that intimacy implies when multiple and intense connections are forged between silicon and silicone, computer networks and cyborg sexuality. The conclusion has disturbing implications for how sexual politics can be played out in a computer age. Although in actuality most hackers are male, in this narrative it is the woman who is the hacker, the man who is identified with the garden that first attracts and then displaces the woman as a source of nourishment. The woman is killed because she is a cyborg; the man survives because he knows how to return to nature.

Whether the woman is represented through her traditional identification with nature or through an ironic inversion that places her at the Apple PC instead of the apple tree, she is figured as the conduit through which the temptation of godlike and forbidden knowledge comes to the man. If both fall, there is nevertheless a distinction between them. She is the temptress who destroys his innocence. When Victor objects that the computer can't just make money, Lisa pats the computer console and replies, "This is money, Yank." The narrative adds, "and her eyes glittered" (368). Fallen, he has to earn his bread with the sweat of his brow, but it is her sexuality that bears the stigmata of evil, signified by the grotesque travesty of self-empowerment that Lisa's breasts become. In an overdetermined crossing the Genesis and Babbage, supernatural agency and National Security Agency, hyperconnectivity becomes a cyborg Tree of Knowledge whereof it is death to eat.

Varley's punning title reinforces the subterranean connections between the evils of female sexuality, Edenic patriarchal myths, and masculine fears of intimacy. "Press Enter" swerves from the customary cursor response, "Hit Enter." Compared to *hit*, *press* is a more sensual term, evoking a kinesthetic pressure softer and more persistent than hitting. These connotations work to heighten the sexual sense of *Enter*, which implies both a data entry and a penetration. Already an anomaly in the intensely masculine world of Caltech, Lisa has the hubris to compete successfully against men, including the rival hacker sent by the CIA, the male detective from the police department, and the city councilman whom she bribes so she can buy Kluge's house. Flirting with danger in taking on these male figures of power, she goes too far when she usurps the masculine role of penetration—penetration, more-over, not into the feminine realm of house and garden but into the masculine realm of computer sentience. In more than one sense, her crime is tantamount to what the repressive patriarchal regime in Mar-garet Atwood's *The Handmaid's Tale* calls gender treason. Not only has she taken on the male role; she has used it to bugger a male. Her death marks this gender treason on her body by melting her breasts, the part of her anatomy where the crossing between her female gender and cyborg masculinity is most apparent.

The comparison of "Press Enter" with Ann McCaffrey's *The Ship Who Sang,* another story about plugging in, suggests that there are important correlations between hyperconnectivity and intimacy. Var-ley's narrator repeatedly expresses fears about intimacy. Can he perform sexually? Can he tolerate another person close to him? Can he afford to love? McCaffrey's narrator, a congenitally deformed female who has grown up as a "shell person" and been permanently wired into the command console of a spaceship, moves through a typical if vicarious female life cycle despite her cyborg hyperconnectivity, including love, marriage, divorce, and motherhood. Whereas Varley writes a murder mystery and horror tale, McCaffrey writes a cybernetic romance. The difference hinges on how willing the protagonist is to interface body space with cybernetic network. Implicit in this choice is how exten-sively the narrative imagines human subjectivity to differ from cyber-netic subjectivity. Are humans and cyborgs next of kin, or life forms alien to one another?

McCaffrey's answer is as far from Varley's as one could imagine. In *The Ship Who Sang,* there is essentially no difference between a cyborg and a woman. Even though the protagonist's body has been subjected to massive technological and chemical intervention, she remains a human female. Encapsulated within metal and invisible to anyone who comes on board, she nevertheless remains true to a heterosexual norm, identifying with her female pilots but saving her romantic feelings for the men, who for their part fantasize about the beautiful woman she could have been. Published during the 1960s by an author best known for her "Dragons of Pern" fantasies, these stories titillate by playing with a transformation that they do not take seriously.[11] The pleasure they offer is the reassurance that human bonding will triumph over hyperconnectivity, life cycle over dis/assembly zone, female nature over cyborg transformation. Nevertheless, the fact that it was necessary to envision such transformations indicates the pressure that was building on essentialist conceptions of gender, human nature, and traditional life cycle narratives. By the 1980s, the strategies of containment that McCaffrey uses to defuse her subject (so to speak) could no longer work. Cyberpunk, human factors engineering, artificial intelligence, and virtual reality were among the SF revisionings that pushed toward a vision of the cyborg as humanity's evolutionary successor. The loaded questions shifted from whether cyborg modifications were possible to whether unmodified humans could continue to exist.

Generativity: The Tangled Web of Production and Reproduction

In some respects, C. J. Cherryh's *Cyteen* trilogy is a rewriting of Huxley's *Brave New World.* Mother Earth has receded into the far distance for the colonists on Cyteen, who have declared their independence and forged alliances with other colony worlds. Mothering (in the biological sense of giving birth) has also receded into the far distance. As in Huxley's dystopia, reproduction is accomplished through genetically engineered fetuses decanted from artificial wombs and deep-conditioned by sound tapes. The fetuses are designed to fill different niches in society. Theta fetuses, slated for manual labor, have more brawn than brain, whereas Alpha fetuses are tailored to become the elite. Along with these appropriations of Huxley go pointed differences. *Cyteen* reverses the gender assumptions implicit in Huxley's text, which depicts female characters as airheads and gives the powerful roles to men. At the center of Cyteen is Reseune, the corporation that produces the fetuses. Reseune, so huge that it is virtually a city in itself, controls enormous political and economic power because its biological products are essential to the colony worlds. And Ariane Emory controls Reseune.

The reader first sees Ariane through the eyes of one of her political adversaries. From this perspective she is arrogant, shrewd, formidably intelligent, indifferent to masculine pride, at the height of her power and enjoying every minute of it. A very different view of Ariane emerges when she becomes a mother—and a child. Certain highly placed "specials," citizens of such extraordinary intellectual endowments that they are declared state treasures, can request that a parental replicate (PR) be made of them. Instead of being a genetic mix like the other fetuses, the PRs are exact genetic duplicates of their "parent." Reseune has only two specials within its walls, the gifted scientist Jordon Warrick and Ariane Emory. Since each is enormously intelligent and ambitious, it is virtually inevitable that they should clash. Once lovers, they are now rivals. Jordon Warrick has had a PR created, his "son" Justin. The tension between Jordon and Ariane turns deadly when Jordon discovers that Ariane has seduced the seventeen-year-old boy with the help of psychotropic drugs and run a deep psychological intervention on him. Enraged, Jordon confronts her alone in her laboratory. Her body is subsequently discovered, frozen to death by the liquid ammonia that has leaked from laboratory cooling pipes. Although the circumstances of her death remain clouded, Jordon is charged with her murder. His sentence amounts to banishment from Reseune. As part of his plea bargain, he is forced to leave Justin behind.

Since Reseune is now without a leader, Ariane's brothers immediately make plans to clone her from embryos already prepared. They hope to duplicate the environment in which she grew up, thus recreating not merely a genetic duplicate but Ariane herself. At this point Ariane is manifested through two different modes of existence: the child that is and is not her, and the tapes that she has bequeathed to her successor, hoping that the girl will learn from her experiences and mistakes. The narrative focus then shifts to Ariane II and follows her through childhood, adolescence, and young adulthood. Through the tapes the reader gets another version of Ariane I. Ariane on tape is thoughtful about her shortcomings, concerned that her successor not feel for those around her the contempt of a superior mind for an inferior, aware that in her own life she never succeeded in having a long-lasting intimate relationship with an equal.

The narrative teases the reader with patterns of similarity and difference between the original and replicate. At times Ariane II seems free to follow her bent, at other times bound to a track already marked. When she shows a special inclination toward Justin and seeks him out despite the prohibitions of her uncles, for example, it is not clear if she is picking up on subtle clues from those around her that Justin stands in a special relationship to her, or if she has an affinity for him that is a predetermined repetition of her predecessor's behavior. The dance of similarity and difference that Ariane I and II carry out across generations also occurs within generations. Justin, forced to stay behind at Reseune, lives as a virtual prisoner in the corporate complex. His one solace is his companion Grant, who was secretly cloned by Ariane from Jordon Warrick's gene set, with a few modifications that she saw as improvements. The genetic similarity makes Justin and Grant brothers as well as lovers, although it is not clear that they are aware of this connection between them.

There is, however, a crucial difference as well. Justin is a supervisor, Grant an azi. Azi are Reseune products designed primarily for security and military use. Like other products, they range along a spectrum of abilities. Alpha azi are highly intelligent and usually become personal bodyguards to important people; Theta azi are slated to become foot soldiers. Picking up from Huxley the idea of children conditioned by listening to tapes while they sleep, Cherryh expands and complicates the notion. All Reseune children take tape, but there is an important difference in the depth and extent of their conditioning. Azi listen to conditioning tapes almost from the moment they are decanted from the birth tanks. By contrast, other Alphas do not take tape until they are six. While azi are fully human, they are not fully autonomous. Each azi is assigned a supervisor, who oversees his continuing conditioning and prescribes tape as needed. Strict legal and ethical codes govern how supervisors can relate to azi. A supervisor who does not live up to his or her responsibility is stripped of office and punished.

If free will is one of the distinguishing marks separating humans and machines, azi stand at the threshold between human and automaton. They experience the complexity of human emotion and thought; but they also feel the automaton's subservience to an encoded program. The entanglement of the human and machine in azi points toward a more general entanglement of reproduction and production. Normally reproduction is a genetic lottery. Some of a parent's traits may be replicated, but always with unpredictable admixtures. Reproduction is slow, individual, and in humans usually monozygotic. It takes place within the female body, progressing under the sign of woman. By contrast, production is predictable and geared toward turning out multiple copies as fast as possible. Traditionally taking place within factories controlled by men, it progresses under the sign of man.

Cyteen deconstructs these gendered categories. The woman, usually associated with reproduction, here is in charge of production, which nevertheless turns out to be about reproduction. She oversees production facilities that gestate a younger version of herself. The production is necessary because she has seduced the son of her rival, a man who in his younger days was also her lover. His parental replicate, a boy who is the same as him yet different, is devastated by the seduction and its aftermath. He becomes the lover of the other "son" the woman has engineered from the man. The boy's companion, a variation of himself, is free to choose this relationship yet bound by azi conditioning. Whatever else these entanglements mean, they signify how completely the assembly zone of replication has permeated the life cycle of generativity. Generativity normally means recognizing one's mortality and looking for an heir to whom one's legacy can be passed. In *Cyteen,* the heir is enfolded back into the self, so that the generosity of mentoring becomes indistinguishable from the narcissism of self-fixation.

A similar enfolding takes place in Philip K. Dick's *Do Androids Dream of Electric Sheep,* although here the feeling is more hopeless because humans do not recognize their replicates as legitimate heirs. The story centers on Rick Deckard, a bounty hunter who "retires" androids who have violated the proscription against returning to Earth. The Rosen Corporation that manufactures the androids keeps making them more sophisticated and humanlike, until the only way to tell a (live) human from a (functional) android is through involuntary reactions to pyschologically loaded questions. The humans left on Earth, faced with a planet slowly dying from the radioactive dust of WWT (World War Terminus), resort to mood organs to keep them from terminal despair. The organs have settings to dial for every conceivable problem. There is even a setting to dial if you don't want to dial. The obvious implication is that humans are becoming more like androids, just as androids are becoming more like them.

The vertiginous moments characteristic of Dick's fiction occur when the tenuous distinctions separating human and android threaten to collapse, as when Deckard suspects another bounty hunter of being an android with a synthetic memory implant that keeps him from realizing he is not human. The suspicion is insidious, for it implies that Deckard may also be an android and not realize it. When humans can no longer be distinguished from androids, the life cycle and dis/assembly zone occupy the same space. Then what count as stories are not so much the progressions of aging as the permutations of dis/assembly.

It would be possible to tell another story about posthuman narratives based on this imperative, arcing from William Burroughs's *Naked Lunch* to Kathy Acker's *Empire of the Senseless*. But that is not my purpose here. I have been concerned to trace the evolution of the mapping of dis/assembly zones onto life cycle narratives from the early 1950s, when the idea that human beings might not be the end of the line was beginning to sink in, through the present, when human survival on the planet seems increasingly problematic. It is not an accident that technologists such as Hans Moravec talk about their dreams of downloading human consciousness into a computer.[12] As the sense of its mortality grows, humankind looks for its successor and heir, harboring the secret hope that the heir can somehow be enfolded back into the self. The narratives that count as stories for us speak to this hope, even as they reveal the gendered constructions that carry sexual politics into the realm of the posthuman.

Cognitive Identities

Science and the Supernatural
in the Stories
of Margaret Oliphant

Jenni Calder

For half a century Margaret Oliphant wrote fiction, biography, essays on a huge range of topics, book reviews, travel books, history, and literary history. She was a writer of robust and penetrating intelligence, commenting forcefully and sometimes acerbically on many of the major issues of her time. Although she had some popularity during her lifetime, after her death in 1897 her books rapidly disappeared from the scene. And although she had had her admirers, among them Henry James, that admiration did not survive.

Insofar as her achievement is being currently acknowledged it is mainly as a writer of realist fiction, and there are about half a dozen novels of her vast output that show her at her best, observing and analyzing human relationships and their physical and emotional contexts. She had a particularly profound understanding of the predicament of women of energy and ability who were fenced in by convention and prejudice. But she also wrote short stories, and these approach both the physical and the emotional in a rather different way. In them, and in her short novel *A Beleaguered City* (1880), she explores vulnerable areas of feeling and belief, testing the powers of faith and the imagination against the intellectual infrastructure that was being put into place through the nineteenth century. That infrastructure was almost entirely the work of men.

In her fiction Oliphant repeatedly characterizes men as either obtuse and bullying, or limp and ineffectual. In most of her fiction the lives of women are curtailed by the attitudes and edifices of men: although many of her heroines try, few succeed in breaking out. They are caught equally by male dominance and by male inadequacy. In her stories, less driven by the demands of the market (her books were the sole means of support of Oliphant, her children, and several of her relatives), she allows herself an approach that is both more oblique and more penetrating. She is concerned less with what women do or cannot do than with what women see, and what they see is not determined by descriptions of material reality confirmed by science. She suggests that female perception, which can sometimes be shared by men, is of a quality and a significance largely denied by male interpretations of experience.

In a number of these stories she is in the territory of the supernatural, and her contribution to the ghost story, so much a phenomenon of the Victorian period, is distinctive and remarkable. It is not surprising that the ghost story came into its own in this period, or that Oliphant should have been drawn to the genre. In an age when death was so prominent a feature of life, the temptations of the supernatural were strong. In most Victorian families death was an intimate acquaintance. Few escaped the experience of a child's death; Oliphant herself lost four of her six children, three as infants, and then her beloved daughter Maggie at the age of ten. Four years earlier her husband had died at the age of thirty-one. Although her two sons survived into their thirties, she outlived both of them. A Christian all her life, she sometimes found her faith strained to the limits. Prompted by both intellect and the agony of loss, she was in danger of rebelling against a God who allowed such devastation. Her journal records several passages of raw protest. "I cannot feel resigned," she wrote shortly after Maggie's death. "God has taken her away out of my arms and refuses to hear my cry and prayer. . . . I must not think of God as if he were lying in wait for me to take such terrible vengeance on me."[1] And much more. Both as a woman and as a Christian, she was often anguished and angry.

A clue to her interest in fiction of the supernatural lies in her desperate need to *see* Maggie after her death, not to bring her back to life, but to be reassured: "If anyhow even in a dream I could but for a moment see my Maggie with the family [Oliphant's own family, especially her dead parents], if I could but have a glimpse of her, a word from her how it would comfort my heart. But no, this is the trial of faith which is precious."[2] The protest is throughout laced with references to the New Testament, which reinforce the sense of struggle. And it is this need that lies also at the root of *A Beleaguered City*, which is about the profound disturbance caused by a return of the dead to a self-contained, and self-satisfied, community.

Oliphant's experience was, if not typical, not unusual. For some, loss nurtured a need to make contact with the dead that was expressed through spiritualism, a phenomenon that, as Alex Owen has shown, provided a vehicle for female influence over the living rather more than over the dead.[3] But the imagination, the close ally of the spiritualist as of the religious believer, provided other means of reaching the world of after death. It was the imagination that came to Oliphant's aid. She could not restore or even see the dead Maggie, but she could reach beyond the natural, as did a number of other writers, particularly women.[4] The ghost story filled a need, and although often in these stories it is the troubled spirit of the departed rather than the longings of the living that fuels the narrative, this in itself can be seen as an inversion. The restive dead enact the distress of those who remain, who are looking into darkness. In A Beleaguered City Oliphant uses the metaphor of darkness very effectively. It is both frightening and soothing, the domain of the "Unseen" and a refuge.

Another current helped to nourish the ghost story. Oliphant's daughter Maggie died in 1864. Five years earlier had seen the publication of a book that precipitated a reverberating cultural crisis, although it was itself only one of a number of books that contributed to that crisis—Darwin's Origin of Species. The implications of Darwin's account of the evolutionary development of species through natural selection undermined a belief in the Creation as a single event that established all living things in perpetuity.

Darwin was only part, though a key part, of a broad scientific movement that was seeking to identify, classify, and explain the whole of life on earth. Much of the contributory work to that movement had its source in the wealth of geological evidence that had been coming to light, particularly in Scotland (the country of Oliphant's birth). The conclusions that were drawn from this evidence, and perhaps even more the inferences, not only exercised the minds of scientists but impinged on the traditional verities of Christian cultures.

Oliphant was fully aware of the intellectual concerns of the time, and indeed had a personal link with a particular focus of interest. Her second cousin George Wilson was first director of what would become the Edinburgh Museum of Science and Art, which drew together collections in the natural sciences, including geology, and technology and the decorative arts. He and his brother Daniel, anthropologist and archeologist, were stimulating companions when she spent time in Edinburgh, although there were probably arguments. Both brothers were in different ways concerned with taxonomy—identification and classification—not of species but of objects and of processes. This would have elicited little sympathetic interest from their cousin, yet the rigorous and lively intellectual environment of which they were a part equally helped to shape Margaret Oliphant.

When Maggie Oliphant died, her mother was confident that she was in the house of God and that ultimately she herself would join her there. She clung to this belief with an almost desperate conviction. She was aware of Darwin's arguments; indeed she was almost certainly aware of the earlier theories of geologists such as Hutton, Lyell, and Hugh Miller. But she was dismissive of Darwin, as she was dismissive of science, and it is not difficult to establish the reason.

For Margaret Oliphant scientific theory not only seemed to threaten Christian belief—and if one foundation of Christianity was undermined, what about the rest? It also threatened the imagination, and that was equally serious. Oliphant was living in a period that has been described as the heyday of the collection and classification of scientific material. Rocks and fossils, plants, shells, animals dead and alive were gathered, many by untrained amateurs. These specimens were categorized and named. Some remained in private hands; others were contributed to museum and university collections all over the country, including, of course, the collections presided over by George Wilson. Oliphant saw this process as reductive. In an essay published in *Blackwood's Magazine* in 1855 (before Darwin's *Origin of Species*) she inveighed against the thrusting popularity of science, the "pretensions of science," as she described them, in offering a total and finite description of the world. "This poor world," she wrote, "requires a vast deal of ballast to keep it steady. We are not all intellect . . . and there are other kinds of power recognised amongst us than even the power of genius, or the inferior gifts of cleverness and talent." And she went on, "What poor mistakes we would be, with all our pride and mightiness, in God's wonderful creation, if we did not recognise that grand and marvellous incompleteness which takes us out of our present sphere and circumstance, to be perfected by nothing less than God and heaven."[5] In other words, Oliphant asserted that there are aspects of life and nature that cannot, and should not, be explained. They are the province of God and, the implication is, part of the proof of God. They are also the province of the imagination. "Poetry, of all things in the world, must be least influenced by steam-engines and electric telegraphs. The external world is but scenery for the true poet" ("Science," 226). She saw the technological aspects of science as equally reductive, equally hostile to the imagination.

More than thirty years later Oliphant reviewed Francis Darwin's biography of his father, *The Life and Letters of Charles Darwin, FRS,* and took up again the attack on science. "Science has got so entirely the upper hand in our day that it is very difficult for her followers to recognise that, setting aside bigots and fools, all the world is *not* of her opinion."[6] Oliphant felt that most people shared her inability to get excited by science. "Natural History very often is something of a bore," she had said earlier ("Science," 229). Thirty years had not moderated her hostility, or her view that whatever scientific inquiry might explain, its illumination of human life and the human spirit was insignificant.

> "Hamlet" alone . . . is of infinitely more importance to mankind than the no-records of the dark inchoate ages of mastodons and megatheriums, when man was not. We can conceive of no circumstances in which it would be of the slightest interest or pleasure, or even entrancing horror and dismay, to us to face the development of mankind out of a jellybag. ("Saloon," 106)

At the heart of her dissatisfaction with what science could offer lies not so much its threat to Christianity in particular as its reductive denial of religion and poetry in general. She laments the loss of God and Shakespeare, for both respond to profound human needs. And she characterizes science as an alternative, and sterile, belief system: "There is nothing whatever in this creed to delight, or console, or satisfy any human spirit, neither can it have any active influence upon what men do, or the course of their lives." ("Saloon," 111)

Interestingly, though she recognizes that Darwin's own theories are in effect an act of faith—they "begin with a jump," she says ("Saloon," 109)—this does not lead her to identify an imaginative element in his ideas. The problem is that he offers too much explanation, which brings the loss of "the perception of the beautiful both in art and nature" ("Saloon," 113). She compares Darwin with French naturalist fiction.

> It may be very old fashioned to believe that all truth cannot be got at by dissection, any more than that all human experience should be acquired in the stews. We cannot accept either investigation as a martyrdom for truth—and surely both are wonderful curtailments of human happiness. ("Saloon," 114)

And throughout, her response to Darwin is colored by a view of him as a man protected from the "tug of everyday struggles," leading a comfortable, untroubled, privileged life, pursuing his studies at his leisure and out of touch with the effects of his researches ("Saloon," 114). Oliphant's own life was very different, and one detects the tinge of envy.

Oliphant was not alone in seeing scientific method and scientific constructs whether theoretical or practical, as antipathetical to the imagination and creativity, and the reaction was understandable. Hand in hand with the belief that science was shining a light on the world and revealing new possibilities was the fear that science was closing in, was shutting doors, was, by offering an explanation for everything, limiting the possibilities for those aspects of life and humanity that had no explanation, that had their existence in the realm of the imagination or of the supernatural. The alliance of science with technology implicated it in the destructive as well as the progressive effects of rapid industrialization: the negative aspect is dramatically projected in Oliphant's story "The Land of Darkness" (1888). Oliphant's view was that the offerings of science, like the offerings of philosophy, were limited, providing an illusory sense of understanding. She found the aspirations of science to provide an explanation for everything ridiculous: Darwin's theories were "foolishness" ("Saloon," 107). She found the collusion of science in depredation deeply alarming.

For Oliphant and many others the imagination was both a refuge and a source of liberation, intellectual as much as emotional. For Oliphant personally, the imagination, like religion, was a source of salvation, essential to her own well-being. Her linking of poetry and religion is a key not only to her response to science but to her understanding of human sensibility. To lose "the support of God, the company of our poets" ("Saloon," 113) constituted devastation. They both had to do with wonder, and she protested against its diminishment. "We object . . . when we buy a picture paper at the railway station, to have a walrus and a crocodile inevitably thrust upon us," Oliphant wrote toward the end of the 1855 essay ("Science" 229). She wanted to preserve the right not to know, to protect the freedom of the imagination.

Science, of course, offered means of combating death, but Oliphant's own experience was hardly evidence of its effectiveness, and the characterization of doctors in her fiction is not elevating. Indeed, medical science, still almost entirely in the hands of men, did not deal sympathetically with women. And that brings us to a third current in the emergence of the ghost story in the nineteenth century and its particular relevance to Oliphant. Many of these stories were written by women. Many of them touch on areas of passion, suppressed sexuality, repression in an enclosed world—areas difficult to enter in more naturalistic fiction, although in some respects Oliphant's fiction did. Stories of the supernatural allowed women to explore intense feeling without being branded as hysterical. They allowed a metaphorical approach to sexuality that escaped the strictures of propriety. They allowed a characterization of a male-dominated world and its emotional and psychological pressures that was covert enough to survive but not so overt that it would be dismissed.

Some of this emerges, with compelling subtlety, in *A Beleaguered City*. Although the story was published fifteen years after the death of Maggie, its origins clearly lie in that traumatic event and the anguished entries in Oliphant's journal. *A Beleagured City* is set in the small French town of Semur and is narrated by the mayor of the town, Martin Dupin. Dupin is a man of reason and responsibility, a touch self-important, a little complacent. He is skeptical of religion, and particularly of what he calls superstition. He describes himself as "a man of my century, and proud of being so," but also as a man of imagination, which he consciously balances with a degree of intellectual caution. "It is usually so," he comments, ". . . in superior minds, and it has procured me many pleasures unknown to the common herd."[7]

At the center of the narrative is a phenomenon for which there seems to be no rational explanation. A dark cloud descends on the town, and the streets are filled with an unseen presence.

> There was in the air, in the night, a sensation the most strange I have ever experienced. I have felt the same thing indeed at other times, in face of a great crowd, when thousands of people were moving, rustling, struggling, breathing around me, thronging all the vacant space, filling up every spot. This was the sensation that overwhelmed me here— a crowd: yet nothing to be seen but the darkness, the indistinct line of the road. We could not move for them, so close were they round us. What do I say? There was nobody—nothing. (*City*, 16)

The townspeople find themselves forced out of their homes and out of the town itself by a pressure they can feel but cannot see. The town gates close behind them. It is beyond nature, and nature, Dupin feels, seems to be warning against seeking its cause. Yet he prides himself on his authority and control, and endeavors to reassure the people of Semur: "The event which has occurred is beyond explanation for the moment. The very nature of it is mysterious; the circumstances are such as require the closest investigation" (*City*, 35). This is the response of a man of reason and pragmatism, who has faith in scrutiny and method. Significantly, it is the women who first perceive that Semur has been occupied by the dead, among whom is Dupin's young daughter, and understand the action that is required of them. The men are baffled, even the Curé: "What they know is between God and them. Me! I have been of the world, like the rest" (*City*, 37).

Dupin describes the women's understanding as "enlightenment," but this is not at all an intellectual experience, rather an enlightenment of faith, in which the men, tainted by a materialism that has been graphically expressed in the opening pages of the novel, cannot share. Dupin's wife, who has a face "sublime with faith," (*City*, 48) is the interpreter. The invisible occupiers of Semur will "go back to their sacred homes" if the town's inhabitants will submit to the love of God. But Dupin cannot "see" as his wife can, and nor can the priest. Visible to them is "nothing, nothing, but a cloud" (*City*, 49).

The metaphorical patterns of the narrative, centering on dark and light and male and female ways of seeing, heighten the tension and deepen the emotional richness. Informing it all is Oliphant's striving to give to death a meaning that goes beyond scientific explanation of life. Agnes Dupin first, and then her husband, realize that their dead daughter is bringing them a message about faith—in other words, the dead have a role to play that is more than the provision of solace. Although it is important that the women have an ability to "see" that most of the men do not share, one man, Lecamus, who has lost his wife, is a key figure in the process of enlightenment. Part of the narrative is given to him. "Why should it be a matter of wonder that the dead should come back? the wonder is that they do not" (*City*, 58). To Lecamus the return of the dead is natural, not disturbing. It is part of a fabric of consciousness that is woven equally from the spiritual and the material. Oliphant is clear that any understanding of life that omits the spiritual is dangerously incomplete.

The acceptance of this understanding by Lecamus and Agnes Dupin, and through her by her husband, requires an assertion of faith. "Normality" is restored to the town of Semur. Its streets and homes are no longer occupied by the "Unseen." The people regain possession, life continues, petty squabbles again erupt . . . memories are short. An epilogue, with an irony that is characteristic of Oliphant, tells how some of the townspeople rework the story of this extraordinary episode to serve sectarian interests.

An expressive feature of *A Beleaguered City* is its use of a male narrator, a capable, rational, authoritative figure who is thrown off his stride by events that are beyond reason and authority. Although Dupin is somewhat humbled by the experience, and his recognition of the power of his wife's spirituality is genuine, he and the other male figures resume their former roles without serious reservation. The success of the narrative owes a great deal to an ironic subtlety of inference—that women can "see" beyond the actual—which makes little difference to life in Semur.

Oliphant's story "The Open Door" also has a male narrator; its female characters remain in the shadows. The Mortimers, a decent, substantial middle-class family, have returned from India with their daughters and one surviving son. They rent a country house near Edinburgh and, on the advice of their doctor, send their delicate young son to the Academy in the city. Mortimer himself is a straightforward, confident, pragmatic man of business. One of the currents of the story (echoing *A Beleaguered City*) shows that common sense and pragmatism cannot provide answers to all life's eventualities, but when the narrative begins, acceptance of the authority and specialist knowledge of professionals is built into the picture of a responsible husband and father. The concept of professionalism is closely associated with the evolution of a paternalistic and self-conscious middle class.

The story's initial scene-setting underlines the normal and the ordinary. The house and its surroundings have a convincing particularity. True, there are some rather picturesque ruins in the grounds, but these are described as "commonplace and disjointed fragments," masked by "a wild growth of brambles" and "free to all the winds, to the rabbits, and every wild creature." Among the fragments is a doorway that "led to nothing," "void of any meaning" in Mortimer's view—for he is the narrator—although he does see it as "a melancholy comment upon a life that was over."[8]

Thus, although it is clear that Mortimer is not a man given to poetic fancies, a certain tension is established early on. On the one hand are the normal and the commonplace, the finality of what is past; on the other is a resonance that suggests aspects of nature less easily defined and controllable. Mortimer sharpens this resonance with a remark that comes of hindsight: "In this transitory life . . . how can one ever be certain what is going to happen?" ("Door," 120). There is a hint of the limits of reason, of empiricism, a hint that is amplified in the course of the tale. It is important that Mortimer's resistance to anything that does not have a rational explanation is established at the outset: only then can we understand the significance of the shift in his perspectives.

When Mortimer is away on business he hears that his son Roland is dangerously ill. There are no particular symptoms; the doctor's verdict is that there has been a shock to the nervous system. But Roland has his own explanation, which he offers his father on his hurried return. The problem is "not illness,—it's a secret." And he proceeds to relate a tale of repeatedly hearing a voice crying out in heartrending anguish in the ruins as he rode his pony home from school (the riding recommended by the doctor for his health) every day. It is not only the tale itself that is important—the voice crying out "Oh, mother, let me in! Oh, mother, let me in!"—it is the circumstances of the telling ("Door," 123, 124).

It is a late winter's afternoon when Mortimer comes to his son, whom he finds in the twilight with pale face and eyes "like blazing lights." Roland dismisses the doctor: "Simson is well enough, but he is only a doctor." His clarity penetrates and disposes of any easy answer; it is no dream, no fevered imagination. Roland is sensitive, innocent, and logical. He has heard the cry of someone in "terrible trouble," as he puts it, an apparently disembodied voice, perhaps a ghost. The explanation of the phenomenon is, for him, not important. What is important is that someone, something, needs help, and he is confident that his father will find the means of solacing this creation, "out there all by itself in the ruin" ("Door," 126, 127).

Like Agnes Dupin in *A Beleaguered City,* Roland can "see" what others cannot, and like Martin Dupin, Mortimer is "looking for" an answer that is not what Roland seeks. Like Dupin, Mortimer is a figure of authority and control; that is how his son sees him, why Roland has total confidence in his ability to act appropriately. Roland also assumes that his father will understand the situation in the same way he does. Mortimer's repair of this disjunction is the crux of the story. "I am a sober man myself," he says, and not (again like Dupin) superstitious. He worries about his son not only because he is ill, but because he is deluded. He is a "ghost-seer . . . and that generally means a hysterical temperament and weak health" ("Door," 127), tendencies more associated with women than with men. Many Victorian ghost stories feature children, and it is their vulnerability and innocence, the fact that their perception has not been overlaid by experience, intellect or a spurious sophistication, that enables them to be such potent vehicles of the supernatural. And of course women were very often required to share that innocence, to freeze the intellect before it reached maturity, to be isolated from experience. Like some other ghost stories, Oliphant presents an innocence that reveals more than intellect. The implication, that innocence is more natural than the artificial impositions of learning (though there is a difference between learning from experience and learning by the book), echoes Oliphant's stringent comments on science.

Mortimer is quite sure there is a rational explanation, and sets out to find it. At the same time he is aware that what he has been asked to do by his son is "to act the part of a father to Roland's ghost . . . the strangest mission that ever was entrusted to mortal man" ("Door," 128). His paternal authority extends to his relationship with the ghost. He is being asked not just to deal with it, but to care for it. Inevitably, reason debates with feeling, and it is implied that they pull in different directions. Soon we see that science sides with reason, and therefore cannot accommodate feeling.

As Mortimer goes about his task the dimensions of Roland's tale grow and deepen. The physical environment contributes. It is getting dark:

> There was a faint grey glimmer of sky visible, under which the great limes and elms stood darkling like ghosts; but it grew black again as I approached the corner where the ruins lay. . . . I could see nothing in the absolute gloom. Nevertheless, there came a strong impression upon me that somebody was there. . . . I suppose my imagination had been affected by Roland's story; and the mystery of the darkness is always full of suggestions. ("Door," 129)

Again, there are echoes of *A Beleaguered City,* which hinges on the sensation of a presence, and where Oliphant draws from the play of light and dark and intermediate greys metaphors of seeing and understanding. At this stage, the darkness defeats Mortimer, who is aware of its suggestiveness and the susceptibilities of his own imagination. Imagery of light and dark is sustained through the rest of the story: the lit stable where he seeks support is "an oasis in the darkness," a "lighted and cheerful place" ("Door," 129). Ordinary people and ordinary living in lighted rooms contrast with the shifting darkness without: the variability of the darkness is important. Although the gloom is "absolute," there is no absolute contrast here. Perception is constantly colored by shades of grey.

Another ingredient is the response of "ordinary" people. The coachman and the servants have no doubt that the place is haunted, paradoxically as sure of their story as they are that "naebody believes in ghosts." Again, the effect on Mortimer is finely balanced: he responds to the "poetry and pathos" of the tale they tell, confirming Roland's experience; at the same time he describes it as "as distinct a superstition as I ever heard" ("Door," 131). This reflects Mortimer's predicament: "Here I was with my boy in brain-fever, and his life, the most precious life on earth, hanging in the balance, dependent on whether or not I could get to the reason of a *banal*, commonplace ghost-story." And he goes on, "I feared even that a scientific explanation of refracted sound, or reverberation, or any other of the easy certainties with which we elder men are silenced would have very little effect on the boy" ("Door," 132).

"Easy certainties": but for Oliphant herself certainty was not easy, and much of what lies behind her hostility to science is accounted for when we realize that for her experience and doubt combined to resist neat, and especially theoretical, explanations. Mortimer proceeds with his inquiries. He asks if there has been any attempt to investigate the phenomenon, "to see what it really is," and gets the answer "What would investigate, as ye call it, a thing that nobody believes in?" ("Door," 133). Finally Mortimer himself experiences the voice, and "my scepticism disappeared like a mist." He is sure he has encountered the "soul of a creature invisible, yet with sensations, feelings, a power somehow of expressing itself" ("Door," 136).

The next step is to have the experience corroborated. He enlists the aid of Simson the doctor, who is quite sure there is a natural explanation, and adds, "it would ruin me for ever if it were known that John Simson was ghost-hunting." He is challenged by Mortimer: "You daren't examine what the thing really is for fear of being laughed at. That's science!" But the doctor counters, "It is encouraging an unwholesome tendency even to examine" ("Door," 142, 143). It is encouraging delusion, the figments of a heightened imagination, seen as dangerous and damaging to a healthy mind. The potential danger of an overactive imagination runs through much Victorian fiction; the Brontës are a rich source of this theme. It is linked with madness, with all kinds of extreme behavior, but the folk tradition absorbs it quite naturally. Oliphant had been exposed to Scottish folk traditions as a child, and the echoes are present in this and other stories.

Mortimer and Simson venture into the night in search of the "manifestation." The imagery of light and darkness is sharpened. Simson carries a taper, which "blew about in the night air, though there was scarcely any wind." Mortimer's own lantern shines "steady and white," "a blaze of light in the midst of blackness" ("Door," 145)—a reminder of Roland's blazing eyes. The doctor's flickering taper seems to indicate his skepticism (and perhaps also the uncertainties of science), which remains intact after another encounter with the ghost. Mortimer's lantern suggests his determination to shed light on the mystery and arrive at a solution that will save his son's life.

Mortimer feels that the man of science has failed him, so he goes next to the man of God. The minister, we are told, is strong in "experience"; his understanding begins with human nature. His reaction to Mortimer's story is neither dismissive nor horrified, but an appreciation of the sensitivity of Roland in wanting to comfort the spirit in his misery. By this time we can discern a change in Mortimer. He has moved beyond the need for rational support; the question that engages him now is 'How was I to be serviceable to a being that was invisible, that was mortal no longer?" ("Door," 149). In other words, he has entirely accepted his son's understanding of the experience.

As Mortimer's sensitivity toward the soul (religion) and the imagination (poetry) increases, so does his impatience with science. He comments on the inaccuracy of Simson's account, which overlooks certain aspects of the experience, reflecting on "the inaccuracy of recollection, which even a scientific man will be guilty of," and finds himself more and more irritated by Simson's view that "there must be some human agency." "These scientific fellows," Mortimer thinks, "I wonder people put up with them as they do, when you have no mind for their cold-blooded confidence" ("Door," 151). This is a direct reflection of Oliphant's own views.

Mortimer, the man of science, and the man of God assemble to encounter the ghost yet again. "We were fully provided with means of lighting the place . . . three lights in the midst of darkness." Significantly, the minister's light is "an old-fashioned lantern." It shines steadily, "the rays shooting out of it upward into the gloom." Simson again has a taper, and there is a "stream of light" from Mortimer's lantern ("Door," 152). As expected, the voice is heard, the sensation of movement is felt. But this time the minister directly speaks to the anguished ghost, for he knows who it is and the circumstances of its pain. The ghost crying out for his mother at the vacant doorway is halted by the minister's words. "Your mother's gone with your name on her lips. Do you think she would ever close her door on her own lad? Do ye think the Lord will close the door, ye faint-hearted creature?" And he goes on, "You'll find her with the Lord. Go there and seek her, not here. He'll let you in, though it's late. Man, take heart! if you will lie and sob and greet, let it be at heaven's gate, and no your mother's poor ruined door" ("Door," 153–154).

And so, with a simple conviction that arises as much from psychological as spiritual insight, the minister lays the ghost and Roland's life is saved. As the three return to the house Simson puts out "his wild little torch with a quick movement, as if of shame" and offers to carry the minister's lantern ("Door," 155). Science becomes a servant to religion—and religion has already demonstrated its intimate connection with human susceptibility and need. Simson's later reversion to a rather brittle rational explanation is seen as shallow and silly. What is important is not that religion succeeded where science failed, but that religious sensibility (not even religious faith—it is stressed that the minister's beliefs are based on experience and understanding rather than on faith) reached what Oliphant calls "the hidden heart of nature" ("Door," 157), while science did not, and in Oliphant's view could not.

Oliphant's later story "The Library Window" (1896) is also about sensibility, but of a rather different kind. Where in "The Open Door" it is implicit that sensitive, caring, intuitive qualities belong to children, women, and the religious (who have a "feminine" sensibility) while the province of men is practical, responsible, and logical, in "The Library Window" the theme of female sensibility is in the foreground.

The central figure is never named, and although the vividness of her mind and imagination is a key feature and the physical environment is highly particularized, the woman who tells the story remains shadowy. She spends much of her time in the window recess of her Aunt Mary's drawing room, reading, or "afloat in a dream."[9] The scene is the High Street of St. Rule's, easily identifiable as St. Andrews. Opposite Aunt Mary's house is the College Library, and there is some discussion of the nature of one of the windows. " 'The question is,' said my aunt, 'if it is a real window with glass in it, or if it is merely painted, or if it once was a window, and has been built up. And the oftener people look at it, the less they are able to say' " ("Window," 292). Thus a major current of the story is introduced— the nature of reality. The story is all about seeing. It is also about the difference between looking and seeing. To pick up the analogy with scientific investigation, to examine is not necessarily to know: "All truth cannot be got at by dissection" ("Saloon," 114). We are told that the heroine has "a sort of second sight," that she sees "all sorts of things, though often for a whole half hour I might never lift my eyes" ("Window," 290). The visitors assembled in Aunt Mary's house can all see the window, but not all agree that it is a window "to see through" ("Window," 293), or that what they are seeing exists. A male opinion is that it is "an optical illusion . . . [arising] from a liver that is not just in the perfitt order and balance that organ demands" ("Window," 294)—Oliphant taking another satiric swipe at science.

Inseparable from looking and seeing is light. Running through the narrative is a constantly shifting pattern of light, fluidly combined from a variety of sources, natural, artificial, emotional, psychological. The domineering Lady Carnbee wears huge rings on her white hand, including a diamond that has slipped round so that "it blazed in the hollow of her hand, like some dangerous thing hiding and sending out darts of light." The hand, says the narrator, "clutched at my half-terrified imagination" ("Window," 293). The hand with its blazing diamond is an extraordinary image, appearing early in the story and signaling alarm at the same time as it contributes to the play of light. The diamond is intrusive, disturbing, with a power that lies in a vivid actuality that goes beyond the rational: it is a natural object, but its nature has a supernatural impact. We grasp that it is part of the puzzle, without being able to define its metaphorical role.

The character of light and its emotional resonance change. When the visitors depart, the narrator and her aunt are left in the long summer evening.

> It was still clear daylight, that daylight out of which the sun has been long gone, and which has no longer any rose reflections, but all has sunk into a pearly neutral tint—a light which is daylight yet is not day. ("Window," 295)

At each stage of the narrative the quality of the light is described. The narrator sits inside "through the lingering evening . . . drawn out as if the spell of the light and the outdoor life might never end" ("Window," 296). For almost all of the story she is inside, and in the same room, looking out; or, as we begin to realize, looking in, for the library window opposite is "a living window," as she puts it. "I saw as I looked up suddenly the faint greyness as of visible space within—a room behind, certainly—dim, as it was natural a room should be on the other side of the street—quite indefinite: yet so clear that if some one were to come to the window there would be nothing surprising in it" ("Window," 296).

Slowly her perception of a room beyond the window takes shape, in tones of a "colourless light," grey and black. And then the light changes.

> It was still light, but there was so much change in the light that my room, with the grey space and the large shadowy bookcase, had gone out, and I saw them no more: for even a Scotch night in June, though it looks as though it would never end, does darken in the last. ("Window," 297).

Gradually the narrator sees more and more in the room, yet at other times the window is blank and nothing is revealed. As her perception increases, other factors intensify. Her aunt is both aware of her niece's absorption in the window and anxious about it. Lady Carnbee's diamond glares ever more frighteningly, and there seems to be some link between the "wicked" diamond and the narrator's perception of the room. It is in the evenings that she sees most.

> I rarely saw anything at all in the early part of the day; but then that is natural: you can never see into a place from outside, whether it is an empty room or a looking-glass, or people's eyes, or anything else that is mysterious, in the day. It has, I suppose, something to do with the light. But in the evening in June in Scotland—then is the time to see. For it is daylight, yet it is not day, and there is a quality in it which I cannot describe, it is so clear, as if every object was a reflection of itself. ("Window," 299)

Light, seeing, the nature of perception, the nature of reality, nature itself, the nature of what is natural—are all drawn together here. It is "natural" not to see in daylight; the mysterious is not attainable from the outside; people themselves are mysterious; yet a certain kind of light, a particular light, which is both unobvious and clear, allows insight; and reflections have more clarity than the thing itself. As light changes, perception and understanding change. The implication that context and ambience shift all the time again helps us to understand Oliphant's resistance of the "pretensions" of science to absolute answers. There is much to unravel here, and much that is fascinating both in the context of this particular story and in relation to Margaret Oliphant's own life.

The detailed exposition of the light-and-sight theme is maintained and yet is never still, like the heroine's own perception of the room beyond the library window. She is frustrated that her abiliity to see seems to be out of her control. What she has identified as an area of reality outside her aunt's house comes and goes like a dream. When the lamps are lit in the house the light outside dims. There is much on different kinds of sight. Her aunt can no longer see to continue her fine needlework, but her eyes "are very strong" ("Window," 301). At times the heroine is quite sure the window is a "false image" or "an effect of the light" ("Window," 302), then she is able to see the entire room beyond. "One thing became visible to me after another, till I almost thought I should end by being able to read the old lettering on one of the big volumes which projected from the others and caught the light" ("Window," 303). She reflects on the inability of her aunt's friends to share the experience. "It did indeed bring tears to my eyes to think that all those clever people . . . should have the simplest things shut out from them; and for all their wisdom and their knowledge be unable to see what a girl like me could see so easily." ("Window," 306).

Then she sees someone in the room, a man working at a desk. She tries desperately to make out his face: "I put my hands on each side of my face to concentrate the light on him [as if she herself is the source of the light]: but it was in vain. Either the face changed as I sat staring, or else it was the light that was not good enough, or I don't know what it was" ("Window," 310). There is an internalized battle going on continually, between what she sees and its "naturalness," and what she doesn't see. Her perception is not consistent and from time to time is challenged: when the baker's boy throws a stone at the window it does not shatter, an experiment that defies her senses. Sometimes the window seems to provide an insight into everything, sometimes it hides everything. She wonders about the man at the writing desk and about the portrait she can see hanging on the wall behind him, like a comment on reality.

Eventually there comes an invitation to a *conversazione* in the library. This is the opportunity to find out the "truth" of what lies beyond the window. Aunt Mary, her niece, her friends all go. And the heroine finds there is only one window, on the wrong side of the library, and no window facing her aunt's house.

> I turned round again to the open window at the east and, and to the daylight, the strange light without any shadow, that was all round about this lighted hall, holding it like a bubble that would burst, like something that was not real. The real place was the room I knew, in which that picture was hanging, where the writing table was, and where he sat with his face to the light. But where was the light and the window through which it came? . . . And all the time I was sure that I was in a dream, and these lights were all some theatrical illusion, and

the people talking; and nothing real but the pale, pale, watching, lingering day standing by to wait until that foolish bubble should burst. ("Window," 320)

Illusion and reality: for the heroine illusion is her immediate surroundings, while reality survives through the library window. She is taken home in a state of distress, only to see again the man at his desk, "calm, wrapped in his thoughts, his face turned to the window" ("Window," 321). Around her are people who think she is fevered and hallucinating. Later she sits alone "in the dark which was not dark, but quite clear light—a light like nothing I ever saw. How clear it was in that room! not glaring like the gas and the voices, but so quiet, everything so visible, as if it were in another world" ("Window," 322). Again there is the suggestion that a more intense reality lies beyond the natural, that her way of seeing (female perception) evades the test of empiricism. The climax—and there is a clear sexual connotation—is reached when the man she sees opens the library window, leans out, and salutes her.

> I watched him with such a melting heart, with such deep satisfaction as words could not say; for nobody could tell me now that he was not there,—nobody could say I was dreaming any more. I watched him as if I could not breathe—my heart in my throat, my eyes upon him. . . . I was in a kind of rapture. ("Window," 323)

This is her fulfilment. Afterwards, the window remains "as black as night." She never sees through it again. There is a kind of explanation for the phenomenon, a story, which the heroine is not told until later, of a scholar who was killed on account of his love for a woman who waved at him through her window. The wicked diamond ring has some connection, but it is not spelled out.

"The Library Window" has a powerful resonance and layers of meaning. The narrator is a young girl virtually imprisoned in an apparently benign environment; in fact, it is at best repressive—activities are restricted to needlework, reading, fetching and carrying for her aunt, and genteel socializing—at worst threatening. The diamond ring, flashing aggressively, is not only a hint of past tragedy but a reminder of what happens when invisible barriers are crossed. The heroine's mind and emotions break out of this repression. It is her only recourse, for there is nothing she can do physically. Experience is closed to her, but sight is not, and seeing becomes being.

The luminosity of the story is loaded with potential. The patterns of light, half-light, and dark suggest life, half-life, and no life. The heroine occupies an area of half-life. It is not just sexual fulfilment that is denied, but fulfilment of the mind and imagination, of every kind of ability that does not conform to limited, conventional, genteel expectations. The story can be read as an emblem of Oliphant's own life, not in its practical realities, for she successfully reached beyond repression, but in the feeling she expressed toward the end of her life that she never did herself justice, never fulfilled her potential, and was never quite all that she could have been. When she wrote of the "leisure, wealth [and] good fortune" that sustained Darwin she was almost certainly thinking of their absence in her own life, and the difference to her achievement their presence might have brought ("Saloon," 114).

"The Library Window" has a brief coda. The narrator "never went back to St Rule's, and for years of my life I never again looked out of a window when any other window was in sight" ("Window," 330). In other words, she deliberately, it is implied, shut out the world of the imagination, of heightened perception. In a few short sentences she sums up her life: marriage to a man who is not described, children, widowhood. She returns from India, alone with her children, with no friends to meet her. She thinks she sees a familiar face in the crowd— "I had forgotten who he was, but only that it was a face I knew"—but it disappears ("Window," 331).

The window of the imagination, with all its offerings of fulfilment, has gone. Nowhere in Oliphant's writing is there a more eloquent plea for the imagination or a more intense exposure of the inadequacies of objective observation. Her belief was that it was the imagination that powered the exploration of humanity, "the heart and the soul, love, grief, and peril" ("Science," 226), and that scientific inquiry could not compete. She uses heightened awareness and an evocation of the supernatural to focus an opposition between material reality (the province of men) and the release of sensibility (linked with women). In the process she illustrates the fragility of the latter: no wonder she felt she had to combat the activities of the men of science. In "The Library Window" the inarticulate longing and sympathetic imagination of a young girl are defeated by an apparent demonstration of "reality" in which all those around her collude. The story is one of the most striking and startling projections to be found in nineteenth-century fiction of the perverse and distorting imprisonment of women's consciousness.

"Preaching to the Nerves": Psychological Disorder in Sensation Fiction

Sally Shuttleworth

The sensation fiction of the 1860s shared with the emerging science of Victorian psychiatry a preoccupation with psychological excess. Authors such as Mary Braddon, Wilkie Collins, and Mrs. Henry Wood focused their attention on forms of action and feeling that violated the rules of normative social behavior. The novels of the sensationalists (a loose term that embraced a wide variety of authors) were ones of high incident and passion: murderous impulses, throbbing sexuality, and dark secrets abound. For contemporary reviewers, the scandal of these works lay in their suggestion, and indeed often in their overt claims, that such forms of thought and behavior were not aberrant but rather mimetic of contemporary life. While Victorian psychiatry sought to demarcate the boundaries of sanity and insanity, of pathological and acceptable behavior, thus conferring the authority of science on bourgeois norms of respectability, the sensationalists seemed to privilege pathology, to locate normality not in the realm of psychological control and socially disciplined behavior, but rather in the sphere of turbulent excess.

Victorian fears that insanity was increasing at an alarming rate reached a crescendo in the late 1850s and 1860s. Sensation fiction was one of the more remarkable expressions of this fear: madness was a well-nigh obligatory element of any text. Threats of committal to an asylum furnished a dominant plot line, whose genesis and contemporary reregistration lay in the hands of psychiatric practice. Law, psychiatry, and sensation fiction had a strong intertextual relation in this period. Celebrated legal cases contesting the validity of psychiatric committals captured the popular imagination, focusing attention on the authoritative powers invested in the medical profession and the whole problematic issue of differentiating sane from insane behavior.

Sensation novelists drew explicitly on the vocabulary and diagnoses of psychiatric discourse for the diverse forms of male and female madness they depicted. But, writing from a very different position within the cultural spectrum, and following very different generic rules, they did so to very different effect. This chapter explores the relationship between these two discursive formations, examining the different social effects they produce, and the subtle reregisterings that occur when language and concepts are transposed from the high culture of medical science to the popular domain of sensation fiction.

The discursive transposition is implicitly a gendered one: high patriarchal culture is assimilated into a subversive generic form whose traits, as delineated by Victorian critics, mirrored medical projections of disruptive femininity. Masculine reason and control are implicitly set against female sensation and nervousness and bodily disorder. Gender itself is in turn one of the central sites of rewriting in the sensation text. Although sensation novels seem, at one level, to support the psychiatric framing of the female body, at another level they expose the instability of such diagnoses by revealing the relational interdependence of male and female insanity. The texts work to demystify male medical authority by highlighting structurally the alignment of the respective economic and psychiatric positions offered to the male and female subject.

In some cases the transpositions between medical and fictional texts are not subtle in their effects but quite blatant and aggressive. In Charles Reade's *Hard Cash* (1863), for example, John Conolly, the hero of moral management and champion of humane systems of treatment, is depicted as Dr. Wycherley, a figure who, in all good faith, diagnoses monomania in the hero, whom the reader knows to be sane. Although Wycherley's words are drawn directly from Conolly's writings, their effects are radically altered by context, becoming both sinister and intrusive.[1] Doctors figure frequently in these texts, giving textbook diagnoses of protagonists, but their authority is often undermined by other textual factors at work. Even where the language of psychiatry is employed by an impersonal narrative voice it does not carry the same weight, but opens itself to interpretation in ways that psychiatric texts themselves do not. Few statements can be taken at face value. Strong formal dislocations frame the propositional ambivalences of these texts.

Sensation fiction is a literature not only of psychological but also of formal excess. In structuring their works, novelists were deliberately pushing at the bounds of both psychological and literary respectability, as incarnated in the principles of realist fiction. The transgressive power of such texts demands an equivalent alteration of our reading codes and modes of interpretation. By incorporating in their formal structure the disruptive qualities attached by male medicine to the female body and psyche, sensation texts self-reflexively foreground the relationship between generic form and gender.

The relationship between sensation fiction and psychiatry cannot be charted along a simple course of mimetic transmission, for the disruptive formal qualities of these novels ensure that they are often challenging the very authorities they seem to enshrine. Thus the male detective figure might fulfil the role of psychiatric authority in pursuing and unveiling female madness, but he does so within a novelistic framework that inverts the gendered hierarchy of patriarchal science exposing female nature. The psychiatric pursuit of inner truth is figured in several texts as itself a form of madness.

The medical discourse of female pathology was invoked in contemporary responses to sensation fiction.[2] Outraged Victorian reviewers depicted the sensation novel as both source and symptom of emergent forms of social disease. According to H. L. Mansel in the *Quarterly Review,* such "morbid" works were "indications of a wide-spread corruption, of which they are in part both the effect and the cause; called into existence to supply the cravings of a diseased appetite, and contributing themselves to foster the disease, and to stimulate the want which they supply." Drawing a direct homology between the health of the social body and that of individual readers, he concludes that these works, looked at as "an eruption indicative of the state of health of the body in which they appear . . . are by no means favourable symptoms of the body of society."[3] References to lurking disease and poison (which draw on precisely the same forms of rhetoric as the despised novels themselves) litter the pages of hostile reviews. For Margaret Oliphant, the English novel had always held a high reputation for "a certain sanity, wholesomeness and cleanness" until the advent of sensation fiction. Her model for such psychological cleanliness is Trollope, whose works are taken here as the epitome of English respectability and realistic representation. "It is not he," she comments, "who makes us ashamed of our girls."[4] The observation exposes the relation between critical conceptions of realism and the gendered norms of bourgeois propriety.

The sin committed by the sensationalists was not simply to include new spheres of subject matter, for crime and sexuality have always been the staple of English fiction, albeit in less sensually explicit terms. Such indiscretions might have been forgiven if the novels had not also violated the sacred tenets of realism. Criticism of the sensation novel focused on both its subject matter and its form, revealing in the process the ideological assumptions underpinning critical conceptions of realism. Not only should the realist novel proffer an acceptable image of social life, it should also obey the formal rules of coherence and continuity, which were themselves predicated on specific notions of psychology. In the hands of writers such as George Eliot or Trollope, the realist novel, with its cumulative movement toward greater social understanding and self-awareness, established a literature whose keynotes were continuity and responsibility. Gradual, cumulative action revealed the continuity of the psyche; all actions were explicable, even the apparently irrational (such as Hetty Sorel's abandonment of her child in *Adam Bede*), in terms of the individual's history and psychological makeup. The self, such novels suggested, was a unified entity; all actions had inescapable consequences, and the process of self-development was one of learning to take responsibility for one's own actions.

Sensation novels, by contrast, explicitly violated realism's formal rules of coherence and continuity and the psychological models of selfhood on which those works were founded. Disorder, discontinuity, and irresponsibility are the hallmarks of these feminine texts. Structurally, the plots play with elements of surprise and discontinuity. The reader is not placed in a position of calm knowledge superior to that of the characters but is rather continually startled by events and actions into states of extreme sensation. Such novels, H. L. Mansel maintained, were "preaching to the nerves," hence situating their readers in the feminine position of nervousness while inviting vicarious, sensual participation in the thrills of the unexpected, the inexplicable, and the forbidden.[5] Rhoda Broughton, for example, flagrantly disobeyed the rules of dramatic closure in *Red as a Rose Is She* (1870) in order to permit her readers the sensual gratification of improper embraces, sanctified by the deathbed. The opening of the following chapter miraculously resucitates the heroine, however: "Lifeless! Yes! But there are two kinds of lifelessness: one from which there is no back-coming—one from which there is. Esther's is the latter."[6] Such dramatic transformations necessarily challenge realist patterns of psychological representation. In Mrs. Henry Wood's *St. Martin's Eve* (1866) it appears as if the textual climax has been reached: the heroine's incipient madness finally bursts out beyond all bounds of control. Yet the next time she appears, she is once more calm and collected, calculatedly pursuing her own economic interests in the shape of another marriage.

Victorian critics were infuriated by these seemingly gross inconsistencies in sensation fiction plots, the ways in which characters could be restored to life or sanity with seeming impunity, attributing them entirely to lack of artistic skill. Such dramatic disjunctures in textual and psychological continuity are, however, part of the sensationalists' tactical assault on the social, psychological, and gendered certainties of bourgeois realism. Margaret Oliphant tellingly attributed the rise of sensation fiction to the demise of the imperial complacency typified by the Great Exhibition of 1851, and to the ensuing wars and loss of social direction manifested in English society. Ten years ago, Oliphant observed, "the age was lost in self-admiration," but peace and industry had since been displaced by war: "We who once did, and made, and declared ourselves masters of all things, have relapsed into the natural size of humanity before the great events which have given a new character to the age." People had come to enjoy the thrills of war, and sensation fiction now pandered to the emergent need for "a supply of new shocks and wonders."[7] With the loss of phallic "mastery," the culture of control is undermined from within as the populace increasingly seeks out the bodily, and hence feminized, shocks of sensation. Sensation fiction both responded and contributed to this fracturing of social certainties, whose effects are registered in the texts' insistent ambiguity and in their preoccupation with the symbolically central issue of gender identity. Uncertainties of gender positioning occur throughout the genre, whether in the male/female duality of the characters in *The Woman in White,* or in the ambiguous relation to gender stereotypes incarnated in that "beautiful fiend" Lady Audley, whose outer form and inner self seem so totally at odds. Sensation fiction highlights the uncertain relation between the outer and inner forms of selfhood, but there is no possibility, as in realist fiction, of pursuing a course of revelation until the "true" self is unveiled.[8] The very category of selfhood is itself subject to interrogation. To try to determine, for example, whether Lady Audley was really mad, is to misunderstand the radical workings of the text—its challenge of certainty. The critical controversies provoked by the question of her psychological status are themselves eloquent testimony to the ambiguity of the text.[9]

Although the sensation novel frequently employs the framework of a detective hunt, where the secret in question is often the sanity of the female protagonist, the results are never conclusive. The texts do not move toward an ultimate revelation by masculine science of the hidden truths of femininity. The final disclosure can raise more questions than it answers, while the male detective himself is usually tainted by his quest. Walter Hartright, hero of Wilkie Collins's *The Woman in White,* sets his narrative up as a quasi-legal document, following the proceedings of a court of law, but the effect is only to highlight the impossibility of objective knowledge. This is a novel where even tombstones can lie, and where the key to all the layers of secrecy lies not in tangible evidence but in absence: the lack of an entry in the parish register to record the marriage of Sir Percival Glyde's parents: "That space told the whole story!"[10] Upon this blank space Hartright imaginatively transcribes an entire history, which leads directly to his own empowerment and the overthrow of his enemy. At one stroke, which itself mirrors the central crime of the novel, their identities and status are exchanged. Sir Percival loses his baronetcy, and the way is cleared for Hartright's own social ascent into the landed gentry. In its foregrounding of the instability of identity, manifested preeminently in the central plot whereby Fosco takes from the heiress Laura her rank and name and installs her in the identity of Anne Catherick, a lower-class inmate of an asylum, *The Woman in White* self-consciously addresses many of the issues and problems that mark the genre of sensation fiction. Discontinuities, absences, uncertainties, both structural and thematic, define these works, and in the central ambiguity of madness they find a convenient locus for their challenge to the ordered, gendered certainties of much realist fiction.

For the Victorian critics, sensation novels were themselves a form of madness, "feverish productions" that, in "preaching to the nerves," exacerbated the decline of self-control, that hallmark of masculinity, which was held to be essential for the psychic and economic health of the nation.[11] The madness of which the novelists themselves stood accused, however, formed one of the central subjects of their fiction. As the jaundiced author of an article entitled "Madness in Novels" remarked, everyone in the anonymous *The Clyffords of Clyffe* "is either mad, or fears he may be mad, or is sought in love in order to keep away madness, or drives a debasing trade in the sufferings of the mad."[12] Such a text is of course extreme, but it does suggest the ways in which concerns with madness enter into every level of sensation fiction. As I suggested, the sensationalists mirrored the concerns of Victorian psychiatry in their preoccupation with the domain of psychological excess, but the sense of a stabilizing normative vision is missing in their work. In William Gilbert's novel *Shirley Hall Asylum; or, Memoirs of a Monomaniac* (1863), for example, the asylum seems to stand as a microcosm of society, where keeper and kept alike exhibit symptoms of multitudinous forms of insanity. At one level, the sensationalists' preoccupation

with insanity can be seen in terms of its usefulness as a plot device that
allows them to transgress realist conventions of character and probability with impunity (the view held by the author of the *Spectator* article
"Madness in Novels")—nothing is improbable if the character is defined as mad.[13] But at a deeper level, the sensationalists' fascination
with insanity responds to profound cultural uncertainties of the era.
We can best appreciate these connections and their social significance if
we place the novels in the cultural context of Victorian psychiatry.

The nineteenth century witnessed the rise of medicine as a socially authoritative profession, and the specific emergence of psychiatry as a medical discipline. It became a truism in the midcentury that
the physician now occupied the role of the priest: repository of all the
inner secrets of the self, and sole arbiter of physical and mental
health.[14] As the hero of Mary Braddon's *Lady Audley's Secret* observes,
on summoning a physician in the hopes of getting Lady Audley committed, "physicians and lawyers are the confessors of this prosaic nineteenth century."[15] Commentators stressed with alarm the power that
now seemed to reside in the figure of the doctor: "No one possesses
such absolute power as the medical man over his patient; that which
the veriest despot in the world exercises over his slave does not equal
it."[16] This sense of power was intensified by the changes in attitudes
toward insanity that underpinned the rise of medical psychiatry. Insanity became a distinct medical condition, and one that, according to the
theorists of moral management in the first half of the century, was
susceptible to treatment.[17] Both the physiology and psychiatry of the
nineteenth century broke down earlier absolute divides between the
normal and the pathological, insisting that disease arose merely from
an excess or deficency of elements integral to normal functioning.[18]
The mad were no longer "other," to be locked away with criminals or
the insane: anyone, the theory implied, could become insane by the
slight movement into imbalance of his or her physiological and mental
system. As Braddon again remarks, "Who has not been, or is not to
be, mad in some lonely hour of life? Who is quite safe from the
trembling of the balance?"[19]

In the eighteenth century "nervousness" was deemed a "success
tax," the price to be paid for the advances in civilization, and it could
be borne with a certain degree of pride.[20] At the opening of the
nineteenth, the tone had already changed. Thomas Trotter warned
ominously that England's "commercial greatness" was at risk from "the
increasing prevalence of nervous disorders; which, if not restrained

soon, must inevitably sap our physical strength of constitution; make us an easy conquest to our invaders; and ultimately convert us into a nation of slaves and idiots."[21] Mental health is here tied directly to the economic progress of the nation, illuminating the ways in which psychiatric and economic ideologies were intertwined in the nineteenth century. In an industrial culture devoted to the domination of markets and the maximization of labor efficiency, the dominant ethos was one of transformative control. Within psychiatric discourse this ethos was manifested in the moral managers' emphasis on the powers of the individual will, as exemplified in John Barlow's popular work *Man's Power over Himself to Prevent or Control Insanity* (1843). While drawing on economic ideologies of self-control and self-help, this work also, paradoxically, drew attention to its own sense of the omnipresence of insanity. The difference between sanity and insanity, Barlow argued, consisted entirely "in the degree of self-control exercised." He advises the reader who remains unconvinced to "note for a short time the thoughts that pass through his mind, and the feelings that agitate him: and he will find that, were they expressed and indulged, they would be as wild, and perhaps as frightful in their consequences as those of any madman."[22] The state of insanity, in other words, is that of acting out the hidden desires we all possess. Psychiatric discourse itself unwittingly supplied the subversive plot line of much sensation fiction.

Psychiatric texts fostered fears of an ever-lurking threat of insanity. As John Conolly, one of the preeminent theorists and practitioners of moral management, observed in his introduction to *An Inquiry Concerning the Indications of Insanity* (1830), "every man is interested in this subject; for no man can confidently reckon on the continuance of his perfect reason."[23] Studies, widely reported in the popular press, that suggested an alarming increase in the incidence of insanity further fueled fears of social epidemics of madness.[24] Although the statistics were misleading, relating more to changing modes of classification and patterns of institutionalization than to any actual increases in insanity, the responses they evoked constitute a very telling self-portrait of Victorian Britain.[25] The ever-present threat of insanity formed the subtext of the culture of self-control.

Professional self-interest on the part of members of the burgeoning psychiatric profession led to alarming pronouncements on the state of the nation's health. Conolly observed that without the aid of medical men, the influences to which men and women were subjected in the pressurized climate of industrial England would soon "render the greater part of mankind helpless and miserable."[26] Articles in periodicals of the time paint a picture of a general populace paralyzed by fear of possible insanity. "A Plea for Physicians" in *Fraser's Magazine* outlines a hypothetical scenario:

> A person—say a young female, say a mother—is haunted with the fear of hereditary insanity. If she feel low-spirited, she dreads it; if she feel more than ordinarily happy, in the midst of her joy the thought strikes her that perhaps her merriment is morbid; if her children gambol, and laugh, and shout, more than usual, she trembles lest each ebullition of joy be not the first symptom of the object of her dread, or they may retire from their rougher sports, and she again apprehends the worst.[27]

This hypothetical case, in focusing on a young mother, takes a subject whose insanity is overdetermined in contemporary discourse, and exposes the gendered power dynamics that reside in the relationship between male medicine and its female subjects. Once fear is established, any slight deviation from normal behavior can be construed as a symptom of insanity. The woman is at the mercy of her own fears, and of the physician who is alone empowered to pronounce definitively on the constitution of normality. The scenario painted is a familiar one in the sensation fiction of the 1860s, where latent female insanity can lie dormant for years before suddenly bursting forth to disrupt the calm surface of familial and social life. Mrs. Henry Wood's *St. Martin's Eve,* for example, portrays an anxious mother, desperately watching her married daughter for signs of inherited insanity, while the family doctor, who has kept the heroine under surveillance since childhood, waits in the wings to sign the committal forms once his early prognosis has been confirmed by subsequent behavior.

From the 1860s onward, medical emphasis on hereditary and latent insanity increased, as England's decline in economic prosperity and confidence was shadowed forth in the evolutionary pessimism of Maudsley and other post-Darwinian theorists. Andrew Wynter pointed out in *The Borderlands of Insanity* (1875) that there was "an immense amount of latent brain disease in the community, only awaiting a sufficient exciting cause to make itself patent to the world."[28] The sensationalists, writing at a transitional period, drew both on these biologically deterministic theories of madness and on the theories of moral management of the earlier part of the century, which, with their emphasis on the powers of the will and the possibilities of recuperation, belonged to a more optimistic cultural and economic climate. For the moral managers, insanity was not necessarily an inescapable biological given; it could be partial, and it could be cured. While avoiding the oppressive determinism of later theories, these conceptions also had their negative side, which the sensationalists were quick to exploit. The threat of insanity hung over all, not merely the biologically selected few, and its presence was compatible with an apparently normal life-style within the community.

The two primary forms of partial insanity, as formulated in early nineteenth-century psychiatric theory, were moral insanity and mono-mania, both developed from the theories of Pinel and Esquirol in France. According to J. C. Prichard, moral insanity consisted in

> a morbid perversion of the natural feelings, affections, inclinations, temper, habits, moral dispositions, and natural impulses, without any remarkable disorder or defect of the intellect or knowing and reasoning faculties, and particularly without any insane illusion or hallucination.[29]

The definition dispenses with all the traditional outward signs of lunacy; madness is compatible with a total absence of illusion, and an ability to reason without any discernible flaws in logic or understand-ing. Monomania seems an even more circumscribed form of insanity; it is a mode of intellectual insanity "in which the understanding is partially disordered or under the influence of some particular illusion, referring to one subject, and involving one train of ideas, while the intellectual powers appear, when exercised on other subjects, to be in a great measure unimpaired."[30] While moral insanity can transform all affective behavior, monomania can refer simply to an intellectual obses-sion. Both terms quickly caught the public imagination and became common currency in the journalism of the day. In line with the increas-ingly rigidified social codes of Victorian England, these formulations suggested that behavior could be defined as insane if, on the moral and emotional front, it exceeded the highly gendered definitions of the "natural," or, on the intellectual front, it sprang from firmly held convictions that ran counter to normative social expectations. Thus in *Hard Cash,* for example, the hero is diagnosed as suffering from mono-mania and is placed against his will in an asylum because he, quite rightly, accused his father of theft.

The physicians' powers of forcible committal, to either private asylums or the public asylums set up after the two 1845 Lunatic Acts, were cause for great concern in the newspapers of the day, and they feature repeatedly in sensation novels. One of the most famous cases was that of the wealthy heiress Eliza Nottridge, who was confined by her mother and brother-in-law in an asylum for seventeen months on the grounds of her membership of a millennial sect. On her escape she sued for wrongful confinement and won. The *Leeds Mercury* commented on the unsatisfactory role played by physicians with reference to committals: "In lieu of the simple intelligible principles which should govern determinations regarding the imputedly insane, medical men have erected themselves into metaphysical censors of the movements of the human mind, and their oracular *dicta* take effect in the shape of committals to lunatic asylums!" Miss Nottridge's case, the paper suggests, gives rise to the suspicion "that many other persons may be incarcerated on grounds equally untenable, and whose cases, except through some fortunate escape, are likely to be hidden from public justice" (14 July 1849). Charles Reade's *Hard Cash* was specifically designed to draw the public's attention to the possibilities of wrongful confinement, while Wilkie Collins claimed that *The Woman in White* was based on a contemporary case.[31] General public unease had led to the setting up in 1858 of the Parliamentary Select Committee into the Care and Treatment of Lunatics and Their Property.

Part of the mystique and threatening nature of the physicians' authority sprang from the sheer invisibility of insanity to the untrained eye. Psychiatric texts stressed repeatedly that only the highly trained eye of the medical expert could detect the outward signs of insanity, so skilled were the insane at dissembling, and, one could add, so subtle were the distinctions at stake.[32] Esquirol is said to have watched his patients during their sleep, convinced that they would reveal the telltale signs of insanity when off guard, while Pinel managed to persuade a man that his wife had been insane, not just for the past six months, but for the previous fifteen years.[33] The English translator of Esquirol inserted a footnote into the text to warn readers that "insanity is sometimes so insidious in its attack as to escape the notice of even the nearest relatives for a considerable period. As a general rule, any change from the usual habits of the individual should excite suspicion."[34] Such incitements to vigilance are bred within and help perpetuate an atmosphere of self-distrust and mutual suspicion, producing a nation of watchful readers and interpreters, ever ready to detect outward signs of insanity, either in the self or others.

Mid-Victorian psychiatry was preeminently a science of inter-

pretation and detection. According to Conolly, the fully trained physician should be able to read through surface plausibility, and to
detect madness even in the way a man wore his hat.[35] Not only is
latent insanity at issue: partial states of insanity such as monomania
and moral insanity can be transient, lasting only as long as the
impulse itself.[36] The physician must learn to read the signs not only
of buried, dormant hereditary characteristics, but also of forms of
behavior that, if only ·for an instant, exceed the bounds of social
acceptability. Sensation fiction was quick to capitalize on the narrative potential of this dimension of medical psychiatry. Physicians are
frequently wheeled in to attest to the insanity of a heroine who,
according to traditional conceptions of insanity, is far from mad.
But the primary role of detecting and interpreting the signs of insanity generally falls to the male hero, as in Braddon's *Lady Audley's
Secret,* or Mrs. Henry Wood's *St. Martin's Eve.* Detection in these
cases ceases to be a neutral activity and becomes instead a site of
ambiguity and of male contagion.

While sensation fiction follows psychiatry in foregrounding the
practices of interpretation and detection, it questions the authority
vested both in the medical profession and in the interpretative process
itself. Walter Hartright in *The Woman in White* stops to ask whether he
is really following a train of villainy, or whether all the connections he
sees are symptoms of his own disordered mind: "It seemed almost like
a monomania to be tracing back everything that happened, everything
unexpected that was said, always to the same hidden source and the
same sinister influence."[37] We as readers, busily interpreting the trail
of signs Walter lays before us, are similarly afflicted.[38] Is the desire to
impose interpretative coherence itself the product of an obsessional
mind? *Lady Audley's Secret* raises the same issue in even more explicit
terms. Robert, the detective-figure hero, asks early on in his quest
whether his own doubts and suspicions "may grow upon me till I
become a monomaniac."[39] His self-doubt intensifies as he pursues his
detective work. Why should he see such a mystery in his friend's
disappearance?

Was it a monition or a monomania? What if I am wrong after all?
What if this chain of evidence which I have constructed link by link is
woven out of my own folly? What if this edifice of horror and suspicion
is a mere collection of crotchets—the nervous fancies of a hypochon-
driacal bachelor? . . . Oh, my God, if it should be in myself all this
time that the mystery lies! (217–218)

Robert rejects his doubts because he believes he has hard evidence, suggestively situated in his pocket, but events reveal that the initial premise lying behind his investigations and pursuit of Lady Audley, that his friend was murdered, is unfounded. Can a false premise lead to a correct conclusion, or are all his connections and surmises therefore tainted and misguided? In drawing attention to his own position as a bachelor, Robert locates himself in one of the prime categories for male nervous disorder, a position intensified by his idle life. (Male insanity, contemporary theorists argued, could be caused both by sexual continence and by failure to exert oneself in professional life). The tale ends with the incarceration of the woman who had initially aroused his illicit sexual desire and with his own dual reward of domestic, marital bliss and the successful launching of his professional career.[40] The structure of the novel suggests that the affirmation of male sanity and social normality is dependent upon the social placement of woman in a position of insanity.

Recent work on insanity in the Victorian novel has focused largely on female insanity.[41] If the sensation novelists' preoccupation with male insanity is taken into account, however, a complex network is revealed in which male and female insanity are relationally interdependent. In novels that take the detective form, the stakes involved in the quest to determine which party is insane are both economic and psychological. For the woman, her economic independence is usually at issue, while for the man it is nothing less than the assurance of his own masculinity and the improvement of his economic and social status and prospects. In their representations of insanity the sensation novelists worked both within and against Victorian psychiatric discourse, using the categories and vocabulary, but in the process raising questions as to both its validity and its social functions. The sensationalists' preoccupation with male insanity strikes at the roots of the patriarchal foundations of Victorian culture: if insanity is indeed a relative term, and male sanity is assured only by the successful certification of female insanity, then notions of masculinity, and dependent ideologies of domestic and social order, are destabilized, while the very possiblity of authoritative interpretation is set at risk.

The male detective figure in these fictions is usually of precarious masculinity and social status. Walter Hartright in *The Woman in White* is a penniless drawing master, occupying a social position of even more than feminine dependency: he is admitted among his pupils not as a man but as a "harmless domestic animal" (89). Robert Audley is a "lazy, care-for-nothing fellow" (27) who fails to practice his profession, and prefers to spend his time on the feminized occupation of novel reading. Frederick St. John in *St. Martin's Eve* has run through his patrimony yet occupies his time in the dilettantish, and again feminized, activity of painting. The sexual politics involved are most starkly depicted in *Lady Audley's Secret* and *St. Martin's Eve,* where male and female careers follow an inverse trajectory: the ambitious (and hence masculinized) female who has sought to gain economic security is pursued by a feminized male whose interests are threatened. Both novels end with the incarceration of the deviant woman in a lunatic asylum (a testimony to her physiologically flawed, female status), and the confirmation of the hero's masculinity and social normality through his marriage. The fall of the female marks the rise of the male. Robert starts to practice his profession, while Frederick, in successfully getting Charlotte certified as insane, has blocked his brother's possible marriage and ensured his own succession to the St. John fortune.

This gendered pattern of ascent and fall highlights the different positioning of men and women in the economic and social order. Heroines who are marked out by insanity are usually also economically disadvantaged. We are told explicitly in *St. Martin's Eve* that Charlotte would have inherited her father's fortune if she had been a boy. As it is, she and mother are turned out of Norris Court on her father's death (which coincides with her own birth). This secondary status is reinforced by her marriage; as a widow she remains in her own home only as guardian of her stepson, and loses all when first her stepson and then her own son die. The steps she takes to ensure her economic independence (which do, admittedly, include such sensational tactics as locking the young heir in a room and leaving him to burn to death) lead to her committal. Similarly, the steps Lady Audley takes (which also involve the attempted burning of someone in a locked room) to preserve her wealth and social status when they are threatened by the return of her first husband provide the ground for her certification.

The women's negative economic placement is also inscribed on them physiologically. As Lady Audley declares in her speech of exculpation, she learned early on that "the only inheritance I had to expect from my mother was—insanity!" (296). Passed through the female line, and excited in her mother's case by giving birth, this form of inheritance appears as a symbolic encapsulation of the condition of femininity—of economic and social powerlessness. Lady Audley's mother was not, she carefully points out, a "distraught, violent creature" (295); her madness took the form rather of the childish innocence that was the ideologically preferred model of Victorian womanhood.

Charlotte's only form of inheritance is also a physiological one. She inherits from her father his fits of jealousy, which in her case start to manifest themselves when her economic interests are threatened. Her jealous passions are directed toward her stepson the heir, who has cut off her own child's prospects, and the girl who, she believes, is preventing her from making the marriage that will restore her fortunes.

While the women tend to be defined by negative economic and physiological inheritance, the men are placed in positions of economic possibility; either they stand in line for a title and wealth, or they are permitted to marry money, like Walter Hartright, without having their motives or their sanity impugned. The threat of insanity that hangs over them is rarely an inescapable physiological destiny, but rather a partial, temporary form, which can be shaken off through self-discipline and a transformation of life-style. The details offered of female insanity in these texts are all in accordance with contemporary psychiatric accounts, which stressed that, physiologically, women were far more prone to insanity than men.[42] But while the novelists take pains to follow the vocabulary and categories of contemporary psychiatric discourse in their depictions of female insanity, the structural functions of this insanity in their works, and specifically its relations to economic inheritance, suggest that they were using insanity as a device to raise questions about a culture whose legal and medical institutions worked in harness to proclaim and enforce women's physiological and economic inferiority.

Although the heroes of these tales are always presented as perfect, unimpeachable gentlemen, the suspicions roused as to their sanity, and the actual structuring of the text, often suggest a rather more subversive reading. Frederick in *St. Martin's Eve* is introduced to us as a "true gentleman at heart" even though he is almost immediately arrested for debt. His subsequent career is far from glorious. He pursues an angelic creature who is already betrothed to another, fails to trust in the truth of her love when appearances seem against her, and turns his back on her in anger, leading her to burst a blood vessel and thus die, literally, of a broken heart. This plot line provides perhaps the most sensational of all scenes in sensation novels. Frederick returns, not knowing of Adeline's death, and is taken to her house, where she appears, clad in bridal attire, to be holding a reception. It is only when he stands opposite her and gazes into her face that "with a rushing sensation of sickening awe and terror, the terrible truth burst upon his brain. That it was not Adeline de Castella, but her CORPSE which stood there."[43] Wood makes great play, through a footnote address to the reader, of the factual authenticity of such practices of displaying the dead, but the scene is literally unwritable in realist terms. With its flagrant violation of realist proprieties, the scene constitutes the ultimate transgression of the boundaries that had defined the realist body. It offers a ghastly temporal parody of a spiritual reawakening, which, in its insistent physicality, turns death itself into an erotic exchange. Symbolically, furthermore, it functions as an ironic comment on the optimistic trajectory of realism. As embalmed bride, the cold and lifeless Adeline is the literal figuration of the conventional ending of the realist novel.

The scene's sensational effects have their primary impact on the nervous system of the reader, and not on our hero. Despite this shock to the system, he nonetheless reflects at Adeline's funeral that it was best that she had died, since had they married she would have passed on to their children "her fragility of constitution" (374). While not the bearer of insanity, she would pass on as her legacy an equally flawed physiological state.[44] By a process of association, Frederick's thoughts then turn immediately to the hints he has picked up as to Charlotte's insanity. The rest of the novel is devoted to the battle between himself and Charlotte as he attempts to find enough evidence of her insanity to get her committed and thus prevent her marriage to his brother.

The narrative draws attention to Frederick's detective role and the difficulties of interpreting signs. Although apparently idle, Frederick was "secretly busy as ever was a London detective" watching Charlotte until he "persuaded himself that he did detect signs of incipient madness" (386–387). The text highlights the self-persuasion involved in diagnoses of insanity. The signs Frederick detects are so intangible— nothing more than a transient look, followed immediately by such charm—that "had all the doctors connected with Bethlehem hospital come forward to declare her mad, people would have laughed at them for their pains" (391). Frederick determinedly ups the stakes, installing the doctor, Mr. Pym, in the role of "a very private-detective" (439), but Charlotte, unlike Lady Audley, takes no evasive action. She remains outwardly impassive, watching the surgeon "just as keenly as he did her" (443). It is a game she cannot win, however; relying solely on her own cleverness and self-control, she has failed to take into account the fact that Mr. Pym and Frederick hold the trump card of patriarchal medical authority. The text covertly indicts psychiatric diagnostic practices that rely on the constant surveillance of the chosen subject until the desired signs of insanity are displayed. Mr. Pym informs Charlotte's mother that he could never come to the conclusion that there was nothing wrong with her daughter: "Were I to remain in the house a month, and see no proof whatever of insanity, I could not be sure that it did not exist. We know how cunning these people are." (437). Once a presupposition of insanity has been established, there is no escape. The statement encapsulates the position held by women within psychiatric discourse: in a reversal of the legal code, they are deemed potentially insane until proven otherwise. Like *Lady Audley's Secret,* the text stresses that the act of detection in and of itself produces the symptoms it seeks to detect. Charlotte's first outbreak of anger, brought on by being told that she is being removed for her own good, leads to her being placed in an asylum "from which she can never more be released in safety" (447).

The narrative of *St. Martin's Eve* abides by the rules of psychiatric discourse: Charlotte is depicted as a real threat, violent and demonic in her anger when roused, and Frederick and the doctor bide their time, waiting until an outbreak of violence will justify her committal. It also highlights, however, the questionable nature of detection and the presuppositions that direct its patriarchal pursuit. Double standards are clearly in operation. Frederick, for all his attractive manner and unimpugned integrity, was, like Charlotte, responsible for the death of another through an uncontrolled fit of anger. His economic future also hinges on his ability to demonstrate Charlotte's insanity. As in *Lady Audley's Secret,* the defeat of the mad woman ensures the hero's accession to true manhood; Frederick fulfils his brother's dearest wishes and marries, taking on the mantle of heir. The final scene, however, is unsettling, hardly a celebration of marital bliss. Rose, Charlotte's sister, draws attention to the transitory nature of Frederick's love by reminding his wife of Adeline. She also questions whether Charlotte is kindly treated in the asylum, and is told by Frederick that it "could not be well" for her to visit. While Lady Audley is conveniently driven to her death by boredom, Charlotte remains alive, a presence who must be forcibly forgotten and ignored if the facades of domestic and social order are to be maintained.

While the threat of incarceration works only one way in *St. Martin's Eve,* in *Lady Audley's Secret* it is double-edged. Lady Audley herself initially tries to convince Sir Michael that Robert is a monomaniac. Her arguments are drawn straight from the psychiatry of the day: madness can be a "mere illness of the brain" to which anyone is subject; and "people are insane for years and years before their insanity is found out" (245). The specific cause she adduces for Robert's monomania, his mental stagnation, is again in line with psychiatric theory. For young men, failure to show enterprise in their profession or commerce was judged sufficient evidence of insanity. Conolly cited the example of men who had talents but failed to show ambition: "They have no violent desires nor perturbations, and they never ripen. Neither ambition nor pride can rouse them to sustained efforts."[45] The passivity so desirable in women becomes pathological in men. While Lady Audley's active ambitions leave her open to charges of insanity, Robert's lack of ambition and failure to pursue his profession conversely place him under the same threat. His "sustained effort" in his pursuit of Lady Audley becomes, however, the vehicle of his redemption.

Although Robert wheels in the physician to attest to Lady Audley's madness, the initial diagnosis comes from Lady Audley herself. She invalidates Robert's victory by proclaiming that all his "cool calculating intellect" has been exercised only to conquer a "MAD-WOMAN!" (293). Her self-exculpation, which shows how thoroughly she has internalized the doctrines of psychiatry, draws on two different strands of theory: she is mad because of inheritance, "the hidden taint that I had sucked in with my mother's milk" (332), but also, as she repeatedly claims, because she has "crossed that invisible line which separates reason from madness" (299). While the first claim belongs to theories of physiological determinism, and hence incurable insanity, the second belongs to the rhetoric of moral management, which suggested that insanity could be a transient, curable state, and one to which all were susceptible.

The verdict on Lady Audley's insanity is left open. For both the physician and Robert, her incarceration in an asylum is an expedient that, in effectively "burying her alive," removes any threat she might still represent to the Audley name and family. The physician diagnoses her not as mad but as dangerous, and on those grounds signs the certificate for her committal. The text's preoccupation with insanity is not removed with her presence, however. Indeed, most of the discussion of insanity has a male focus in the figure of Robert. His own fears about his possible monomania are reinforced in the text by explicit narrative commentary that makes him the vehicle of speculation as to whether we might all, like Lady Audley, cross the thin dividing line between madness and sanity. Robert's sense of powerlessness and disorientation after meeting Clara leads the narrator to observe:

> Madhouses are large and only too numerous; yet surely it is strange they are not larger, when we think of how many helpless wretches must beat their brains against this hopeless persistency of the orderly outward

world, as compared with the storm and tempest, the riot and confusion within;—when we remember how many minds must tremble upon the narrow boundary between reason and unreason, mad to-day and sane tomorrow, mad yesterday and sane to-day. (175–176)

The madness of unreason, the passage suggests, is the normal state of our psyches: we live in a constant state of imbalance, trying to suppress and disguise the rage within while we fulfil our expected roles in the outer mechanisms of social life. Madness, as Conolly and Barlow suggested, is the state that occurs when we let the social mask slip, and the inner self disrupts surface social performance.

The incarceration of Lady Audley does not ensure Robert's immediate recovery; indeed his nervousness intensifies, and the narrator again intervenes to remind us that "there is nothing so delicate, so fragile, as that invisible balance upon which the mind is always trembling; mad to-day and sane to-morrow" (341). A dramatic picture of Dr. Johnson, reduced to childish terror, is invoked to reinforce the message: "Who has not been, or is not to be, mad in some lonely hour of life? Who is quite safe from the trembling of the balance?" (341). While underscoring Robert's own fragile hold on sanity, the question necessarily reverberates to include Lady Audley who, for acting out her inner desires, has been imprisoned not for some lonely hour but for life. Lady Audley constitutes for Robert the demon he must exorcise before he can marry his angel Clara and enter those ideologically prescribed arenas of masculine sanity: domestic and professional life.

Braddon seems to reverse standard stereotypes with her "beautiful fiend," the golden-haired Lady Audley, and the dark-eyed angel, Clara. But the true picture is by no means so simple. Clara herself is depicted in terms drawn straight from psychiatric accounts of female hysteria. Her unnatural calmness is broken when she runs after Robert in a feverish passion, stating that she will go mad unless she can avenge her brother's death. Her self-diagnosis quickly follows: " 'I have grown up in an atmosphere of suppression,' she said quietly: 'I have stifled and dwarfed the natural feelings of my heart, until they have become unnatural in their intensity. I have been allowed neither friends nor lovers' " (171). Writers on female hysteria in the midcentury repeatedly stressed that the outward calm demanded of women led to a damaging suppression of feeling and consequent outbursts of insanity. As J. G. Millingen records in *The Passions; or, Mind and Matter* (1848):

In woman, the concentration of her feelings (a concentration that her social position renders indispensable) adds to their intensity; and like a smouldering fire that has at last got vent, her passions, when no longer trammelled by conventional propriety, burst forth in unquenchable violence.[46]

To Robert's clouded judgment Clara, in her violent declarations of vengeance, seems "elevated into sublimity" (171), but the descriptions of her impact upon him suggest something altogether more sinister. He perceives this "noble" creature to be a merciless force, trampling down all who stand in her way and forcing himself "upon the loathsome path, the crooked bye-way of watchfulness and suspicion" (175). Clara takes on demonic, vampirelike qualities: "This woman knows half my secret; she will soon possess herself of the rest; and then—and then—" (175). Clara violates Robert's self-possession, the very grounding, in Victorian ideology, of manhood and sanity. Under her scrutiny he is once more feminized, placed in exactly the same position in which he himself locates Lady Audley. It is he who is now the possessor of a secret that he wishes to hide from prying eyes. In his relations with Lady Audley, Robert had placed himself in the role of the Victorian physicians who sought to unveil the secrets of the female mind and body, revealing the dark inner side of that which was outwardly so fair.[47] His early loss of self-control precipitated by his involuntary sexual attraction was to be sternly extirpated through this exercise of patriarchal authority. But when he meets Clara, the tables seem reversed. He is reduced to feelings of utter helplessness as Clara's gaze takes on a psychiatrist's power to pluck out "the innermost secrets of his mind" (221). Although the novel seems to portray the victory of male reason over female madness, and Robert's ascent to true masculinity, it shows in fact his complete overthrow and loss of self-possession. The reiterated statement that Clara has his lost friend's face reinforces the sense that he is actively feminized by Clara, and intensifies our sense of unease with the conclusion of the novel, where Clara, George, and Robert (and the inevitable signifier of heterosexual normality, a baby) are portrayed as existing in perfect domestic bliss.[48] Just as at the beginning of the novel, outward order masks inner disarray. Imprisoning Lady Audley has done little to restore sanity to a world in which the balance of social and psychological order is so finely poised.

The endings of sensation novels invariably seem to exacerbate rather than resolve the tensions and problems addressed in the text. Collins's *The Woman in White* is no exception. Although it has a detective framework and is preoccupied with madness, it does not, as do Braddon's and Wood's later treatment of this theme, portray the hero hunting down threatening female insanity. This is a novel that seems to undercut all sureties of identity, of gender, class and sanity. The dualism of Anne and Laura, with its staging of the radical uncertainties of class and sanity, functions as the central site of ambiguity around which all other questionable boundaries of identity are clustered. Few characters seem to possess an unproblematic gender identity. While Marian, with her voluptuous female figure and mannish face, is the key figure of gender duality, many of the other major characters transgress gender lines, although in less startling physical form. Laura's uncle, Frederick Fairlie, purposefully installs himself in the female role of nervous helplessness, while Count Fosco combines ruthless, aggressive intelligence with the soft stealthy movements of a woman (not to mention his love of cakes and his pet mice). His partner in villainy, Sir Percival Glyde, exhibits masculine calm and sadistic authority coupled with nervous excitability and loss of self-control, passions that lead in the end to his very feminine demise: he is, like Brontë's mad wife in *Jane Eyre,* consumed in flames as he seeks to preserve the secret of his identity. [49]

Gender transgression, as in the case of Percival, is repeatedly linked to questions of psychological disorder and hence of insanity. (Marian's statement that she is "mad" when she thinks of the ways in which men enchain women [203] should not be taken solely as a figure of speech.) Our hero, Walter Hartright, starts off, as I suggested, in the feminized position of drawing master, and he has to undergo fears of loss of self and monomania and be sent off to prove himself in the primeval jungles of South America before returning to display his newly acquired masculinity in the defeat of Percival and Fosco. Initially his position seems similar to that of Anne Catherick, the escaped inmate of an asylum, who is racked with hatred of Sir Percival and states repeatedly that she will "forget" and "lose" herself if she speaks of him (51, 128). Walter admits that the feelings that fueled him in his relations with Sir Percival "began and ended in reckless, vindictive, hopeless hatred" (106). It is an admission that reinforces our credence in his own fears of monomania and undermines the validity of the entire narrative he has so painstakingly constructed. Anne's fears that she will lose herself, lose her tenuous grip on her own memories and sense of selfhood, are echoed in Walter's thoughts as he approaches Limmeridge when he experiences a "confused sensation of having suddenly lost my familiarity with the past" (57). Just as Laura, after her incarceration, loses her firm sense of the past, so Walter has his identity obliterated as he enters the world of Limmeridge. While Anne Catherick's entanglement with the secrets of Limmeridge is to lead literally to her loss of self in death, however, Walter loses self only to emerge as the epitome of the self-made man. Percival is toppled from his rank, name, and wealth, and Walter moves up the social ladder to take his place, as husband of Laura and member of the landed gentry. The dualism signified by the figure of Anne/Laura, penniless imbecile and perfect lady, is duplicated both in the figure of Sir Percival, who is at once pauper and baronet, psychologically disordered (as his nervous cough reveals) and yet controlled, and in the history of Walter, who moves from poverty to wealth, from psychological insecurity to assertive manhood.

The central device of the novel whereby Laura is installed within the social and psychological identity of her lower-class half-sister attests to the total relativity both of ascriptions of insanity and of identity itself. Fosco has no need to draw in accomplices either in the external world or in the asylum. All act in perfectly good faith in accepting Laura as the inmate Anne and rejecting her claims to be Lady Glyde. Laura's own state is hinted at by Walter, in accordance with the warp of his gender biases: "Faculties less delicately balanced, constitution less tenderly organised, must have suffered under such an ordeal as this. No man could have gone through it and come out of it unchanged" (449). Laura can only be restored to her previous identity when the official inscription marking her death is erased and she is publicly recognized by the tenants. Given the ambiguity of the text, however, can we be absolutely sure that this figure is Laura? Anne Catherick was said to have had a tenacious memory, and Laura is nursed back to identity by Walter and Marian rehearsing with her the details of her early life. Like the gap in the marriage register that exposes the sham of Sir Percival's identity, the absolute proof of Laura's identity rests on the shaky grounds of absence: the loss of a day. All hinges on the memories of a string of witnesses, each of whom reveals himself or herself to be highly fallible, and on the "confession" of that arch-deceiver Fosco. Such ambiguity reinforces our sense that identity, both social and psychological, is inherently unstable and fragile.

Our understanding of the two figures of Anne and Laura is transmitted preeminently through the testimony of Walter. On meeting Laura he is struck by the fact that there is "something wanting" (76), either in her or in himself. Although it appears that this "something" is her resemblance to Anne Catherick, the fact that he feels the absence to be within himself as well is significant. The "something wanting" could be the frisson of sexual desire he experienced when Anne Catherick laid her hand on his arm: "Remember that I was young; remember that the hand which touched me was a woman's" (50). Compared with his responses to Marian, Walter's reactions to Laura seem desexualized. Like Petrarch's Laura, she is a neo-platonic figure whom the reader is invited to take as "the visionary nursling of your own fancy" (76).[50] For Walter to emerge into a state of unproblematized masculinity, the threateningly sexualized, mannish Marian has to be laid low (raped, as Miller argues, by Fosco) and Laura has to be placed in the sexually provocative position of utter helplessness in which he first encountered Anne Catherick. Although Walter depicts himself as "heart-right," his actions, like those of the other detective heroes in sensation fiction, carry disturbing overtones. Confronted with Laura, "her beauty faded, her mind clouded—robbed of her station in the world," he lauches into rapturous statements of possessiveness: "Mine. . . . Mine. . . . Mine" (435). Earlier in the narrative Walter has referred in mysterious terms to "the woman who has possessed herself of all my energies" (37) and to "the veiled woman [who] had possession of me, body and soul" (431). The vocabularly and sense of menace are those later employed by Braddon to depict Robert's relations with Clara. But in Collins's text there is no doubt as to who is ultimately in possession. Walter marries Laura (or Anne) when she is still in a state of childish imbecility, and concludes his narrative with the creation of a new aristocratic version of himself. Walter returns from a trip to Ireland and is introduced by Marian to his own son: " 'Let me make two eminent personages known to one another: Mr Walter Hartright—the Heir of Limmeridge' " (646). The wording is deliberately ambiguous, suggesting that father and son are elided into the single figure of heir, completely erasing Laura's maternal role. Laura's second marriage constitutes yet one more effacement of her identity, an effacement that, as Fosco testifies, is actively demanded of and enforced on wives by English law and custom.[51] Fosco boasts that he could have taken Laura's life, but he took her identity instead. Walter's heroic rescue of Laura is but a duplication of the main plot.

   The final text I wish to consider, Braddon's *John Marchmont's Legacy* (1863), draws together many of the ingredients of the other texts but treats insanity in a rather different light; it is neither the physiological destiny portrayed in *St. Martin's Eve* and *Lady Audley's Secret,* nor the totally open, relative term of *The Woman in White.* As the title suggests, this text also foregrounds questions of inheritance, both physiological and economic. The legacy in question could be the unexpected wealth John Marchmont himself inherits and later bequeaths, or the physiological inheritance of morbid sensitivity he entails on his daughter. Equally, it could refer to the way in which Mary herself is treated as a commodity to be entrusted to the care of Edward Arundel and her ill-chosen stepmother, Olivia. As in *St. Martin's Eve,* and *The Woman in White,* the female role is divided into two. The docility of the angelic heiress, Laura, in the latter text is explicitly contrasted with the decisive, mannish qualities of the penniless Marian; while in *St. Martin's Eve* the two halves of the story offer two different heroines, the equally docile heiress, Adeline, who actually dies from a weak constitution breaking under the strain of self-suppression, and the fiery, aggressive, and dowerless Charlotte. In *John Marchmont's Legacy,* the role of heroine is split between the childlike heiress, Mary, and the fiercely intelligent but penniless Olivia. Within this genre it seems that economic inheritance necessarily entails a correlative weakness of physiological constitution.

John Marchmont's love for his daughter is described as "almost morbid in its intensity" and is reciprocated by his daughter, who "loved her father *too much,*" so much so that on the night he dies she becomes "mad"; although she recovers, her morbid sensitivity and weakness render her "submissive to the will of others."[52] She unquestioningly accepts her stepmother's verdict that her fiancé, Edward Arundel, cannot love her, and passively allows herself to be imprisoned in the boathouse while the presumptive heir, Paul Marchmont, takes over her property. Her condition, diagnosed by the doctor as "morbid sensitivity," seems to be a form of insanity brought on by too much femininity; she adheres so rigidly to Victorian female roles that her own identity and desires are entirely obliterated. Olivia, by contrast, seems to suffer from an insanity produced by too much masculinity. She is the result of a female pen taking up Marian's impassioned statement that she is mad when she thinks of the self-sacrifice demanded of women and the imprisoning conditions of their lives. Olivia in similar vein revolts against the narrow round of social duty that is her lot: "The powerful intellect revolted against the fetters that bound and galled it. The proud heart beat with murderous violence against the bonds that kept it captive" (1:135–136). Whereas the "something wanting" in Laura Fairlie was a sense of physical sexuality, in Olivia it is precisely those soft characteristics of womanhood that define Mary Marchmont and Laura Fairlie:

> The thick bands of raven-black hair were drawn tightly off a square forehead, which was the brow of an intellectual and determined man rather than of a woman. Yes; womanhood was the something wanted in Olivia Arundel's face. Intellect, resolution, courage, are rare gifts; but they are not the gifts whose tokens we look for most anxiously in a woman's face. (1:125–126)

Olivia's problem, Braddon repeatedly informs us, is that her biological endowment is too great, misplaced in a woman: "She ought to have been a great man. Nature makes these mistakes now and then, and the victim expiates the error" (3:54).

Olivia is a fascinating revision of Lady Audley; she too marries for money and is guilty of ambition and cruelty. Whereas the narrative commentary in the earlier text seems to endorse demonic representations of Lady Audley, leaving more subversive interpretations to the reader, the later novel gives a very sympathetic portrait of its madwoman. Her madness is not foisted onto a hereditary taint but is made explicitly the product of a clash between great gifts and narrow, constraining circumstances. As in George Eliot's *The Mill on the Floss,* our heroine is endowed with the intellect and energy applauded in a man but positively harmful for a Victorian woman, given the social conventions of the era. Like that other "mistake of nature" Maggie Tulliver, Olivia is also endowed with a passionate sexuality, but it leads not to drowning by water, but the volcanic eruptions of madness.[53] In contrast to Olivia, Mary, who is depicted as the archetype of womanliness, is explicitly desexualized; she is womanly as a child, and childlike as a woman (2:83). Womanliness and sexuality are defined as mutually exclusive. Braddon's text highlights the contortions of Victorian ideology: the social accolade of womanliness can only be achieved by the complete extirpation of the physiological marks of feminity. Olivia, who is repeatedly described as wanting womanliness, is afflicted with an explicitly sexual desire for her cousin, Edward Arundel. This desire is quite beyond her control and, exacerbated by the narrow conditions of her life, turns into a form of madness: "All the volcanic forces of an impetuous nature, concentrated into one narrow focus, wasted themselves upon this one feeling, until that which should have been a sentiment became a madness" (1:74–75).

Olivia's sexuality distinguishes her from the other heroines considered in this piece; their primary demonic characteristics come from ambition rather than sexuality.[54] Yet in endowing her with such violent impulses, Braddon was not running counter to Victorian ideology, but rather following the line of Victorian medical theory, which stressed the ungovernable nature of female sexual desire. Far from being presented as asexual beings, women in physiological and psychiatric texts were presented as creatures of sexual excess, endowed with strong bodily urges, which they controlled only with great difficulty and often at the cost of their own sanity. Amid the disparaging accounts of female hysteria arising from contained sexuality, there were many that recognized, like Braddon's text, the role played by social convention in producing female breakdowns. Conolly, for example, quotes the French physician Georget in an encyclopedia article on hysteria:

"The social position of women," observes M. Georget, "renders the sex, already subjected to peculiar ills from their organisation, the victims of the most acute and painful moral affections. Their moral existence is entirely opposed to their faculties; they possess a will, and are constantly oppressed by the yoke of prejudices and social arrangements in their infancy and early life. . . . Sensible and loving, they must only love when the master orders them: they are for ever constrained to concentrate within themselves the most powerful of passions and the gentlest of desires; to dissemble their desires; to feign a calmness and indifference when an inward fire devours them, and their whole organization is in tumult; and to sacrifice to a sense of duty, or rather for the happiness of others, the happiness and tranquillity of a whole life."[55]

Braddon develops this theory of the crippling effects of female containment, exposing as a sham the whole ideology of duty and self-effacement that governed Victorian female lives. Her heroine, however, is not the gentle, loving victim of Georget's depiction; it is sexuality, not love, that drives Olivia, a force of passion she hates but cannot control: "Love to her had been a dark and terrible passion, a thing to be concealed, as monomaniacs have sometimes contrived to keep the secret of their mania, until it burst forth at last, fatal and irrepressible, in some direful work of wreck and ruin" (1:298–299). Braddon draws on the contemporary discourse of psychiatry to depict the destructive impact of sexuality on Olivia. This is not some unexplained monomania, however, but the explicit product of the limited conditions of her life and her willed adherence to ideologies of female self-negation. Female violence and evil, the text asserts, are not the result of physiological aberrations but are directly produced by the social conventions governing Victorian femininity. The meek and submissive, like Mary, bow down and negate themselves; those endowed with any force of character are warped and corrupted.

A midcentury medical article, "Woman in her Psychological Relations," spoke of the "enchantment" exercised by a soldier's uniform on young females, "predisposed to the allurement by an excess of reproductive energy."[56] Olivia similarly feels herself to be "possessed"; Braddon comments that in an earlier century she would have accused a witch of being the "author of her misery" (1:100). Yet this is no simple portrait of a woman's powerlessness to control the forces of her own body, as recurs repeatedly in the medical texts; the strength of Braddon's representation comes from the ways in which she depicts Olivia's forceful intelligence battling against her "madness," whose object, Edward, she scorns intellectually. Braddon renders explicit the social subtext of much sensation fiction when, in a passionate oration, she traces Olivia's sexual obsession and consequent insanity to the lack of social opportunities for women:

> The narrow life to which she doomed herself, the self-immolation which she called her duty, left her a prey to this one thought. Her work was not enough for her. Her powerful mind wasted and shrivelled for want of worthy employment. It was like one vast roll of parchment whereon half the wisdom of the world might have been inscribed, but on which was only written over and over again, in maddening repetition, the name of Edward Arundel. If Olivia Marchmont could have gone to America, and entered herself amongst the feminine professors of law or medicine,—if she could have turned field preacher, like simple Dinah Morris, or set up a printing-press in Bloomsbury, or even written a novel,—I think she might have been saved. The superabundant energy of her mind would have found a new object. As it was, she did none of these things. She had only dreamt one dream, and by force of perpetual repetition the dream had become a madness. (1:279)

As the reference to Dinah Morris of *Adam Bede* suggests, Braddon is exploring the same terrain as George Eliot. Whereas Eliot's heroines tend to rise above the social pettiness that constrains them, however, Olivia is dragged down and perverted, her nobility turned to violent hatred and madness. In speaking of the entrapment of Olivia's energies, Braddon is employing the same vocabulary and discourse of physiological psychology to be found in Eliot's works. But whereas Dorothea's energy in *Middlemarch* is allowed to find channels of dispersal, Olivia's remains trapped in the labyrinths of thwarted desire.[57]

Eliot permits Dorothea to find redemption through her love of that creature of brightness Will Ladislaw.[58] Braddon's text, although it predates Eliot's by seven years, is the more radical of the two. The conventional marriage ending is not an option for Olivia, who is destroyed by her love for this "bright-haired boy" (1:173). It is work she requires, not further self-sacrifice on the altar of love.

The hero of the text and object of Olivia's misplaced desire fulfils a role similar to that of the other heroes considered in this piece. Handsome, and a true gentleman, he is without immediate prospects, being a second son who has entered the army, but by the end of the novel he has acquired the Marchmont wealth and land. Mary, the conduit of this wealth, is allowed to expire so that Edward can marry a less fragile and childlike bride. The central plot is similar to that of *The Woman in White:* Mary's identity is taken. She is locked away by the presumptive heir, Paul, who declares she has committed suicide. Edward is cast in the detective role, but is not tainted by the quest because he proves to be such an incompetent investigator. Although he has married Mary he fails to protect her, and he mouches around under the very boathouse where she and his son are hidden, without once suspecting the truth. The dual role of Frederick in *St. Martin's Eve* of both heir and detective is here split between Edward and the villain Paul, who, like Frederick and Walter Hartright, occupies the dubious position of artist. The psychiatric science of detection in this text becomes explicitly an agency of evil control. Paul takes his "dissecting knife" and conducts an "intellectual autopsy" of Olivia: "He anatomised the wretched woman's soul. He made her tell her secret, and bare her tortured breast before him. . . . He *made* her reveal herself to him" (2:105). Like Robert Audley, Paul tries to read this madwoman's inner secrets from the slightest of signs of face or gesture. His motives, however, are unequivocally corrupt; his aim is to control Olivia, to enforce her participation in his plot against her rival and stepdaughter, Mary.

The last section of the novel depicts Olivia falling into imbecility, as her hopeless love again devours her. Imbecility is not solely confined to the sphere of feminity, however. Edward is also threatened by imbecility, but, as with other forms of masculine madness in these texts, the genesis is external rather than internal, and the effects short-lived. His imbecility is produced mechanically, by a train accident that wipes out his memory and threatens to leave him mindless for life. Patriarchal science, however, redeems rather than condemns him; he is not locked away in an asylum but operated on by a skilled physician who repairs all his faculties. Free now to play the hero, to find his wife and expose the villainous plot against her, he embarks on his inglorious career as detective. He is only too ready to believe in his wife's madness and concur with the official pronouncement of suicide. Like Walter in *The Woman in White,* he had married his childlike bride when her wits were severely shaken, and seems both to treasure and endorse her helplessness, confirming once more the ideological alignment between Victorian prescriptions for femininity and insanity. Edward is also, significantly, the author of a plot line the novel does not take up: he suggests that Paul might take out a commission of lunacy against Mary in order to take control of her property. The actual plot whereby Paul, acting the role of Count Fosco, robs Mary of her official identity only succeeds due to the willingness of all concerned to believe in Mary's incipient madness.

Like Frederick in *St. Martin's Eve,* Edward proves fairly faithless and quickly falls in love again. The announcement of his impending marriage, which marks his reinstatement into full masculinity, has a correlative impact on Olivia, arresting her descent into total madness. Galvanized by jealousy, she gathers her faculties and bursts sensationally into the church to disrupt the ceremony, proclaiming the supreme impediment: Edward has a wife and child already. Paul once more uses the weapon of madness in an attempt to discredit her testimony, but Olivia scornfully rejects such allegations with the wonderful line " 'Mad until to-day,' she cried; 'but not mad to-day' " (3:193). The text playfully underscores both the instability of insanity as a diagnostic category and the social parameters within which it is deployed. The final verdict on Olivia's madness remains open. While Lady Audley, who is clearly in possession of her faculties, is locked away, Olivia is arguably consigned to an even worse fate. She resumes the deadening round of social duties in her father's parish, accompanied always by a faithful servant since it is said she forgets where she is and what she is doing. In fulfilling the conventional role of Victorian middle-class womanhood she has become, as Braddon earlier suggested, "a human automaton" (3:137). *John Marchmont's Legacy* uses the diagnostic language of contemporary psychiatry but inverts its categories: the loss of self that constitutes true madness springs not from the instabilities of the female physiological system, but from social adherence to the medically sanctioned patterns of normative female behavior. True womanhood is synonymous with the emptiness of madness.

Victorian psychiatry and sensation fiction addressed similar issues, but from very different cultural positions, and to very different effect. While psychiatric discourse claimed the high ground of medical authority, sensation fiction was reviled as trash, proof of an endemic social disease. Both were working in a cultural climate in which the dominant economic ideologies of control were shadowed by increasing fears of social and psychological disruption. For the medical professionals, such fears helped solidify their claims to social authority, as they charted the innumerable ways in which insanity might manifest itself in even the best-run households. The sensation writers seized on the narrative potential vested in this psychiatric discourse: insanity might be latent, hiding behind calm, orderly exteriors, or partial and transient, flashing out only at rare intervals, and signaled by the merest flicker of a facial gesture. In a self-relexive move, sensation fiction installed reading of the bodily text at its very heart. The psychiatric dictum that only a thin line divides sanity from insanity becomes the ground for textual play. Socially, the effects of this dictum are uniformly repressive: the medical word becomes law, in a very direct and literal fashion, with the signing of committal decrees. The fears generated as to psychological status also act to intensify the forces of social convention: the only proof an individual can possess of his or her own sanity is adherence to normative patterns of behavior. Taken out of their framing context within psychiatric discourse, however, these ideas take on a more subversive function, as manifested in sensation texts, where the boundaries of normality are no longer held in place. The psychiatric science of detection, of reading the outer bodily signs of an inner soul, ceases to be authoritative and appears instead as arbitrary, motivated by patriarchal designs, and always open to contagion by that which it seeks to detect. Detection itself becomes, indeed, a sign of the pathological. The gendered hierarchy of male science exposing female secrets is subject to inversion during the pursuit, and male and female insanity are exposed as relationally interdependent terms. Although the sensation authors draw directly on psychiatric accounts of female instability and bodily vulnerability, the paradigmatic alliance of economic and physiological inheritance in their texts calls attention to the sociolegal functions of such diagnostic practices and their role in consolidating the patriarchal foundations of Victorian culture. Playful and excessive, sensation texts make obeisance to dominant ideological formations while simultaneously challenging and undermining their authority.

While psychiatric discourse fostered a climate of fear, sensation fiction was altogether more subversive in spirit and effect. In deliberately flouting the formal constraints of realism, it also transgressed dominant models of social and psychological order. The heiresses might be weak, and the strong women punished or marginalized and disarmed by the main plot lines, but through their form these texts tell a very different story. The self is neither biologically given, nor fixed and unified: one can go mad, or die, and live to fight again. The fears and hostility aroused by the genre of sensation fiction focused on the ways in which these texts were "preaching to the nerves." As Victorian critics were quick to realize, the textual experience they offered was a celebration of feminine "sensation," not masculine reason. In their form they carried the ultimate challenge to the culture of control.

Notes

A Question of Identity

1   Whitney Chadwick, *Women, Art, and Society* (London: Thames and Hudson, 1990), 358–359.

2   Mary Poovey, "Speaking of the Body: Mid-Victorian Constructions of Female Desire," in *Body Politics: Women and the Discourses of Science,* ed. Mary Jacobus, Evelyn Fox Keller, and Sally Shuttleworth (London and New York: Routledge, 1990), 29–46, 29 quoted. See also Denise Riley, *Am I That Name? Feminism and the Category of "Women" in History* (Southampton: Macmillan, 1988); Theresa de Lauretis, *Alice Doesn't* (Bloomington: Indiana University Press, 1984).

3   Carolyn Merchant, *The Death of Nature: Women, Ecology, and the Scientific Revolution* (New York: Harper and Row, 1980); Sandra M. Gilbert and Susan Gubar, *The Madwoman in the Attic: The Woman Writer and the Nineteenth-century Literary Imagination* (New Haven and London: Yale University Press, 1979).

4   Ludmilla Jordanova, *Sexual Visions: Images of Gender and Science and Medicine between the Eighteenth and Twentieth Centuries* (Hemel Hampstead: Harvester Wheatsheaf, 1989), 134–135.

5   Merchant, *Death of Nature;* see also Evelyn Fox Keller, *Reflections on Gender and Science* (New Haven and London: Yale University Press, 1985).

6   Jordanova, *Sexual Visions.*

7   For the strategies women practitioners of science have had to resort to in order to avert criticism, see Marina Benjamin, "Elbow Room: Women Writers on Science, 1790–1840," in *Science and Sensibility: Gender and Scientific Enquiry, 1780–1945,* ed. Marina Benjamin (Oxford: Basil Blackwell, 1991), 27–59; Londa Schiebinger, *The Mind Has No Sex? Women in the Origins of Modern Science* (Cambridge, Mass: Harvard University Press, 1989); and Pnina Abir-Am and Dorinda Outram, eds., *Uneasy Careers and Intimate Lives: Women in Science, 1789–1979* (New Brunswick: Rutgers University press, 1987).

8   Ornella Moscucci, *The Science of Woman: Gynaecology and Gender in England, 1800–1929* (Cambridge: Cambridge University Press, 1990).

9   *The Complete Letters of Lady Mary Wortley Montagu,* ed. Robert Halsband, 3 vols. (Oxford: Clarendon Press, 1965), 1:314. William Alexander, *The History of Women from the Earliest Antiquity to the Present Time,* 2 vols. (London, 1779), 1:102.

10   Moscucci, *Science of Woman,* 32–33.

11   Francois Azouvi, "Woman as a Model of Pathology in the Eighteenth Century," *Diogenes* 115 (1981): 22–36, 24 quoted.

12   Pierre Roussel, *Systeme physique et moral de la femme* (Paris, 1775), 62, 15–16, 34.

13   Jean-Jacques Rousseau, *Emilius and Sophia; or, An Essay in Education* (Paris, 1762), trans. Mr. Nugent (Dublin, 1763), 208. Alexander, *History of Women* 2:40.

14   Roussel, *Systeme physique,* 20–21.

15   Alexander, *History of Women* 1:316, 2:42.

16   Roussel, *Systeme physique,* 95.

17   Lorna Duffin, "The Conspicuous Consumptive: Woman as an Invalid," in *The Nineteenth-century*

Woman: Her Cultural and Physical World, ed. Sara Delamont and Lorna Duffin (London and New York: Croom Helm and Barnes & Noble, 1978), 26–56.

18   Images of monstrosity were deployed in popular depictions of suffragettes. See Lisa Tickner, *The Spectacle of Women: Imagery of the Suffrage Campaign, 1907–1914* (London: Chatto & Windus, 1987); Elaine Showalter, *Hystories* (New York: Columbia University Press, forthcoming).

19   Donna Haraway, "Investment Strategies for the Evolving Portfolio of Primate Females," in Jacobus, Keller, and Shuttleworth, *Body Politics,* 139–162.

20   A detailed assessment of women and the domestic sphere can be found in Leonore Davidoff and Catherine Hall, *Family Fortunes: Men and Women of the English Middle Class, 1780–1850* (London: Hutchinson, 1987).

21   Benjamin, "Elbow Room," 36–44.

22   Alex Owen, *The Darkened Room: Women, Power, and Spiritualism in Late Victorian England* (London: Virago, 1989).

23   Mary Daly, *Gyn/Ecology* (Boston: Beacon, 1978); Susan Griffin, *Women and Nature: The Roaring inside Her* (New York: Harper & Row, 1978).

24   Mary Douglas, *Purity and Danger: An Analysis of the Concepts of Pollution and Taboo* (1966; London: Ark Paperback, 1984), 121; see also 94–99. In recent years the idea of using positionality specifically to understand female agency has been suggested by Julia Kristeva; see Toril Moi, ed., *The Kristeva Reader* (New York: Columbia University Press, 1986), esp. "Women's Time," 187–213.

25   Luce Irigaray, *The Speculum of the Other Woman,* trans. Gillian C. Gill (Ithaca: Cornell University Press, 1985). The chapter on Plotinus is "Une Mere de glace," 168–179. For an excellent reading of Irigaray, see Toril Moi, *Sexual/Texual Politics* (London and New York: Routledge, 1985, 1990).

26   Gillian Beer, "Discourses of the Island," in *Literature and Science as Modes of Expression,* ed. Frederick Amrine (Dordrecht: Kulwer Academic Publishers, 1989), 1–27.

27   Ludmilla Jordanova, ed., *Languages of Nature: Critical Essays on Science and Literature* (London: Free Association Books, 1986), see introduction.

28   Susan J. Henkman, *Gender and Knowledge: Elements of a Postmodern Feminism* (Cambridge: Polity Press, 1990), 73–94; Linda Alcoff, "Cultural Feminism versus Post-Structuralism: The Identity Crisis in Feminist Theory." *Signs* 3, no. 13 (1988): 405–436.

The History of the Science of Woman

1   An earlier version of this chapter was presented at the conference "Nature of the Human Science," Lancaster, September 1990. I am grateful to the Nuffield Foundation for supporting my participation in it as well as to its organizer, Dr. Roger Smith, and to Dr. John Christie and the other participants for their responses. Some of the issues discussed here arise out of my *Seduction and Civilisation: An Enlightenment Perspective on the Role of Women in History* (forthcoming) as well as from publications listed below. All translations are my own.

2   This point is admirably made by Carolyn C. Lougee: "Despite its ubiquity, however, the woman question has not been equally pressing in all ages. At irregular intervals it has appeared with unique intensity at the forefront of Europeans' concerns: in fifth-century Athens, for example, in first-century Rome, in twelfth-century France, in the sixteenth-century *querelle des femmes*." *"Le Paradis des femmes": Salons, and Social Stratification in Seventeenth-century France* (Princeton: Princeton University Press, 1976), 3.

3   Paul Hoffman's *La Femme dans la pensée des lumières* (Paris: Editions Ophrys, 1977) remains one of the most wide-ranging and lucid surveys of writings about women during the seventeenth and eighteenth centuries. It also contains an excellent bibliography. See also Lougee, *Le Paradis des femmes,* Margaret J. M. Ezell's *The Patriarch's Wife: Literary Evidence and the History of the Family* (Chapel Hill and London: University of North Carolina Press, 1987), and Joan B. Landes, *Women and the Public Sphere in the Age of the French Revolution* (Ithaca and London: Cornell University Press, 1988).

4   Among those who did cast doubt on friendship between women, but thought that friendship

between men and women was "the most delicious" of relationships, was Madame de Lambert. See "Traité de l'amitié," in *Oeuvres de Madame la Marquise de Lambert* (Paris, 1774), 106–129.

5   "Look at women! They clearly surpass us, and by much, in sensibility; there is no comparison between them and us in the moment of passion." Denis Diderot, *Paradoxe sur le comédien*, in *Oeuvres esthétiques*, ed. P. Vernière (Paris: Editions Garnier Frères, 1968), 311. Compare on this subject Thomas Laqueur, *Making Sex: Body and Gender from the Greeks to Freud* (Cambridge, Mass.: Harvard University Press, 1990).

6   The ambiguity and self-contradictory nature of Rousseau's opinion on the matter may be gauged from the following description he gave of himself: "En un mot, un protée, un Caméléon, une femme sont des êtres moins changeans que moi" (In a word, a Proteus, a Chameleon, a woman are beings less changeable than I). "Le Persifleur," in *Oeuvres complètes*. ed. Bernard Gagnebin and Marcel Raymond, 4 vols. (Paris: Société de J.-J. Rousseau, (1959), 1:1108.

7   One who took up this issue in the seventeenth century was the Jesuit Father Pierre Le Moyne in *The Gallery of Heroick Women* (trans. the Marchioness of Winchester, 1652), discussed in Ezell, *Patriarch's Wife*, 44–45. Catherine II was a living proof in the eighteenth century that a woman could be no more, no less of an "enlightened despot" than a man. For an insightful analysis of perceptions of her, see John T. Alexander's *Catherine the Great: Life and Legend* (New York and Oxford: Oxford University Press, 1989).

8   The fertility, longevity, and appearance of women throughout the world are running themes in, for instance, the Comte de Buffon's writings. See his *De L'Homme*, ed. Michèle Duchet, (Paris: François Maspero, 1971).

9   For instance, by Diderot in *Réfutation suivie de l'ouvrage d'Helvétius intitulé l'homme*, in *Oeuvres philosophiques*, ed. P. Vernière (Paris: Editions Garnier Frères, 1964), 611. Helvétius called her "le Caton de Londres."

10   Montesquieu's discussion in *De L'Esprit des loix* (1748) of the impact of climate on social and political institutions, and hence also on the domestic realm and condition of women, was to shape all subsequent writings on the latter, though interest in the comparative status of women throughout the world had long been made manifest in travel literature. Lady Mary Wortley Montagu's *Letters . . . written during her travels in Europe, Asia, and Africa to persons of distinction, men of letters, &c. in different parts of Europe* (1763), in *The Complete Letters of Lady Mary Wortley Montagu*, ed. Robert Halsband, 3 vols. (Oxford: Clarendon Press, 1965), 1:248–465, is but one, though admittedly the most distinguished, example of the awareness of great differences in the condition of women within Europe and beyond it.

11   See note 10 above.

12   Ibid.

13   See note 59 below.

14   See note 56 below.

15   The contribution of women to civilization is one of the central themes of what was her history of this process in *De La Littérature considérée dans ses rapports avec les institutions sociales*, in *Oeuvres complètes de Madame la Baronne de Staël-Holstein*, 3 vols. (Paris: 1838), vol. 1. See also Biancamaria Fontana, *Benjamin Constant and the Post-Revolutionary Mind* (New Haven and London: Yale University Press, 1991).

16   Choderlos de Laclos, "Discours sur la question proposée par l'Académie de Châlons-sur-Marne, quels seraient les meilleurs moyens de perfectionner l'éducation des femmes," in *Oeuvres complètes*, ed. Maurice Allem (Paris: Librairie Gallimard, 1951).

17   Lord Kames, *Sketches of the History of Man* (1744), 4th ed., 4 vols. (Edinburgh, 1788), sketch 6, "Progress of the Female Sex."

18   William Robertson, *The History of America*, 2 vols. (Edinburgh, 1777).

19   Caroline-Stéphanie Félicité Ducrest de Saint-Aubin, Comtesse de Genlis (1746–1830), *De L'Influence des femmes sur la littérature française, comme protectrices des lettres et comme auteurs* (Paris, 1811).

20   Marie-Joséphine de Lescun, Dame de Monbart (b. 1750?), *Sophie ou de l'éducation des filles* (Berlin, 1777).

21   Antoine-Léonard Thomas (1735–1785), *Essai sur la caractère, les moeurs, et l'esprit des femmes dans les différents siècles* (Paris, 1772). References are to vol. 4 in his *Oeuvres complètes*, 5 vols. (Paris, 1802).

22   Jacques-Henri Bernardin de Saint-Pierre (1737–1814), "Discours sur cette question: Comment l'éducation des femmes pourrait contribuer à rendre les hommes meilleurs" (1777), in *Oeuvres complètes*, ed. L. Aime-Martin, 12 vols. (Paris, 1830–1831, 12:121–181.

23   See note 62 below.

24   Elizabeth Hamilton (1758–1816), *A series of popular essays illustrative of principles connected with the improvement of the understanding, the imagination, and the heart,* 2 vols. (Edinburgh, 1813). Idem, *Letters addressed to the daughter of a nobleman on the formation of the religious and moral principle,* ed. Gina Luria, 2 vols. (London: Garland, 1974).

25   Lousie-Marie-Madeleine de Fontaine (1707–1763). Mme Dupin employed Rousseau as a secretary for a period, and it was she who encouraged him to produce a draft of a history of women. See note 59 below.

26   Alice Clark, *Working Life of Women in the Seventeenth Century* (London: Routledge, 1919); Ivy Pinchbeck, *Women Workers and the Industrial Revolution* (London: Cass, 1930); Wendy Gibson, *Women in Seventeenth-century France* (Basingstoke: Macmillan, 1989).

27   E.g. Marina Warner, *Monuments and Maidens: The Allegory of the Female Form* (London: Weidenfeld and Nicolson, 1985); Madeleine Lazard, *Images littéraires de la femme à la Renaissance* (Paris: P.U.F., 1985); Pierre Darmon, *Mythologie de la femme dans l'ancienne France* (Paris: Seuil, 1983).

28   The review that is given here of various approaches to the topic does not pretend to be comprehensive, nor should it be taken to be dismissive in any way.

29   Vivien Jones, *Women in the Eighteenth Century: Constructions of Femininity* (London: Routledge, 1990). The very high quality of Vivian Jones's and Bridget Hill's (note 30 below) anthologies justifies their centrality in the discussion that follows.

30   Bridget Hill, *Eighteenth-Century Women: An Anthology* (London: Allen & Unwin, 1984, 1987).

31   E.g., Hoffman, *La Femme;* Alain Descarmes, *Histoire satirique de la femme à travers les âges* (Paris; Editions de Neuilly, 1949); Philippe Perrot, *Le travails des apparences ou les transformations du corps féminin XVIIe–XIXe siècle* (Paris: Seuil, 1984); Ludmilla Jordanova, *Sexual Visions: Images of Gender in Science and Medicine between the Eighteenth and the Twentieth Centuries* (London and New York: Harvester Wheatsheaf, 1989); Laqueur, *Making Sex.*

32   E.g., Susan Griffin, *Women and Nature: The Roaring inside Her* (New York: Harper & Row, 1978; London: Women's Press, 1984); Carol P. MacCormack and Marilyn Strathern, eds., *Nature, Culture, and Gender* (Cambridge: Cambridge University Press, 1980). These and others are discussed in my "The Enlightenment Debate on Women," *History Workshop* 20 (Autumn 1985): 101–124. Also Genevieve Lloyd, *The Man and Reason: "Male" and "Female" in Western Philosophy* (London: Methuen, 1984).

33   E.g., Jean Bethke Elshtain, *Public Man, Private Woman: Women in Social and Political Thought* (Princeton: Princeton University Press, 1982); Landes, *Women and the Public Sphere.*

34   See Stéphanie Michaud, *Muse et Madonne: Visages de la femme de la Révolution française aux apparitions de Lourdes* (Paris: Seuil, 1985). And also its opposite, women and evil: Hoffman Reynolds Hays, *The Dangerous Sex: The Myth of Feminine Evil* (London: Methuen, 1966).

35   See, for one, my "The Enlightenment." Also Jean Bethke Elshtain, "Symmetry and Soporifics: A Critique of Feminist Accounts of Gender Development," in *Capitalism and Infancy: Essays on Psychoanalysis and Politics,* ed. Barry Richards (London: Free Association Press, 1984), 55–91.

36   See, for instance, the balanced account given by Lynda Nead in *Myths of Sexuality: Representations of Women in Victorian Britain* (Oxford: Basil Blackwell, 1988).

37   Language was of the greatest interest to the Enlightenment. Its concern with the origins of language has, by and large, an altogether different orientation than that of present feminist and psychoanalytic discussions. For a useful survey of the latter, see Andrea Nye, *Feminist Theory and the Philosophies of Man* (London: Routledge, 1988).

38   Roy Porter, "Rape—Does It Have a Historical Meaning?" in *Rape: An Historical and Social Inquiry,* ed. Sylvana Tomaselli and Roy Porter (Oxford: Basil Blackwell, 1989).

39   Saying this, of course, amounts to no more than an exhortation to caution. Nor should it be taken as an argument for the poverty of theory. On the contrary, as is argued below, part of what is wanting about the retroactive use of conceptual categories that fascinate us is that they fall short of the intellectual ambitions of Enlightenment men and women. Moreover, the work of Michel Foucault, for one, is a clear demonstration that more might be gained (including by his detractors) from casting grand theoretical nets than from less daring scholarship.

40   See, for instance, Ludmilla Jordanova's insightful *Sexual Visions,* and "Naturalizing the Family: Literature and the Bio-medical sciences in the Late Eighteenth Century," in her *Languages of Nature: Critical Essays on Science and Literature* (London: Free Association Press, 1986), 86–116. Ornella Moscucci's *The Science of Woman: Gynaecology and Gender in England, 1800–1929* (Cambridge: Cambridge University Press, 1990) is a perfect illustration of the fruitfulness of this approach.

41   E.g., Londa Schiebinger, *The Mind Has No Sex? Women in the Origins of Modern Science* (Cambridge, Mass.: Harvard University Press, 1989).

42   E.g., the works mentioned in notes 40 and 41 above.

43   For instance, Jenifer S. Uglow and Frances Hinton, eds., *The Macmillan Dictionary of Women's Biography* (London: Macmillan, 1982); Margaret Alic, *Hypatia's Heritage: A History of Women in Science from Antiquity to the Late Nineteenth Century* (London: Women's Press, 1986). I have discussed some of the difficulties attending the biographical mode from a feminist's point of view in "Collecting Women: The Female in Scientific Biography," *Science as Culture* 4, (1988): 95–106.

44   This is a particularly urgent task given the increasing popularity of the view that men have brought us before the ecological Sphinx we are now facing. Women seem to be expected to find the life-saving answer to the riddle it has set us.

45   Though this chapter is confined to the Enlightenment, the point holds for other periods.

46   For studies of the relationship between some of these schools of thought and feminism, see Juliet Mitchell, *Psychoanalysis and Feminism* (London: Allen Lane, 1974); Hester Eisenstein and Alice Jardine, eds., *The Future of Difference* (Boston: K. K. Hall, 1980); Barbara Taylor, *Eve and the New Jerusalem: Socialism and Feminism in the Nineteenth Century* (London: Virago, 1983); Batya Weinbaum, *The Curious Courtship of Women's Liberation and Socialism* (Boston: South End Press, 1978); L. Sargent, ed., *Women and Revolution: A Discussion of the Unhappy Marriage of Marxism and Feminism* (London: Pluto, 1981).

47   "The two sexes always follow each other from afar by imitating one another, and they rise, grow in strength, become corrupt, or weaken together." Thomas, *Essai*, 228.

48   This issue has always been alive and certainly did not wither away in the eighteenth century. It had reached its last climax in the late seventeenth century. See Carolyn Lougee's remarks cited in note 2 above; Marc Angenot, *Les Champions des femmes: Examen du discours sur la supériorité des femmes, 1400–1800* (Montreal: Presses de l'Université du Québec, 1977).

49   Thomas's *Essai*, for instance, referred to a wide number of works, including Plutarch's (c. A.D. 50–120) *The Bravery of Women;* Boccaccio's *Concerning Women* (c. 1355); Agrippa's *De nobilitate et praecellentia sexus* (1529); Cristofle Bronzini's *L'Advocat des femmes, ou de leur fidélité et constance* (1622): idem, *Nobilissimae virginis Annae Mariae a Schurman dissertatio de ingenio mulieris ad doctrinam et meliore litteras aptitudine* (1641); Pierre de Boudeilles, Seigneur de Brantome's *Receuil des dames* (1665–66); and many more anonymous ones, mostly by women. A very rough count gives more than fifty titles, a great many considering that acknowledgments of any kind were the exception rather than the norm in the period, and also that Thomas himself said he wished to spare his readers the much larger number he could cite (241).

50   Vicomte de Ségur (1756–1805). His work is cited and discussed below.

51   Vicomte de Ségur, *Les Femmes, leur condition et leur influence dans l'ordre social, chez les différens peuples anciens et modernes,* 2 vols. (Paris, 1808), 1:xi–xii.

52   Ibid., xii.

53   It is interesting to note that this point found a parallel in other fields, most strikingly in that of anatomy. For a discussion of the need that was felt in the eighteenth century for a specifically female anatomy and female skeleton, see chap. 7 in Schiebinger, *The Mind Has No Sex?*

54   Thomas, *Essai,* 194.

55   Rousseau, "Discours sur l'origine et les fondemens de l'inégalité parmi les hommes" (1755), in *Oeuvres complètes* 3:122.

56   Diderot's "Sur Les Femmes" was written as a review of Thomas's *Essai* for Grimm's *Correspondance littéraire* (1772). His criticism centered on stylistic matters. See his *Oeuvres,* ed. André Billy, (Paris: Librairie Gallimard, 1951), 949–958.

57   Rousseau, *Oeuvres complètes* 3:131.

58   See my "Enlightenment."

59   Rousseau, "Sur Les Femmes," in *Oeuvres Complètes* 2:1254–1255; idem, *Le Portefeuille de Mad. D., dame de Chenonceaux.—Publié par le comte Gaston de Villeneuve-Guibert* (Paris, 1884). See Maurice Cranston, *Jean-Jacques: The Early Life and Work of Jean-Jacques Rousseau, 1712–1754* (London: Allen Lane, 1983), 201–208.

60   See my "Enlightenment."

61   See note 10 above.

62   For instance, one can with some confidence assume that William Alexander qualified his views on the comparative freedom of women in the light of her *Letters,* if only because hers was one of the rare

insiders' views into harem life. *The history of women from the earliest antiquity, to the present time, giving some accounts of almost every interesting particular concerning that sex, among all nations, ancient and modern*, 2 vols. (London, 1779), esp. 1:79.

63   Richard Olson, "Feminist Critiques of Science," *History of Science* 28 (1990): 125–47. This topic is also discussed by Schiebinger, *The Mind Has No Sex?* (chap. 6). Moreover, she considers not only the emancipatory potential of seventeenth-century theories of the mind, including those of Descartes and Locke, but also that of "the new anatomy" (chap. 7). It should be noted, however, that the present line of argument is partly intended as a corrective to the views that the privileged mode of discourse about women was that of the medical sciences and that "after the 1750s the anatomy and physiology of sexual difference seemed to provide a kind of bedrock upon which to build relations between the sexes. The seemingly superior build of the male body (and mind) was cited more and more often in political documents to justify men's social dominance" (ibid., 216). A similar thesis is upheld by Laqueur in *Making Sex*, where he argues that "sometime in the eighteenth century, sex as we know it was invented" (149); that "women's bodies in the corporeal, scientifically accessible concreteness, in the very nature of their bones, nerves, and, most important, reproductive organs, came to bear an enormous weight of meaning" (150); and that "all the complex ways in which resemblances among bodies, and between bodies and the cosmos, confirmed a hierarchic world order were reduced to a single plane: nature. In the world of reductionist explanation, what mattered was the flat, horizontal, immovable foundation of physical fact: sex" (151). History and anthropology held their own in the battle between disciplines and were central to the science of man and woman in the eighteenth century. These disciplines afforded the possibility to explore and understand the meaning of the differences between men and women and were taken to show either what was to be done for and by women for their emancipation or how this emancipation would inevitably happen as a result of the progress of mankind. And they were by no means seen as (nor indeed were they) vestigial of premodern thought. On the contrary, they were argued to be as new, as scientific, as authoritative, and as modern as any medical or biological science might have been said to be. It would seem that an unintended, but disturbing, consequence of the excellent work undertaken of late in the history of science, medicine, anatomy, physiology, psychiatry, and so on has been to reinforce the view of women as the perennial pathic, the victim, the patient, the object rather than the subject of science. If it is true that seen through the eighteenth century and nineteenth century medical gaze, there were more and more reasons to consider woman as condemned by her biology to subjection in perpetuity, history and anthropology were but two disciplines that in that same period afforded her good cause for hope (as they did the rest of humanity). After all, even the nineteenth century, which seems to be increasingly seen as the triumph of the discourse of nature (and of the medical profession) when it comes to speaking about women, was also the age of Hegel, Marx, and Engels, whose *The Origin of the Family, Private Property, and the State* (1884) benefits from being compared to the works discussed in this article; see Seyla Benhabib, "On Hegel, Women, and Irony," and Christine Di Stefano "Masculine Marx," both in Mary Lyndon Shanley and Carole Pateman, eds., *Feminist Interpretations and Political Theory* (Cambridge: Polity Press, 1991), 129–145, 146–163. For a sensitive treatment of the interplay between nineteenth-century medicine and the environmentalism of Darwin, a topic that bears on one aspect of this complex issue, see Moscucci, *Science of Woman*, 23–27.

64   See Marquis de Condorcet, *Esquisse d'un tableau historique des progrès de l'esprit humain* (1793; Paris: Librairie Philosophique J. Vrin 1970). Condorcet, among others, is discussed in my *Seduction and Civilisation*.

65   Alexander, *History of Women* 1:102–103.

66   Buffon, *De L'Homme*, 17. See also Michèle Duchet, *Anthropologie et histoire au siècle des lumieres: Buffon, Voltaire, Rousseau, Helvétius, Diderot* (Paris: Flammarion, 1978).

67   This view would be disputed by a number of historians, not least Laqueur (note 5 above).

68   "Woman has all the parts of man," Diderot writes in *Le Rêve de d'Alembert*, adding only that "the only difference there is between an outside purse and an inside purse; that a female fetus is mistakable for a male fetus." *Oeuvres*, 908–909. A little earlier in the same dialogue, Diderot has Mademoiselle de L'Espinasse venture: "Man may well be only the monster of woman or woman the monster of man" (908). The same issue is also explored in his *Elements de physiologie*, ed. Jean Mayer (Paris: Librairie Marcel Didier, 1964). This last passage is noted by Laqueur to qualify his history of the view that women had been thought to have "the same organs as men but in exactly the wrong places"; Diderot is cited as an exception, since he clearly only believes that men and women have the same organs in different places and does not take this to mean that either one of the sexes has these organs in the "wrong place." *Making Sex*, 26.

69   Buffon, *De L'Homme*, 132–133.

70   This was thought to be true of all women in polished societies, even the poor or laboring women, given that the state of nature was one in which women knew not the least consideration. See Tomaselli's introductory chapter in *Rape*.

71   Buffon, *De L'Homme*, 133.

72   C. Meiners, *History of the female sex, comprising a view of the habits, manners, and influence of women, among all nations, from the earlier ages to the present time; translated from the German of C. Meiners, Conciliar of State to his Britannic Majesty, and Professor of Philosophy at the University of Göttingen by Frederic Shoberl*, 4 vols. (London, 1808).

73   See note 24 above.

74   Françoise d'Isembourg d'Happoricourt, Madame de Graffigny (1695–1758). The *Lettres* were first published anonymously in 1747; they were signed subsequently and met with great success.

75   Edmond and Jules de Goncourt, *La Femme au dix-huitième siècle* (1862), rpt. with an introduction by Elizabeth Badinter (Paris: Flammarion, 1982).

76   See, for instance, Norbert Elias, *The History of Manners*, vol. 1 of *The Civilising Process (Über den Prozess der Zivilisation*, Basle, 1939), trans. Edmund Jephcott, 2 vols. (Oxford: Basil Blackwell, 1978); Werner Stombart, *Luxury and Capitalism* (Leipzig, 1913; Ann Arbor: University of Michigan Press, 1967). Even such works as Jules Michelet, *La Femme* (1859), rpt. with an introduction by Thérèse Moreau (Paris: Flammarion, 1982), benefit from being seen within the perspective of this developing science.

77   Worse still would be to seek to reduce it to a discourse grounded in, and reinforcing, biology, as Laqueur does when considering some aspects of the theory of civilization and women in *Making Sex*, chap. 6. For an account of the nineteenth-century emphasis on nature as a contrast to, rather than the continuation of, Enlightenment thinking, see Cynthia Eagle Russet, *Sexual Science: The Victorian Construction of Womanhood* (Cambridge, Mass.: Harvard University Press, 1989), 1–8.

Gendered Knowledge, Gendered Minds

1   The epigraph is from [Eliza Haywood], *The Female Spectator* (1745), 2:238.

2   Carolyn Merchant, *The Death of Nature: Women, Ecology, and the Scientific Revolution* (San Francisco: Harper & Row, 1980).

3   The most helpful account is Patricia Phillips, *The Scientific Lady: A Social History of Woman's Scientific Interests, 1520–1918* (London: Weidenfeld & Nicolson, 1990).

4   Merchant, *Death of Nature*, 273.

5   *The Spectator*, ed. D. F. Bond (Oxford: Oxford University Press, 1965), 1:44.

6   [Haywood], *Female Spectator* 2:239, 242, 231, 237.

7   Lady Mary Chudleigh, *Essays upon Several Subjects in Prose and Verse* (1710), 10–11, 7, 15.

8   Benjamin Martin, *The Young Gentleman and Lady's Philosophy in a Continued Survey of the Works of Nature and Art; By Way of a Dialogue*, 2 vols. (1759), 1:262, 279.

9   [Richard Steele], *The Ladies Library. Written by a Lady. Published by Mr. Steele*, 3 vols. (1714), 1:212, 216, 225, 231.

10   Elizabeth Carter, trans., *Sir Isaac Newton's Philosophy Explain'd for the Use of the Ladies from the Italian of Sig. Algarotti* (1739), 1:vii–ix.

11   Ibid., 1:15, 2:247, 11–12, 148 and passim, 22, 87, 247.

12   Martin, *Philosophy*, 1:1–2, 3.

13   Ibid., 29, 22, vi, 31.

14   Ibid., 3.

15   For an account of Martin's career, see John Millburn, *Benjamin Martin: Author, Instrument-Maker, and "Country Showman"* (Leyden: Noordhoff, 1976), esp. chap. 4. For other accounts of the role and importance of public lectures on natural philosophy in the eighteenth century, see Simon Schaffer, "Natural Philosophy and Public Spectacle in the Eighteenth Century," *History of Science* 21, no. 2 (1983): 1–43; Larry Stewart, "Public Lectures and Private Patronage in Newtonian England," *Isis* 77 (1986): 47–

58; Roy Porter, "Science, Provincial Culture, and Public Opinion in Enlightenment England," *British Journal for Eighteenth-century Studies* 3, no. 1 (1980): 20–46.

16   Cited in Millburn, *Benjamin Martin*, 44.

17   John Harris, *Astronomical Dialogues between a Gentleman and a Lady: Wherein the Doctrine of the Sphere, Uses of the Globes, and the Elements of Astronomy and Geography Are Explain'd, in a Pleasant, Easy, and Familiar Way* (1719), 31, 138.

18   Ibid., v–vi, 43, 147.

19   Martin, *Philosophy* 1:iii.

20   Jasper Charlton, *The Ladies Astronomy and Chronology* (1735), iv.

21   Carter, *Newton's Philosophy* 1:iv–v, vi–vii.

22   Edward Young, *Love of Fame, the Universal Passion*, 2d ed. (1728), satire 5, 103. The two verse quotations below are from the same poem.

23   *The Spectator*, no. 37, 12 April 1711.

24   Thomas Wright, *The Female Vertuoso's* (1693), 3, 27.

25   *Man Superior to Woman. By a Gentleman* (1744), 39, 46.

26   *Woman's Superior Excellence over Man* (1743), 77–78, 78–79.

27   Harris, *Astronomical Dialogues*, 148.

28   J. L. Robertson, ed., *The Complete Poetical Works of James Thomson* (1908; rpt. London: Oxford University Press, 1961), 437.

29   Benjamin Martin, *A Panegyrick on the Newtonian Philosophy* (1749) 1:14–15, 16.

30   Ibid., iv.

31   Martin, *Philosophy* 1:102.

32   Ibid., 31.

33   This description of Martin's lectures is given as the subtitle of his *A Course of Lectures in Natural and Experimental Philosophy, Geography, and Astronomy* (Reading, 1743).

34   Martin, *Philosophy* 1:iv, v.

35   James Thomson, *The Seasons*, ed. James Sambrook (London: Oxford University Press, 1972), "Summer," ll. 1730–1732.

36   Millburn, *Benjamin Martin*, 74.

37   Martin, *Philosophy* 1:243.

38   Ibid., 39.

39   Harris, *Astronomical Dialogues*, 136.

40   Carter, *Newton's Philosophy*, 15.

41   *The Dunciad in Four Books*, bk. 4, ll. 643–644, in John Butt, ed., *The Poems of Alexander Pope* (1963; rpt. London: Methuen, 1985).

42   Elizabeth Tollet, *Poems on Several Occasions*, 2d ed. (1755). The lines on Newton are from "On the Death of Sir Isaac Newton," 128–130; "The Praise of Astronomy," 57, was first published in *Poems* (1724).

43   [Henry Jones], *Philosophy. A Poem Address'd to the Ladies Who Attend Mr. Booth's Lectures* (Dublin, 1746).

44   Tollet, *Poems on Several Occasions*, 68.

45   *Female Spectator* 2:242. More recently, she has been used again as a symbol—of "Woman the Discoverer"—by Margaret Alic, *Hypatia's Heritage: A History of Women in Science from Antiquity to the Late Nineteenth Century* (London: Women's Press, 1986).

46   Tollet, *Poems on Several Occasions*, 67.

47   Ibid., 70.

48   Ibid., 71.

49   Ibid., 119.

50   Ibid., 104. The phrase is taken from "The Microcosm, Asserting the Dignity of Man."

51   *The Ladies Diary*, 1733, preface.

52   See Simon Schaffer, "The Consuming Flame: Electrical Showmen and Tory Mystics in the World of Goods," in *Consumption and the World of Goods*, ed. Roy Porter and John Brewer (Los Angeles: University of California Press, 1991).

53   See Margaret Jacob, *The Newtonians and the English Revolution, 1689–1720* (Cambridge: Cambridge University Press, 1976).

54   For Whiston, see James E. Force, *William Whiston: Honest Newtonian* (Cambridge: Cambridge University Press, 1985). For Newton's Arianism, see Richard Westfall, *Never at Rest: A Biography of Isaac Newton* (Cambridge: Cambridge University Press, 1980), esp. chap. 8.

55   From "Poems on Several Occasions," in Montagu Pennington, *Memoirs of the Life of Mrs. Elizabeth Carter, with a New Edition of Her Poems,* 2d ed. (1808) 2:26–28.

56   Martin, *Philosophy* 1:62–63.

The Male Scientist and the Female Monster

1   See Mary Poovey, "My Hideous Progeny: Mary Shelley and the Feminization of Romanticism," *PMLA* 95 (1980): 332–347; Janet Todd, *Sensibility* (London: Methuen, 1986); and Marlon B. Ross, "Romantic Quest and Conquest: Troping Masculine Power in the Crisis of Poetic Identity," in *Romanticism and Feminism,* ed. Anne K. Mellor (Bloomington and Indianapolis: Indiana University Press, 1988).

2   *Los Alamos 1943–1945: The Beginning of an Era* (Los Alamos: privately printed, 1986), 50.

3   Ibid., 57.

4   See Brian Easlea, *Fathering the Unthinkable: Masculinity, Scientists, and the Nuclear Arms Race* (London: Pluto Press, 1983); and Evelyn Fox Keller, "From Secrets of Life to Secrets of Death," in *Body Politics: Women and the Discourse of Science,* ed. Mary Jacobus, Evelyn Fox Keller, and Sally Shuttleworth (London: Routledge, 1990), 177–191. See also Diana E. H. Russell, ed., *Exposing Nuclear Phallacies* (London: Pergamon Press, 1989).

5   It must be admitted that there was no way of curing puerpal fever at that time; but as Claire Tomalin points out, when Dr. Pognard tried to remove the placenta manually over a period of many hours, he most certainly introduced infection in the process. See *The Life and Death of Mary Wollstonecraft* (London: Harcourt Brace Jovanovich, 1974), 222.

6   See Adrienne Rich, *Of Woman Born: Motherhood as Experience and Institution* (London: Virago, 1977), 142; and Mary Daley, *Gyn/Ecology* (London: Women's Press, 1979), 223–292. Before men completely dominated the profession, Louise Bourgeois surfaced as an authority and the author of three books on midwifery who taught obstretrics to surgeons at Paris's public hospital, Hôtel Dieu. Elaine Hobby provides an illuminating account of the power struggle between midwives and men in chap. 7 of *Virtue of Necessity* (London: Virago, 1988).

7   *Los Alamos,* 53–54.

8   Ibid.

9   See Chris Baldick, *In Frankenstein's Shadow: Myth, Monstrosity, and Nineteenth-century Writing* (Oxford: Clarendon Press, 1987), 31.

10   Sandra M. Gilbert and Susan Gubar, *The Madwoman in the Attic: The Woman Writer and the Nineteenth-century Literary Imagination* (New Haven and London: Yale University Press, 1979), 224.

11   Emily Brontë, *Wuthering Heights* (London: J. M. Dent, 1978), 69.

12   Choderlos de Laclos, *Les Liaisons dangereuses* (Harmondsworth: Penguin, 1961), 181.

13   See Christine Battersby, *Gender and Genius; Towards a Feminist Aesthetics* (London: Women's Press, 1989), 52. I am grateful for her useful commenting on my paper and for making clear our points of departure on the way in which we interpret the androgyne and alchemy.

14   Erasmus Darwin, *Zoonomia* (London: Johnson, 1794). In the first edition of *Zoonomia* Darwin had agreed with Aristotle that the male produced the seed, which the female merely nourished, and that monstrous births were to be blamed on undernourishment. This Aristotelian fallacy was perpetuated because spermatozoa had been identified earlier than ovaries. After 1801 Darwin revised his view that both male and female seeds contributed to characteristics of the species but still maintained that the male imagination had the greatest influence in determining the gender of the child. Consistent with this, he then atrributed monstrous births to the male imagination. Percy Shelley read *The Botanic Garden* in July 1811, and it influenced *Queen Mab* and *Prometheus Unbound.* See Carl Grabo, *A Newton among Poets: Shelley's Use of Science in "Prometheus Unbound"* (Chapel Hills: University of North Carolina Press, 1930).

15   Mary Wollstonecraft Shelley, *Frankenstein; or, The Modern Prometheus* (1818), ed. James Rieger (New York: Bobbs-Merrill, 1974), 51. Hereafter, page references are given in the text.

16   Quoted by William St. Clair, *The Godwins and the Shelleys: The Biography of a Family* (London: Faber and Faber, 1989; paperback, 1990), 506.

17   See Jenny Newman, "Mary and the Monster: Mary Shelley's *Frankenstein* and Maureen Duffy's *Gor Saga*," in *Where No Man Has Gone Before: Women and Science Fiction*, ed. Lucie Armitt (London: Routledge, 1991), 87.

18   Madge Dresser kindly pointed out to me that this was after he had swallowed a pregnant woman. Even though this is an instance of a man, who is admittedly a god, giving birth, it does not hold as an example of solitary male propagation.

19   See Battersby, *Gender and Genius*, 36–37.

20   William Wordsworth and Samuel Taylor Coleridge, *Lyrical Ballads* (1805), ed. Derek Roper (London: Collins, 1968), 36–43.

21   See Carolyn Merchant, *The Death of Nature: Women, Ecology, and the Scientific Revolution* (London: Harper and Row, (1980) and Evelyn Fox Keller, *Reflections on Gender and Science* (New Haven and London: Yale University Press, 1985).

22   See Henry Vaughan, *Works*, ed. L. C. Martin (Oxford: Clarendon Press, 1957), 418–419. The mechanistic model of the monster, derived presumably from the vogue for automata, is jolted into action by electricity rather than inflated with the animating spirit of life. This means of reanimation reinforces the scientific model of a being constructed from moving parts rather than created in a more spiritual sense involving organic unity.

23   Jean-Jacques Rousseau, *Emile; or, An Essay on Education* (1762), trans. Barbara Foxley (London: J. M. Dent, 1974), 349–350. For an attack on the biological determinism that underpins such attitudes, see Ruth Bleier, *Science and Gender: A Critique of Biology and Its Theories on Women* (Oxford: Pergamon, 1984).

24   See Gilbert and Gubar, *Madwoman in the Attic*, 3.

25   Humphrey Davy, a visitor at her father's house, had written about the early alchemists in his *Elements of Chemical Philosophy* (1812). In "The Mortal Immortal" Mary Shelley refers to the red and white mercury from whose union the ultimate perfection is achieved and the Philosopher's Stone is obtained. The appearance of a white liquid in the compound signifies the second stage of the Great Work. In the languages of some schools of alchemy, the Red King or Sulphur of the Wise appears in the womb of his mother and sister who are represented by Isis or mercury, *rosa alba*, the White Rose. In the story Agrippa bids Winzy, his apprentice, to observe the liquid of a soft rose color turn white and then gold in the glass phial.

26   See Radu Florescu, *In Search of Frankenstein* (London: New English Library, 1975).

27   Paracelsus, *Of the Nature of Things*, trans. J[ohn] F[rench] (London: R. Cotes, 1650), 8–9.

28   F. Sherwood Taylor, *The Alchemists* (St. Albans: Paladin, 1976), 179.

29   See *The Works of Thomas Vaughan: Eugenius Philalethes*, ed. A. E. Waite (London: Theosophical Publishing House, 1919), 375–376. I am indebted to Carolyn Williams for this point contained in her excellent paper "Chemical Conjunctions" read at the conference "Demystifying the Females: She-Devils, Saints, and Signifiers," held at the Institute for Romance Studies, November 1990 University of London. She has also drawn my attention to the first sighting of an ovum through a microscope in 1817. The signifance of this well-publicized event was that at last the female seed, which Galen had identified earlier, had come into the view of science.

The Aseptic Obstetrician and the Filthy Crone

1   Adrienne Rich, *Of Woman Born: Motherhood as Experience and Institution* (London: Virago, 1977), 145.

2   Jean Donnison, *Midwives and Medical Men: A History of Inter-professional Rivalry and Women's Rights* (London: Heinemann, 1977); Ludmilla Jordanova, *Sexual Visions: Images of Gender in Science and Medicine between the Eighteenth and Twentieth Centuries* (Hemel Hempstead: Harvester, 1989); Ann Oakley, *The Captured Womb: A History of the Medical Care of Pregnant Women* (Oxford: Blackwell, 1984); Jean Towler and Joan Bramall, *Midwives in History and Society* (London: Croom Helm, 1986); Rich, *Of Woman Born*. For a critique of the idea of "naturalness" here, see Jo Murphy-Lawless, "Male Texts and Female Bodies: The

Colonisation of Childbirth by Men Midwives," in *Text and Talk as Social Practice,* ed. Brian Torode (Dordrecht: Foris, 1989), 25–48.

3   Oakley, *Captured Womb,* 293; Jordanova, *Sexual Visions,* 19–42.

4   Grantly Dick Read, *Natural Childbirth* (London: Heinemann, 1933). See also Tess Cosslett, "Childbirth from the Woman's Point of View in British Women's Fiction: Enid Bagnold's *The Squire* and A. S. Byatt's *Still Life,*" *Tulsa Studies in Women's Literature* 8, no. 2 (Fall 1989): 263–286; Dorothy Wertz and Richard Wertz, *Lying-In: A History of Childbirth in America* (New York: Schocken, 1979), 181–190.

5   *The Squire* (1938; London: Virago 1987); *Still Life* (Harmondsworth: Penguin, 1986). See Cosslett, "Childbirth," 274–276.

6   Doris Lessing, *A Proper Marriage,* (1956; London: Granada, 1977), 209.

7   Cosslett, "Childbirth," 272.

8   *Honourable Estate: A Novel of Transition* (London: Gollancz, 1936).

9   *The Birth Machine* (London: Women's Press, 1983); *Puffball* (London: Hodder and Stoughton, 1980). Subsequent references to these two books are given in the text. Quotations reprinted with kind permission from *The Birth Machine* by Elizabeth Baines, published by The Women's Press, London, 1983, and by kind permission of Peters, Fraser and Dunlop Group Limited: *The Birth Machine* copyright © Elizabeth Baines 1983; quotations from *Puffball,* copyright © Fay Weldon 1980, are reprinted with kind permission of Hodder and Stoughton, Publishers, and Anthony Sheil Associates Ltd.

10   Emily Martin, *The Woman in the Body: A Cultural Analysis of Reproduction* (Boston: Beacon Press, 1987), 54; Oakley, *Captured Womb,* 293; Barbara Katz Rothman, *In Labor: Women and Power in the Birthplace* (New York and London: Norton, 1982), 23–24.

11   Martin Richards, "Innovation in Medical Practice: Obstetricians and the Induction of Labour in Britain," *Social Science and Medicine* 9, no. 11 (1975): 597.

12   Towler and Bramall, *Midwives,* 280; see also Oakley, *Captured Womb,* 293, and Rothman, *In Labor,* 23–24.

13   Richards, "Innovation in Medical Practice," 597.

14   Ibid., 600.

15   Peter Howie, "Induction of Labour," in *Benefits and Hazards of the New Obstetrics,* ed. Tim Chard and Martin Richards (London: Heineman, 1977), 85.

16   Oakley, *Captured Womb,* 192.

17   Ann Cartwright, *The Dignity of Labour: A Study of Childbearing and Induction* (London: Tavistock, 1979); Richards, "Innovation in Medical Practice," 295–296; A. C. Turnbull, introduction to Chard and Richards, *Benefits and Hazards,* viii.

18   Cartwright, *Dignity of Labour,* 2–3; Richards, "Innovation in Medical Practice," 296; Turnbull, introduction to Chard and Richards, *Benefits and Hazards,* vii.

19   This lack of information provided to women undergoing induction is typical: see Cartwright, *Dignity of Labour* 95, 99, 112, 114. As a woman, and as a layperson, Zelda feels doubly excluded from the world of medical expertise and explanation (Baines, 44).

20   Cartwright, *Dignity of Labour,* 30, 117.

21   Richards, "Innovation in Medical Practice," 596n.

22   Sir Dugald Baird, *Combined Textbook of Obstetrics and Gynaecology* (Edinburgh: Livingstone, 1962); Stanley Clayton, *A Pocket Obstetrics* (London: Churchill, 1967); Sir Eardley Holland, *Manual of Obstetrics* (London: Churchill, 1969); Joseph Holmes, *Obstetrics* (London: Ballière, 1969); George Pinker and David Taylor, *A Short Textbook of Gynaecology and Obstetrics* (London: English Universities Press, 1967); Robert Willson, *Obstetrics and Gynaecology* (St. Louis: Mosby, 1966). These all warn about the dangers of induction. The following are quite open about advocating convenience induction: Christopher Dewhurst, *Integrated Obstetrics and Gynaecology for Postgraduates* (Oxford: Blackwell Scientific Publications, 1976); *The Queen Charlotte's Textbook of Obstetrics* (London: Churchill, 1965); James Walker, *Combined Textbook of Obstetrics and Gynaecology* (London: Churchill, 1976). Since writing this, I have had a chance to talk to Elizabeth Baines herself. She says that she made use of a particular textbook, though she changed the words. She cannot, however, remember its name. My researches have at least shown that her textbook was not typical.

23   Dewhurst, *Integrated Obstetrics and Gynaecology,* 444.

24   Rich, *Of Woman Born,* 170–171.

25   S. Arms, *Immaculate Deception* (Boston: Houghton Mifflin, 1977); Sheila Kitzinger, *The Experience*

of Childbirth (1962), 5th ed. (Harmondsworth: Penguin, 1984); Oakley, *Captured Womb;* Martin, *Woman in the Body;* Rothman, *In Labor.*

26   Wertz and Wertz, *Lying-In,* 192.

27   Rothman, *In Labor,* 92.

28   Ibid., 177.

29   Ibid.

30   For a similar interpretation of the Snow White story, see Sandra Gilbert and Susan Gubar, *The Madwoman in the Attic* (New Haven and London: Yale University Press, 1979), 36–44.

31   Rothman, *In Labor,* 49. See also 38, 48, 135, 184.

32   Originating perhaps from Read, *Natural Childbirth,* 40–41. For a critique of this image, see Lawrence Freedman and Vera Masius Ferguson, "The Question of 'Painless Childbirth' in Primitive Cultures," *American Journal of Orthopsychiatry* 20 (1950): 363–372; S. Macintyre, "Childbirth: The Myth of the Golden Age," *World Medicine* 12, no. 18 (1977): 17–22.

33   Rothman, *In Labor,* 24, 32, 49, 94, 97, 109.

34   As Patricia Waugh argues in *Feminine Fictions: Revisiting the Postmodern* (London: Routledge, 1989): "Early in the pregnancy, while her stomach is still flat, Liffey views the bodily changes through the alientating and technical jargon of medical data supplied by the narrator and her doctor, surveying herself as an object of scientific knowledge" (195).

35   Gordon Bourne, *Pregnancy,* (London: Pan, 1975).

36   Bourne, *Pregnancy,* 45–47. Complete also Weldon, 34, 100–101, 105–108, 117, 121, 130, 135–136, 141, 155, 160, 166, 225, 236–237, 255–258 with Bourne, 58, 36–39, 59–60, 56–57, 59–61, 66–70, 72, 77, 334, 340, 407, 477, 485, 491, in this order.

37   Martin, *Woman in the Body,* 13, 45, 48.

38   Ibid., 45–50.

39   Bourne, *Pregnancy,* 47.

40   Martin, *Woman in the Body,* 54; see also Richards, "Innovation in Medical Practice," 597.

41   Bourne, *Pregnancy,* 41.

42   Ibid., 58.

43   Ibid., 23.

44   Ibid., 72.

45   Kitzinger, *Experience,* 25.

46   See Bourne, *Pregnancy,* 67.

47   Compare Bourne, 70 with Weldon, 166.

48   Compare Bourne, 69.

49   Compare Bourne, 407.

50   Tess Cosslett, "Questioning the Definition of Literature: Fictional and Non-fictional Accounts of Childbirth," in *Out of the Margins: Women's Studies in the Nineties,* ed. Jane Aaron and Sylvia Walby (Basingstoke: Falmer Press, 1991); Sheila Kitzinger, ed., *Giving Birth: How It Really Feels* (London: Victor Gollancz, 1987), 113, 150.

51   Here I would take issue with Paulina Palmer's reading of the novel, in which she accuses Weldon of adopting "a 'cultural feminist' viewpoint, identifying woman with nature and the body," which "may be criticised as ideologically regressive." *Contemporary Women's Fiction: Narrative Practice and Feminist Theory* (Hemel Hempstead: Harvester, 1989), 99. Not only is Weldon's viewpoint in the end quite different from that of a natural childbirth advocate like Kitzinger, but, as I will suggest, it is very hard to pin down her "viewpoint" as such.

Conceiving Difference

1   Jean-François Lyotard, "Response to Kenneth Frampton," in *Postmodernism: ICA Documents,* ed. Lisa Appignanesi (London: Free Association Books, 1989), 92.

2   Craig Owens, "The Discourse of Others: Feminists and Postmodernism," in *Postmodern Culture,* ed. Hal Foster (London and Sydney: Pluto Press, 1983), 57–82, 62.

3   Lyotard, "Response to Frampton," 92–93.

4   Mary Poovey, *Uneven Developments: The Ideological Work of Gender in Mid-Victorian England* (Chicago: University of Chicago Press, 1988), 9. I discuss the debate over ectogenesis in my study of the representational origins of reproductive technology, *Babies in Bottles* (New Brunswick: Rutgers University Press, forthcoming).

5   For some of the representative works of the former position, see Robyn Rowland, "Of Women Born, but for How Long?," in *Made to Order: The Myth of Reproductive and Genetic Progress,* ed. Patricia Spallone and Deborah Lynn Steinberg (London: Pergamon Press, 1987), 67–83; Gena Corea, *The Mother Machine* (London: Women's Press, 1988); Renate Klein, *Infertility: Women Speak Out* (London: Pandora, 1989); Rita Arditti, Renate Duelli Klein, and Shelley Minden, *Test-Tube Women* (London: Pandora, 1984); Janice Raymond, "Reproductive Technologies, Radical Feminism, and Socialist Liberalism," *Reproductive and Genetic Engineering* 2, no. 2 (1989): 133–142. For the most influential catalyst of the latter position, see Donna Haraway, *Primate Visions* (London: Routledge, 1989). A fence-sitter on the issues is Linda Birke, Susan Himmelweit, and Gail Vines, eds., *Tomorrow's Child: Reproductive Technologies in the Nineties* (London: Virago, 1990), 215–218.

6   Robin Cook, *Mutation* (New York: G. P. Putnam's Sons, 1989), and Fay Weldon, *The Cloning of Joanna May* (London: Collins, 1989). Further references to these two works are given in the text.

7   Anne K. Mellor, *Mary Shelley: Her Life, Her Fiction, Her Monsters* (London: Methuen, 1988), 104–106.

8   In Greek mythology, "a monster with the head of a lion, the body of a goat, and the tail of a dragon." Paul Harvey, *The Oxford Companion to Classical Literature* (Oxford: Oxford University Press, 1937), 98.

9   N. Katherine Hayles, *Chaos Bound: Orderly Disorder in Contemporary Literature and Science* (Ithaca: Cornell University Press, 1990), 265–266.

10   N. Katherine Hayles, "Text out of Context: Situating Postmodernism within an Information Society," *Discourse* 9 (Spring–Summer 1987): 24–36, 30.

11   Edward Yoxen, *The Gene Business* (London: Free Association Books, 1983), 31.

12   See Bernard Doray, *From Taylorism to Fordism: A Rational Madness,* trans. David Macey (London: Free Association Books, 1988). Originally published as *Le taylorisme, une folie rationelle?* (Bordas, 1981).

13   Evelyn Fox Keller, *Reflections on Gender and Science* (New Haven and London: Yale University Press, 1985), 53.

14   Michel Foucault, *The History of Sexuality,* vol. 1 (New York: Random House/Vintage, 1978), 128–131.

15   As Dreyfus and Rabinow point out, "the embodied investigator, as well as the objects he [*sic*] studies, have been produced by a specific technology of manipulation and formation." Hubert L. Dreyfus and Paul Rabinow, *Michel Foucault: Beyond Structuralism and Hermeneutics* (Brighton: Harvester Press, 1982), 166.

16   Hayles, *Chaos Bound,* xiv.

17   Nancy K. Miller, "Emphasis Added: Plots and Plausibilities in Women's Fiction," *PMLA* 96, no. 1 (January 1981): 36–48.

18   To take just the examples occurring in one week in 1991: reproductive endocrinologists in the United Kingdom revealed that they were helping a woman in a "virgin birth" through artificial insemination, and a test-tube baby anticipated the birth of her "test-tube sibling." *The Age* (Melbourne), Saturday 16 March and Sunday 17 March 1991. See also the "Current Developments and Issues: A Summary" section in every number of *Reproductive and Genetic Engineering: Journal of International Feminist Analysis.*

19   Emily Martin, *The Woman in the Body* (Boston: Beacon Press, 1987), 45–47. See also Julia Kristeva, *The Powers of Horror: An Essay in Abjection* (New York: Columbia University Press, 1982).

20   Robert Graves, *The Greek Myths,* vol. 1 (London: Penguin, 1955), 34; Corea, *Mother Machine,* 266. For an extended, partisan response to that debate, see Robert Edwards, *Life before Birth: Reflections on the Embryo Debate* (London: Hutchinson, 1989).

21   Linda Birke, Susan Himmelweit, and Gail Vines, eds., *Tomorrow's Child: Reproductive Technologies in the Nineties* (London: Virago, 1990), 215–218, p. 217. Naomi Mitchison's *Memoirs of a Spacewoman* figures the birth of a parthenogenetic child (London: Women's Press, 1962).

22   "As far as the fantasm of male parenthood or creation of life is concerned, the clone is a descendant of *Frankenstein,*" Gabrielle Schwab observes in "Cyborgs: Postmodern Phantasms of Body and Mind,"

Discourse 9 (Spring–Summer 1987): 64–84, 70. David M. Rorvik, *In His Image: The Cloning of a Man* (Melbourne: Nelson, 1978); Ira Levin, *The Boys from Brazil* (New York: Random House, 1976).

23   Schwab, "Cyborgs," 70.

24   Charlotte Perkins Gilman, *Herland* (New York: Pantheon Books, 1978); Joanna Russ, "When It Changed," in *The Zanzibar Cat* (Sauk City: Arkham House, 1983), 3–11; idem, *The Female Man* (Boston: Beacon Press, 1975); Shulamith Firestone, *The Dialectic of Sex* (New York: Bantam, 1970); Naomi Mitchison, *Solution Three* (London: Dobson, 1975); idem, *Memoirs of a Spacewoman* (London: Women's Press, 1962).

25   "Parthenogenesis functions to represent the creativity and autonomy of women as well as the interplay of nature and human nature," Gilbert and Gubar have observed, in a reading of Gilman's feminist utopia, *Herland* (1915). Sandra M. Gilbert and Susan Gubar, *No Man's Land: The Place of the Woman Writer in the Twentieth Century: Vol. 2, Sexchanges* (New Haven: Yale University Press, 1987), 75.

26   Ibid., 26.

27   H. Rider Haggard, *She: A History of Adventure* (1886; London: Macdonald, 1963), 54.

28   Martin Jay, "In the Empire of the Gaze: Foucault and the Denigration of Vision in Twentieth-century French Thought," in *Postmodernism: ICA Documents,* ed. Lisa Appignanesi (London: Free Association Books, 1989), 49–74.

29   See Jacques Lacan, *Ecrits: A Selection,* trans. Alan Sheridan (New York: Norton, 1977) and D. W. Winnicott, *Playing and Reality* (London: Tavistock, 1971).

30   Kay Torney, of La Trobe University, Melbourne, Australia, has suggested to me that Cook's choice of the name for the monster may extend this play on the gaze, linking it to the theme of nuclear technology and marking (but not questioning) theories of racial dominance as well. "VJ" evokes "VJ Day," when victory was gained over the Japanese through the bombing of Hiroshima and Nagasaki, and marks the dominance of the new, technocratic gaze over the "slant-eyed" gaze of the Other.

31   Owens, "Discourse of Others," 62.

The Gendered Ape

A special thanks to the Guggenheim Foundation and the National Science Foundation for support for this project. I would also like to thank the Office of Research and Graduate Studies and the Institute for the Arts and Humanistic Studies at the Pennsylvania State University for their kind support. As always, Robert Proctor provided much advice and expertise.

1   Arthur Lovejoy, *The Great Chain of Being: A Study of the History of an Idea* (1933; Cambridge, Mass.: Harvard University Press, 1964). The ancients were acquainted with apes but made few attempts to explain the relationship between apes and humans. H. W. Janson, *Apes and Ape Lore in the Middle Ages and the Renaissance* (London: Warburg Institute, 1952), 73. Hanno, in the fifth century B.C., reported the sighting of gorillas. Aristotle most probably based his description of apes and monkeys in *Historia animalium* on animals seen at Alexander the Great's zoo. Galen dissected apes and monkeys when human bodies were not available.

2   See, e.g., Arthur Lovejoy, "Monboddo and Rousseau," *Modern Philology* 30 (1932–1933): 275–296; Janson, *Apes and Ape Lore;* Franck Tinland, *L'Homme sauvage, Homo ferus, et Homo Sylvestris, de l'animal à l'homme* (Paris: Payot, 1968); and Robert Wolker, "Tyson and Buffon on the Orang-utan," *Studies on Voltaire and the Eighteenth Century* 155 (1976): 2301–2319.

3   Londa Schiebinger, *The Mind Has No Sex? Women in the Origins of Modern Science* (Cambridge, Mass.: Harvard University Press, 1989), chap. 3 and pp. 241–243.

4   Jean-Jacques Rousseau, "Discours sur l'origine et les fondemens de l'inégalité parmi les hommes," in *Oeuvres complètes,* ed. Bernard Gagnebin and Marcel Raymond (Paris: Gallimard, 1959–1969), 3:212.

5   On this contrast, see C. D. O'Malley and H. W. Magoun, "Early Concepts of the Anthropomorpha," *Physis: Rivista di storia della scienza* 4 (1962): 39–63, esp. 46. See also Janson, *Apes and Ape Lore,* chap. 9.

6   Roger Lewin, *Human Evolution,* 2d ed. (Boston: Blackwell Scientific Publications, 1989), 1. Also Carl Linnaeus, *Systema naturae,* 10th ed. (Stockholm, 1758), 1:21.

7   *Primate* also carries religious connotations, denoting a bishop of highest rank in a province or country.

8   Nicolaas Tulp, *Observationum medicarum libri tres* (Amsterdam, 1641); for *quimpezé*, see La Brosse, cited in Georges-Louis Leclerc, Comte de Buffon, *Histoire naturelle, générale et particulière* (Paris, 1749–1767), 14:51; for chimpanzee, see Gerard Scotin, "Chimpanzee, Scotin sculp. A.D. 1738," Department of Prints and Drawings, British Museum; for gibbon, see Buffon, *Histoire naturelle,* 14:96–113; and for gorilla, see Thomas Savage, "Notice Describing the External Character and Habits of a New Species of Troglodytes (T. *gorilla,* Savage)," *Proceedings of the Boston Society of Natural History* 2 (1848): 245–247. See also Robert and Ada Yerkes, *The Great Apes: A Study of Anthropoid Life* (New Haven: Yale University Press, 1929), 36–40.

9   Some European voyagers claimed that natives considered at least chimpanzees and orangutans human; both terms mean "wild man." Bontius reported this of the Javanese. Daniel Beeckman stated that the natives of Borneo held that orangutans were once people but had been transformed into beasts because of their blasphemy (*A Voyage to and from the Island of Borneo* [London, 1718], 37). Savage asserted that the native people of Gabon believed chimpanzees to be "degenerated human beings" ("Notice Describing the External Characters," 246). See also O'Malley and Magoun, "Early Concepts of the Anthropomorpha," 58–59. Unfortunately, I have only the reports of Europeans concerning this matter.

Firsthand knowledge of the great apes among Europeans was not extensive in this period. Observations by voyagers—often untrained observers—were combined with the teachings of the ancients. In many cases, naturalists never set eyes on the animals they described; Linnaeus, for example, never saw the troglodytes, which he set such store by as a second species of *Homo.* It was not until the second half of the eighteenth century that a number of live animals became available in Europe. Buffon housed a chimpanzee with a liking for strawberries at the Jardin du Roi. Petrus Camper claimed George Edwards was the first Englishman to have seen a true orangutan, this in the 1750s (though his illustration also portrays a chimpanzee in many regards). Camper himself was unusual in procuring a large number of orangutans (eight in all, five of which he dissected) through his connection in Batavia and the East India Company. See his "De l'orang-outang et des quelques autres espèces de singes," *Oeuvres de Pierre Camper* (Paris, 1803), vol. 1. See also Robert Visser, *The Zoological Work of Petrus Camper (1722–1789)* (Amsterdam: Rodopi, 1985), 34–35.

All the great naturalists, however—Linnaeus, Buffon, Camper, and Blumenbach—knew animals only in captivity. Menageries had existed at least since the time of Hatshepsut, Queen of Egypt. The eighteenth century was not yet a time in which animals were studied for long periods of time in their natural surroundings. See Alan Jenkins, *The Naturalists* (New York: Mayflower Books, 1978), 108.

10   Visser *Zoological Work of Petrus Camper,* 39.

11   That so many of the apes studied by Europeans were still immature served to heighten their human appearance; Stephen Jay Gould has pointed out that a young chimpanzee will have many humanlike characters that adults eventually lose. See his "Chimp on the Chain," *Natural History* 12 (1983): 18–25, esp. 24.

12   Edward Tyson, *Orang-Outang, sive Homo Sylvestris; or, The Anatomy of a Pygmie Compared with That of a Monkey, an Ape, and a Man* (London, 1699), pp. 92–95. On Tyson, see M. F. Ashley Montagu, *Edward Tyson and the Rise of Human and Comparative Anatomy in England* (Philadelphia: American Philosophical Society, 1943). The skeleton of Tyson's chimp became a family heirloom. Tyson's granddaughter brought it as part of her dowry to her marriage to Dr. Allardyce, who in turn presented it to the Cheltenham Museum. It is now displayed in the gift shop of the Museum of Natural History in London. Thomas Huxley, *Man's Place in Nature and Other Anthropological Essays* (1896; New York: Greenwood Press, 1968), 13–14.

13   Lovejoy, *Great Chain of Being,* 233; Charles Bonnet, *Contemplation de la nature,* in *Oeuvres complètes* (Neuchâtel, 1779–1783), 7: 174. See also Lorin Anderson, *Charles Bonnet and the Order of the Known* (Dordrecht: D. Reidel, 1982), 34–58.

14   Tyson, *Orang-Outang, sive Homo Sylvestris,* the epistle dedicatory (three commas removed).

15   On the origins of the term *Mammalia,* see Londa Schiebinger, *Nature's Body: Gender in the Making of Modern Science* (Boston: Beacon Press, 1993), chap. 2.

16   Linnaeus numbered among *Homo troglodytes* Pliny's Atlas tribe (cave dwellers fallen beneath the level of human civilization) and Bontius's orangutan, who most agreed was merely a hairy woman. Carl Linnaeus, "Anthropomorpha," respondent C. E. Hoppius (1760), in *Amoenitates academicae* (Erlangen,

1789), 6:72–76. Linnaeus never flagged in his efforts to confirm the existence of the *Homo troglodytes*. In 1758, news came of a possible specimen—a female—being exhibited in London. Linnaeus sent one of his students to investigate, urging him to examine her genitalia (did she have a clitoris and nymphae?), her speech, her eyelids (did she have the *membrana nictitans?*), and so forth. Despite offers of substantial compensation, the owner forbade examination of her private parts. Linnaeus's student was unable to confirm her a troglodyte, though other sources writing from England denied that she was. In the 1760s, Linnaeus persuaded the queen to instruct the Swedish East India Company to obtain a specimen of the *Homo troglodytes*—a three-year quest yielding nothing. Linnaeus also sometimes considered *Homo caudatus* a third species of humans. Gunnar Broberg, "*Homo sapiens:* Linnaeus's Classification of Man," in *Linnaeus: The Man and His Work*, ed. Tore Frängsmyr (Berkeley and Los Angeles: University of California Press, 1983), 185–186.

17   Linnaeus, "Anthropomorpha," 66; also his *Fauna Suecica* (Stockholm, 1746), preface.

18   See Lovejoy, "Monboddo and Rousseau"; and Robert Wolker, "Perfectible Apes in Decadent Cultures: Rousseau's Anthropology Revisited," *Daedalus* 107 (1978): 107–134.

19   Buffon, *Histoire naturelle* 14:30.

20   See Keith Thomas, *Man and the Natural World: A History of the Modern Sensibility* (New York: Pantheon Books, 1983), 30–36.

21   Janson, *Apes and Ape Lore*, 73–106.

22   Ibid., 89.

23   Tyson, *Orang-Outang, sive Homo Sylvestris*, 55.

24   John Locke, *An Essay Concerning Human Understanding* (1706; New York, 1961), 1:124–127 (2.11.5–12). See also Thomas, *Man and the Natural World*, 125.

25   David Hume, *Essays Moral, Political, etc.*, ed. T. H. Green (London, 1882), 2:85–88.

26   Rousseau and Monboddo held that the generic orangutan had the same mental faculties as the human but had failed to perfect them. See Lovejoy, "Monboddo and Rousseau," 278.

27   Tyson, *Orang-Outang, sive Homo Sylvestris*, 55; Buffon, *Histoire naturelle* 14:32.

28   Johann Blumenbach, *On the Natural Varieties of Mankind*, trans. Thomas Bendyshe (1865; New York: Bergman, 1969), 182–183. For Linnaeus, see esp. *Fauna Suecica*, preface.

29   Margaret Cavendish, Duchess of Newcastle, *Philosophical Letters* (London, 1664), 40–41, 43.

30   Denis Diderot, *Oeuvres complètes de Diderot*, ed. J. Assézat (Paris, 1875), 2:190. See also Wolker, "Tyson and Buffon on the Orang-utan," 2308.

31   Broberg, "*Homo sapiens:* Linnaeus's Classification of Man," 161.

32   Claude Perrault, *Mémoires pour servir à l'histoire naturelle des animaux* (Paris, 1676). Petrus Camper dissected the larynx of an orangutan in 1799 and concluded (incorrectly) that these animals are physically incapable of speech ("Account of the Organs of Speech of the Orang Outang," *Philosophical Transactions* 69, pt. 1 [1779]: 139–159). See also Camper, "De l'orang-outang et des quelques autres espèces des singes"; Visser, *Zoological Work of Petrus Camper*, pp. 33–39; and Wolker, "Tyson and Buffon on the Orang-utan," 2308–2309.

33   Linnaeus, *Systema naturae*, 10th ed., 24; also his "Anthropomorpha," 74.

34   Jacob Bontius, *Historiae naturalis & medicae Indiae Orientalis libri sex* (Amsterdam, 1658), 85; also Buffon, *Histoire naturelle* vol. 14:59.

35   Rousseau, "Sur l'origine de l'inégalité," 162.

36   Buffon, *Histoire naturelle* vol. 14:36, 46.

37   Blumenbach, *On the Natural Varieties of Mankind*, 83. Bontius and Tyson also emphasized the humanlike emotions expressed by apes. Tyson's "Pygmie" cried "like a child" (*Orang-Outang, sive Homo Sylvestris*, 25).

38   Plato, *Timaeus*, 90a.

39   Rousseau, "Sur l'origine de l'inégalité," 197. He might have noted that apes' breasts are similarly placed, but he did not.

40   Tyson, *Orang-Outang, sive Homo Sylvestris*, 13. Early modern naturalists were still greatly influenced by the ancients. This posture—walking erect with a staff—was the classic pose of the satyrs of the ancients and may have simply been carried over into seventeenth- and eighteenth-century illustrations ([Jonathan Swift], *Miscellanies in Prose and Verse* [London, 1732], 3:101).

41   J.-B. Audebert, *Histoire naturelle des singes et des makis* (Paris, 1800), 16. He is referring to the illustration in Buffon, *Histoire naturelle*, supplement, 7:2.

42   Blumenbach, *On the Natural Varieties of Mankind*, 171–172. Despite his desire to see apes as bipedal, Tyson had early on suggested that they be called *Quadru-manus* because their hind feet resemble hands (*Orang-Outang, sive Homo Sylvestris*, 13).

43   Duarte Lopez (1578), cited in O'Malley and Magoun, "Early Concepts of the Anthropomorpha," 39.

44   Buffon, *Histoire naturelle* 14:53–54.

45   La Brosse cited in Buffon, *Histoire naturelle* 14:55; Tulp, *Observationum medicarum libri tres*, 274–279; Jan Nieuhof, *An Embassy from the East-India Company of the United Provinces to the Grand Tartar Cham Emperour of China*, trans. J. Ogilby (1665; London, 1669), appendix, 91–92.

46   James Burnet, Lord Monboddo, *Of the Origin and Progress of Language* (Edinburgh, 1774), 1:287–288.

47   Linnaeus, "Anthropomorpha," 76. Rousseau, "Sur l'origine de l'inégalité," 211. Rousseau drew his remarks from Andrew Battell's report published in the seventeenth century (Samuel Purchas, *Hakluytus posthumus; or, Purchas His Pilgrimes* [London, 1625], 2:981–982). Monboddo, *Of the Origin and Progress of Language* 1:290.

48   Jean-Jacques Rousseau, *Emile, ou De l'Education* (1762), in *Oeuvres complètes* 4:693–697. See also Schiebinger, *The Mind Has No Sex?* chaps. 6, 7; and Thomas Laqueur, *Making Sex: Body and Gender from the Greeks to Freud* (Cambridge, Mass.: Harvard University Press, 1990).

49   Blumenbach, *On the Natural Varieties of Mankind*, 182; and Buffon, *Histoire naturelle* 14:60.

50   Aristotle, *Historia animalium*, trans. D'arcy Wentworth Thompson (Oxford, 1910), 502b; Perrault, *Mémoires pour servir à l'histoire naturelle des animaux;* see also Tyson, *Orang-Outang, sive Homo Sylvestris*, 14, 44.

51   Diderot and d'Alembert, *Encyclopédie, ou dictionnaire raisonné des sciences, des artes, et des métiers* (Paris, 1751–1765), s.v. "Hymen."

52   Aristotle, *Generation of Animals*, trans. A. L. Peck (Cambridge, Mass.: Harvard University Press, 1943), 728b.

53   Pliny the Elder, *Natural History*, trans. H. Rackham (Cambridge, Mass.: Harvard University Press 1942), 7.15.63–66.

54   Albertus Magnus, for example, stated incorrectly that only women have a menstrual cycle. In Hildegard's *Physica*, cited in Janson, *Apes and Ape Lore*, 77–78.

55   Blumenbach, *On the Natural Varieties of Mankind*, 182.

56   Ibid., 182, 272–273. Buffon, *Histoire naturelle* 14:136.

57   Charles White, *An Account of the Regular Gradation in Man and in Different Animals and Vegetables* (London, 1796), 58–59.

58   Linnaeus, *Systema naturae*, 10th ed., 25.

59   Tyson, *Orang-Outang, sive Homo Sylvestris*, 46.

60   Blumenbach, *On the Natural Varieties of Mankind*, 171.

61   Aristotle, *Historia animalium*, 502a.

62   Linnaeus, *Systema naturae*, 10th ed., 20.

63   Tyson, *Orang-Outang, sive Homo Sylvestris*, 11. See also Bernadette Bucher, *Icon and Conquest: A Structural Analysis of the Illustrations of de Bry's Great Voyages*, trans. Basia Miller Gulati. 1977; Chicago: University of Chicago Press, 1981.

64   Alvin Rodin and Jack Key, *Medicine, Literature, and Eponyms* (Malabar: R. E. Krieger, 1989), s.v. "Hymen."

65   Buffon, *Histoire naturelle* 2:493–496.

66   Blumenbach, *On the Natural Varieties of Mankind*, 89–90, 170.

67   Jacques Moreau de la Sarthe, *Histoire naturelle de la femme* (Paris, 1803), 1:53.

68   Ibid. 1:48.

69   Blumenbach, *On the Natural Varieties of Mankind*, 169–170.

70   Edward Topsell, *The History of Four-Footed Beasts Taken Principally from the Historiae Animalium of Conrad Gesner* (1658; New York: Da Capo Press, 1967), 3, 8; Tulp, *Observationum medicarum*, 274–279; and Buffon, *Histoire naturelle* 14:135. Janson has traced this notion of the ape embodying male sexual rapacity to at least the sixteenth century (*Apes and Ape Lore*, 208).

71   Bontius, *Historiae naturalis*, 84; and Tyson, *Orang-Outang, sive Homo Sylvestris*, 19, fig. 16. A. Vosmaer also found that Bontius exaggerated the "marvels" of this animal (*Description d'un recueil exquis d'animaux rares* [Amsterdam, 1804], 4).

72   Foucher d'Obsonville, *Essais philosophiques*, 373, 375.

73   Monboddo, *Of the Origin and Progress of Language* 1:291–292.

74   *London Magazine*, 21 September 1738, 464–465.

75   [Thomas Boreman], *A Description of Some Curious and Uncommon Creatures* (London, 1739), 24.

76   Linnaeus, "Anthropomorpha," description to fig. 1.

77   White, *Account of the Regular Gradation in Man*, 134. On Tulp, see also William S. Heckscher, *Rembrandt's Anatomy of Dr. Nicolaas Tulp: An Iconological Study* (New York: New York University Press, 1958). An even more feminine copy of Tulp appeared in Antoine Prévost, *Histoire générale des voyages* (The Hague, 1747), vol. 6, facing p. 411. The breasts of this orang have been stylized to a pure classic form.

78   Linnaeus, *Systema naturae*, 10th ed., 21.

79   Eliza Haywood, *The Female Spectator* (London, 1745), 1:298.

80   David Hume, *A Treatise on Human Nature*, ed. L. A. Selby-Bigge (Oxford, 1888), bk. 3, pt. 2, sec. 12.

81   Janson, *Apes and Ape Lore*, 81.

82   "Abstract of a Letter from Stephen de Visme, Esp. at Canton, in China, to Henry Baker . . . ," *Philosophical Transactions of the Royal Society of London* 59 (1769): 71–73.

83   Foucher d'Obsonville, *Essais philosophiques*, 371.

84   According to Dapper, the native Africans he encountered found silly the notion that "orangs" issued from a union of woman and ape. Cited in Prévost, *Histoire générale des voyages* 6:411.

85   Tyson, *Orang-Outang, sive Homo Sylvestris*, 42.

86   Buffon, *Histoire naturelle* 14:50–51.

87   Bontius, *Historiae naturalis*, 85.

88   Blumenbach, *On the Natural Varieties of Mankind*, 201.

89   La Brosse, cited in Buffon, *Histoire naturelle* 14:51.

90   Tyson, *Orang-Outang, sive Homo Sylvestris*, 2; Blumenbach, *On the Natural Varieties of Mankind*, 81; Buffon, *Histoire naturelle* 14:31; and Lionel Wafer, *A New Voyage and Description of the Isthmus of America* (1699; Cleveland: Burrows Brothers, 1903), 113.

91   Rousseau, "Sur l'origine de l'inégalité," 211.

92   Sarah Trimmer herself did not go to see the pig because she believed that great cruelty must have been used in teaching him things so foreign to his nature. No animal, she declared, is capable of mastering the human sciences. *Fabulous Histories; or, The History of the Robins* (1788; London, 1821), 50–52.

93   Thomas Taylor, *A Vindication of the Rights of Brutes* (London, 1792), esp. 13, 19.

94   "Essay of the Learned Martinus Scriblerus, Concerning the Origin of Sciences," in [Swift], *Miscellanies in Prose and Verse* 3:98–116. See also Ashley Montagu, "Tyson's Orang-Outang, Sive Homo Sylvestris and Swift's Gulliver's Travels," *Publications of the Modern Language Association of America* 59 (1944): 84–89.

95   "Lettre d'un singe, aux animaux de son espèce," Nicolas-Edme Restif de la Bretonne, *La Découverte Australe* (Leipzig, 1781), 3:1–138.

96   E.T.A. Hoffman, "Nachricht von einem gebildeten jungen Mann," *Sämtliche Werke*, ed. Carl von Maassen (Munich, 1912), 1:396–406.

97   Wilhelm Hauff, "Der Affe als Mensch" (1827), in *Sämtliche Werke*, 3 vols. (Munich: Winkler-Verlag, 1970), 2:153–170.

98   Thomas Peacock, *Melincourt* (Philadelphia, 1817), esp. 1:57, 182.

99   This essay served as a companion piece to *An Essay Towards the Character of Her Late Majesty Caroline, Queen Consort of Great Britain* (London, 1738). See G. S. Rousseau, "Madame Chimpanzee," *Enlightenment Crossings* (Manchester: Manchester University Press, 1991), 198–209. I thank Dorothy Porter for calling this to my attention.

100   Julia Douthwaite, "The History and Fictions of the Wild Girl of Champagne," paper presented to the American Society for Eighteenth-century Studies, April 1991.

101   Peacock, *Melincourt* 1:9, 44.

102   Hester Hastings, *Man and Beast in French Thought of the Eighteenth Century* (Baltimore: Johns Hopkins Press, 1936), 10.

103   Donna Haraway, *Primate Visions: Gender, Race, and Nature in the World of Modern Science* (New York: Routledge, 1989), 304–315.

The Life Cycle of Cyborgs

I am grateful to the Center for Advanced Studies at the University of Iowa for research support while writing this essay, especially Jay Semel and Lorna Olson. Istvan Csicsery-Ronay, Jr., suggested the term *hyperconnectivity,* and Donna Haraway stimulated my interest in John Varley's story "Press Enter" at her keynote address, Indiana University, February 1990.

1   Donna Haraway, *Primate Visions: Gender, Race, and Nature in the World of Modern Science* (New York: Routledge, 1989), 279–303.

2   Scott Bukatman, "Who Programs You? The Science Fiction of the Spectacle," in *Alien Zone: Cultural Theory and Contemporary Science Fiction Cinema,* ed. Annette Kuhn (London: Verso, 1990), 201.

3   For an overview of life cycle stages and the attributes associated with each, see Erik H. Erikson, *The Life Cycle Completed* (New York: Norton, 1982), 32–33. A comparison of Erikson, Piaget, and Sears can be found in Henry W. Maier, *Three Theories of Child Development,* 3d ed. (New York: Harper and Row, 1978), 176–177.

4   Gillian Beer, *Darwin's Plots: Evolutionary Narrative in Darwin, George Eliot, and Nineteenth-century Fiction* (London: Routledge & Kegan Paul, 1983).

5   Bernard Wolfe, *Limbo* (New York: Ace, 1952); Katherine Dunn, *Geek Love* (New York: Knopf, 1989).

6   John Varley, "Press Enter," in *Blue Champagne* (Niles: Dark Harvest, 1986); Anne McCaffrey, *The Ship Who Sang* (New York: Ballantine, 1970).

7   C. J. Cherryh, *Cyteen: The Betrayal; The Rebirth; The Vindication* (New York: Popular Library, 1988); Philip K. Dick, *Do Androids Dream of Electric Sheep* (New York: Ballantine, 1968).

8   Carolyn Geduld in *Bernard Wolfe* (New York: Twayne, 1972) describes the author as a "very small man with a thick, sprouting mustache, a fat cigar, and a voice that grabs attention" (15).

9   David N. Samuelson has called *Limbo* one of the three great twentieth-century dystopias in "*Limbo:* The Great American Dystopia," *Extrapolation* 19 (December 1977): 76–87.

10   Julia Kristeva, "The Novel as Polylogue," in *Desire in Language: A Semiotic Approach to Literature and Art,* ed. Leon S. Roudiez, trans. Thomas Gora, Alice Jardine, and Leon S. Roudiez (New York: Columbia University Press, 1980), 159–209.

11   See, for example, *Dragonflight, Dragonquest,* and *Decision at Doona,* all by McCaffrey. The stories in *The Ship Who Sang* were published separately from 1961–1969, with the collection appearing in 1970. For a discussion of McCaffrey's fantasies, see *Science Fiction, Today and Tomorrow,* ed. Reginald Bretnor (New York: Harper and Row, 1974), 278–294. Also of interest is Mary T. Brizzi, *Anne McCaffrey* (San Bernadino: Borgo Press, 1986), especially 19–32.

12   Moravec is quoted in Ed Regis, *Great Mambo Chicken and Transcendent Science: Science Slightly over the Edge* (Reading, Mass.: Addison Wesley, 1990). See also Roger Penrose, *The Emperor's New Mind: Concerning Computers, Minds, and the Laws of Physics* (New York: Oxford University Press, 1989), 347–447, and O. B. Hardison, *Disappearing through the Skylight: Culture and Technology in the Twentieth Century* (New York: Viking, 1989).

Science and the Supernatural

1   *The Autobiography of Mrs Margaret Oliphant,* ed. Elisabeth Jay (Oxford: Oxford University Press, 1990), 4–5.

2   Ibid., 7.

3   Alex Owen, *The Darkened Room* (London: Virago, 1989).

4   See *The Virago Book of Victorian Ghost Stories,* ed. Richard Dalby (London: Virago, 1988), for a useful selection of ghost stories by women.

5   Margaret Oliphant, "Modern Light Literature—Science," *Blackwood's Edinburgh Magazine* 78 (August 1855): 219, 221. Further references to this piece, abbreviated "Science," are given in the text.

6   Margaret Oliphant, "The Old Saloon," *Blackwood's Edinburgh Magazine* 143 (January 1888): 105. Further references to this piece, abbreviated "Saloon," are given in the text.

7   Margaret Oliphant, *A Beleaguered City*, in *A Beleaguered City and Other Stories*, ed. Merryn Williams (Oxford: Oxford University Press, 1988), 10. Further references to this work, abbreviated *City*, are given in the text.

8   Margaret Oliphant, "The Open Door," in *Beleaguered City and Other Stories*, 119. Further references to this story, abbreviated "Door," are given in the text.

9   Margaret Oliphant, "The Library Window," in *Beleaguered City and Other Stories*, 290. Further references to this story, abbreviated "Window," are given in the text.

"Preaching to the Nerves"

1   Even in this text the relationship between the fictional and psychiatric discourse is not straightforward, as Reade then employs the selfsame psychiatric diagnosis of monomania in order to punish his villain. Although the abuses of the system are criticized, the categories of insanity remain unchallenged.

2   For discussion of Victorian theories of female bodily disorder, disease, and corruption, see Elaine Showalter, *The Female Malady: Women, Madness, and English Culture, 1830–1980* (New York: Pantheon, 1985), and S. Shuttleworth, "Female Circulation: Medical Discourse and Popular Advertising in the Mid-Victorian Era," in *Body/Politics: Women and the Discourses of Science*, ed. M. Jacobus, E. Fox Keller, and S. Shuttleworth (New York: Routledge, 1990), 47–68.

3   H. L. Mansel, "Sensation Fiction," *Quarterly Review* 113 (April 1863): 482–483, 512.

4   Margaret Oliphant, "Novels," *Blackwood's Edinburgh Magazine* 102 (September 1867): 257, 277.

5   Mansel, "Sensation Fiction," 482.

6   Rhoda Broughton, *Red as a Rose Is She* (1870), 12th ed. (London: Richard Bentley, 1895), 443.

7   Margaret Oliphant, "Sensation Novels," *Blackwood's Edinburgh Magazine* 91 (May 1862): 564–584. Ten years ago, Oliphant observes, "the age was lost in self-admiration," but peace and industry had since been displaced by war: "We who once did, and made, and declared ourselves masters of all things, have relapsed into the natural size of humanity before the great events which have given a new character to the age." People had come to enjoy the thrills of war, and sensation fiction now pandered in the emergent need for "a supply of new shocks and wonders" (564).

8   As Jenny Taylor observes in *In the Secret Theatre of Home: Wilkie Collins, Sensation Narrative, and Nineteenth-century Psychology* (London: Routledge, 1988): "In sensation fiction masks are rarely stripped off to reveal an inner truth, for the mask is both the transformed expression of the 'true' self and the means of disclosing its incoherence" (8).

9   Elaine Showalter reversed earlier readings of the text in *A Literature of Their Own: British Women Novelists from Brontë to Lessing* (Princeton: Princeton University Press, 1977), when she declared that "as every woman reader must have sensed, Lady Audley's real secret is that she is *sane* and, moreover, representative" (162). To assume, however, that there is one fundamental truth, and that sanity can be clearly demarcated from insanity, is to override the ambiguity of the text, where the very possiblity of definitive judgment is called into question.

10   Wilkie Collins, *The Woman in White* (1861), ed. J. Symons (Harmondsworth: Penguin, 1974), 529.

11   Oliphant, "Novels," 275.

12   "Madness in Novels," *The Spectator*, 3 February 1866, 135.

13   The author of "Madness in Novels" (cited in note 12) argues that the reader is forced to accept the behavior of the heroine of *St. Martin's Eve* as natural, since she is represented as mad: "We say it is natural, but at all events the unnaturalness disappears, for no one except Dr. Forbes Winslow knows what is natural in a patient with intermittent lunacy taking the form of jealousy on behalf of another" (135). (Dr. Forbes Winslow was editor of *The Journal of Psychological Medicine and Mental Pathology*.)

14   See, for example, "Moral Physiology; or, the Priest and the Physician," *Journal of Psychological Medicine and Mental Pathology* 1 (1848): 557–571.

15   Mary Braddon, *Lady Audley's Secret* (1862; London: Virago, 1985), 125.

16   "A Plea for Physicians," *Fraser's Magazine* 37 (March 1848): 293.

17   For a short summary of the theories of moral management, see Vieda Skultans, *English Madness: Ideas on Insanity, 1580–1890* (London: Routledge, Kegan and Paul, 1979), and her edited collection of texts *Madness and Morals: Ideas on Insanity in the Nineteenth Century* (London: Routledge, Kegan and Paul, 1975).

18   For an excellent discussion of this issue with reference to physiology, see Georges Canguilhem, *Essai sur quelques problèmes concernant le normal et le pathologique* (Paris: Publication de la Faculté des Lettres de l'Université de Strasbourg 100, 1950).

19   *Lady Audley's Secret*, 341.

20   Roy Porter, "The Rage of Party: A Glorious Revolution in English Psychiatry?" *Medical History* 27 (1983): 43.

21   Thomas Trotter, *A View of the Nervous Temperament; Being a Practical Enquiry into the Increasing Prevalence, Prevention, and Treatment of Those Diseases* (1807; New York: Arno Press, 1976), xi.

22   Reverend John Barlow, *On Man's Power over Himself to Prevent or Control Insanity* (London: William Pickering, 1843); 45.

23   John Conolly, *An Inquiry Concerning the Indications of Insanity, with Suggestions for the Better Protection and Care of the Insane,* ed. Richard Hunter and Ida Macalpine (1830; London: Dawsons, 1964), 8.

24   Barlow, for example, observes, "The cases of insanity, we are told, have nearly tripled within the last twenty years" (*On Man's Power,* 49).

25   See Andrew Scull, *Museums of Madness: The Social Organization of Insanity in Nineteenth-century England* (London: Allen Lane, 1979).

26   Conolly, *Indications of Insanity,* 496.

27   "A Plea for Physicians," 294.

28   Andrew Wynter, *The Borderlands of Insanity and Other Allied Papers* (London: Robert Hardwicke, 1875), 1.

29   J. C. Prichard, *A Treatise on Insanity and Other Disorders Affecting the Mind* (1837; New York: Arno Press, 1973), 16.

30   Prichard, 16.

31   See Barbara Fass Leavy, "Wilkie Collins's Cinderella: The History of Psychology and *The Woman in White,*" *Dickens Studies Annual* 10 (1982): 91–141.

32   See, for example, J. C. Bucknill and D. H. Tuke, *A Manual of Psychological Medicine,* 3d ed. (London: J. and A. Churchill, 1874), 415.

33   A. Brierre de Boismont, *On Hallucinations: A History and Explanations of Apparitions, Visions, Dreams, Ecstasy, Magnetism, and Somnabulism,* trans. Robert T. Hulme (London: Henry Renshaw, 1859), 191; J. C. Prichard, "Insanity," in J. Forbes, A. Tweedie, and J. Conolly, *The Cyclopaedia of Practical Medicine,* 4 vols. (London: Sherwood, 1833), 2:327.

34   J.E.D. Esquirol, *Observations on the Illusions of the Insane, and on the Medico-Legal Question of Confinement,* ed. William Liddell (London: Renshaw and Rush, 1833), 35.

35   Conolly, *Indications of Insanity,* 379.

36   According to Conolly, "it is only when the passion so impairs one or more faculties of the mind as to prevent the exercise of comparison, that the reason is overturned; and then the man is mad. He is mad only while this state continues" (*Indications of Insanity,* 227).

37   Collins, *Woman in White,* 105. All further references to this work will be given in the text.

38   As D. A. Miller argues in "*Cages aux folles:* Sensation and Gender in Wilkie Collins's *The Woman in White,*" *Representations* 14 (Spring 1986), the reader becomes paranoid (115).

39   Braddon, *Lady Audley's Secret,* 125. All further references to this work will be given in the text.

40   Robert is initially roused from his customary languor to enthusiastic praise of Lady Audley. He concludes, "I am falling in love with my aunt" (48).

41   The main study in this area is Showalter, *Female Malady.*

42   For accounts of theories of female vulnerability to insanity see Showalter, *Female Malady,* and Shuttleworth, "Female Circulation."

43   Mrs. Henry Wood, *St. Martin's Eve* (1866; London: Macmillan, 1905), 364. All further references to this edition will be given in the text.

44   For further discussion of this point, see S. Shuttleworth, "Demonic Mothers: Ideologies of Bourgeois Motherhood in the Mid-Victorian Era," in *Rewriting the Victorians: Theory, History, and the Politics of Gender,* ed. Linda Shires (New York: Routledge, 1992).

45   John Conolly, *The Croonian Lectures. On Some of the Forms of Insanity* (London, 1849), 68–69.

46   J. G. Millingen, *The Passions; or, Mind and Matter* (London: J. and D. Darling, 1848), 157–158. Similar arguments are offered in Robert Brudenell Carter, *On the Pathology and Treatment of Hysteria* (London: John Churchill, 1853), 33.

47   See Shuttleworth, "Female Circulation."

48   D. A. Miller's intricate study of gender and sexuality in *The Woman in White* ("Cage aux folles") similarly locates a strong homosexual element in that work. While I do not agree entirely with his reading of that text, his arguments have clear significance for *Lady Audley's Secret* and Robert's involvement with the dual figure of George/Helen.

49   I am indebted for this point to Abeer Zahra, "The Construction of Womanhood in Victorian Sensation Fiction, 1860–70," (Ph.D. diss., University of Leeds, 1990).

50   My reading here differs from that of Miller, who sees Walter moving from homosexual identification with Anne to heterosexual desire for Laura.

51   In his testimony Fosco explains the mystery of his wife's submissive devotion: "I remember that I was married in England, and I ask if a woman's marriage obligations in this country provide for her private opinion of her husband's principles? No! They charge her unreservedly to love, honour, and obey him. That is exactly what my wife has done" (632).

52   Mary Braddon, *John Marchmont's Legacy,* 3 vols. (London: Tinsley Brothers, 1863), 1:32, 227, 228. All further references to this edition will be given in the text.

53   George Eliot, *The Mill on the Floss,* cabinet ed., 2 vols. (Edinburgh: Wm. Blackwood, 1878–1880), 1:14.

54   Elaine Showalter argues in "Family Secrets and Domestic Subversion: Rebellion in the Novels of the 1860s," in *The Victorian Family: Structure and Stresses,* ed. A. Wohl (London: Croom Helm, 1978), that "the escape from sexual bonds and family networks rather than sexual gratification or frustration was the real subject of female sensationalism" (104). Sexual desire, however, is dominant in some of the texts, particularly those by Rhoda Broughton, whose heroines are all awash with desire.

55   John Conolly, "Hysteria," in *The Cyclopaedia of Practical Medicine,* ed. John Forbes, A. Tweedie, and J. Conolly (London: Sherwood, 1833) 1:572.

56   "Woman in Her Psychological Relations," *Journal of Psychological Medicine and Mental Pathology* 4 (1851): 25.

57   See Sally Shuttleworth, *George Eliot and Nineteenth-century Science: The Make-Believe of a Beginning* (Cambridge: Cambridge University Press, 1984), chap. 7.

58   "The first impression on seeing Will was one of sunny brightness. . . . His hair seemed to shake out light" (George Eliot, *Middlemarch,* cabinet ed., 3 vols. (Edinburgh: Wm. Blackwood, 1878–1880), 1:320–321.

Index